Back Through the Veil:
A Brief History of African-Americans Living in Mansura, Louisiana

"But who can remember pain, once its over? All that remains of it is a shadow, not in the mind even, in the flesh. Pain marks you, but too deep to see. Out of sight, out of mind."
— Margaret Atwood, The Handmaid's Tale

Donald G. Prier, PhD

Back Through the Veil - A Brief History of African Americans Living in Mansura Louisiana

CreateSpace

Nonfiction/Reference/Publishing

First Edition

ISBN-13: 978-1536892932

ISBN-10: 1536892939

DEDICATION

The people of African descent mentioned in this book represent but a tiny fraction of the millions who lost their lives during the horrible **Passage** from Africa following their capture into slavery, the tens of thousands who were tortured and died during their hell on earth and those who lived lives in constant fear of violence against themselves and their families. Most had lives that meant nothing to those who captured and held them in bondage, treating them as creatures no higher than animals and beasts of burden and, ultimately, disposed of their remains will little or no civility. There exists no evidence of their existence on this earth. No picture. No names. Nothing. Only God has preserved images of their earthly bodies, their names, and their souls.

To those poor souls is this book dedicated.

PREFACE

The focus of this book is on the town of Mansura and the surrounding areas. This focus is based on the following five reasons:

1. I was born and grew up in Mansura, where I attended Our Lady of Prompt Succor and Cardinal Cushing Elementary schools. My parents, Oliver Prier and Beulah Walters, were also born there. Most of my ancestors on the American continents were also born (and died) as slaves in or near Mansura. In addition, I have many relatives still living there.

2. There is a general lack of awareness among the African-Americans in the Mansura area of their family history: i.e., who their ancestors were, where they came from, how they were impacted by slavery and who might have held them in slavery against their will.

3. Mansura represents a microcosm of the world where most of the current African-American citizens and their families developed. It was impacted by most of the important events in the history of North America to include the early exploration of America, the American Revolution, the growth and demise of slavery, the American Civil War, Reconstruction, two world wars, and natural disasters such as the Great Flood of 1927 and the Great Depression.

4. My wife, Mary Bernell Augustine Prier, has a wealth of local African-American historical and genealogical information stored in her memory that has been invaluable to me in writing this book. She inherited that gift from her mother, Laura Barker Augustine, who, herself, was a noted oral historian.

5. Finally, this book would have been much more difficult to write without the slave birth and death records developed and maintained by the priests of St. Paul the Apostle Catholic Church of Mansura.

I chose the title, "***Back Through the Veil - A Brief History of African-Americans Living in Mansura, Louisiana***", for this book because our memories of history are like looking through a car's rearview mirror: Everything we see continues to shrink, and eventually vanish, as we travel down the road. Soon, the images we saw begin to become blurred as the newer events cover the earlier ones. Eventually, all we see is a composite picture, miniature in size and with few details. If we add additional information to that picture that is meant to create a distorted image, then we can't really know what the real picture should be. The history of our travels becomes lost or seriously changed.

Thus it is with the history of African-Americans. Many of the historical events, slave and Slave Holder names and families, event locations, etc. have been, either on purpose or via accident, distorted or completely destroyed. What remains is a clouded view of our history that resembles a view through a **veil**.

Few of us are able to travel back through that veil and accurately recreate our history. We do not know the names of our African ancestors, how they manage to survive the passage from Africa to the Americas, where they landed, who their Slave Holders were, what their lives were like living in slavery, and how they reacted when freedom finally came. Hopefully, this book will remove parts of that veil.

The use of the word, *Brief*, in the title was to recognize the fact that everyone has their own family story. This book is about **My Story** and includes not only my own experiences but those of my family, my wife's family and those of close friends and relatives. By adding some of the factual information that I have included in this book, the final product is a composite story or picture, where my own experience is at its center.

Anyone else can produce a similar composite story using the same process and resources that I did. However, their story would be significantly different from mine. It would, indeed, be **Their Story**.

If it were possible for every living person who has lived in Mansura to write **Their Story** and then combine them all into a single volume publication, that combined work would be a volume much too large to publish. Compared to such a large body of knowledge, this book is clearly, *Brief*.

By writing this book, I hope to capture and convey to the reader as much information on the "Veiled" subjects as possible. Hopefully, others will be encouraged to write **Their Story**. The value of such a product to future generations is immeasurable.

At first, I set out to learn more about my family and my ancestors. That early work occurred while I was a graduate student, studying for my doctorate in chemistry at LSU during the late 1970's. At that time, there were no such things as searchable databases, genealogy tools like Ancestry.com or well-organized genealogy collections in most public libraries, as exist today.

LSU's library did have a large and fairly well organized collection of U.S. census data on microfiche. However, building a simple family tree required considerable amounts of time peering into the microfiche readers and then printing whole pages of information, even when only one person's information was needed.

Clearly, I had little time for this wonderful distraction from my research projects and the result was a relatively short version of my family tree. Nevertheless, it was accepted by several of my family members as groundbreaking since most of us knew so little about our family history.

After about 20 years of inactivity, I gradually began to revisit some of my notes and copied information from the earlier work at LSU. By then, many libraries had yielded to the public demand for genealogy information, mostly stimulated by the book and mini-series, *Roots*, authored by Alex Haley (Haley). Those 20 years also allowed the public access to two more sets of U.S. census data, from 1930 and 1940. These new data helped me to go much further in developing my own family tree as well as that of my wife's, Mary Bernell Augustine.

This takes us to my current project, which is using my knowledge about the history of so many African-American families in Mansura to develop some sort of narrative of them. My information is in no way thorough and I will likely miss some key people or events. For this I apologize in advance. Since this is planned to be the first in a series, if you have information that you feel is important to add, please let me know and I will try to include it in the next book in the series.

I relied heavily on data publicly reported in the various editions of the U.S. Census. This allowed me to use information that provided a certain level of personal privacy that is restricted to those records. Thus, the scope of these discussions contained in this work are limited to the timeframe from the beginning of slavery in Louisiana to 1940, the year when the last U.S. Census data were published. Also included are numerous references to historical publications that have some bearing on the history of Mansura, Louisiana, the parish of Avoyelles, and the state of Louisiana. In addition, several references to family oral histories are included, many of which have been communicated from one generation to the next over the past 150 years or so.

Of singular importance in this work are numerous references to slave baptisms performed under the directions of the various priests who pastored St. Paul the Apostle Catholic Church during its early history in central Louisiana. Their persistence in recording the birth and baptism dates, the names of the slave mothers of the children being baptized, and their godparents, is of enormous historical importance (A. R. Ducote).

Table of Contents

Introduction

In this book, we will explore some of the historical events that have occurred over the past 200 years in North America, the state of Louisiana, the parish of Avoyelles and the town of Mansura. This will allow us to get some perspective on how these events impacted the lives of everyone living in Mansura today and why the racial barriers are just beginning to weaken and, hopefully, disappear.

FIGURE 1. VIEW OF L'EGLISE STREET IN MANSURA (HUNTER AND ROSENTHAL)

A second book in this series will go into much more details regarding the family histories of several specific African-American families in the Mansura area.

Mansura, Louisiana (Wikipedia-Staff) is one of nine incorporated areas within the parish of Avoyelles and is about 4 miles south of Marksville, the parish seat of government. It is a typical Louisiana small town, located near the geographical center of the state. The town lies on mostly flat land, with the Mississippi River about 40 miles to the northeast, the Red River about 15 miles to the west, and generally flat plains and marshland to the south. The area between Mansura and the Mississippi River includes large areas of swampland, whose denizens include alligators, a variety of poisonous and non-poisonous snakes, numerous types of fish and wild animals, and some of the most aggressive and deadly insects around.

Mansura's population in the year 2010 was about 1419 (Decuir). It is a town whose economy, for well over 200 years, has been supported by the huge cotton, corn, sugar cane and sweet potato fields that stretched in every direction, as far as the eyes could see. The large expanses of pecan, oak, cypress and pine trees provided valuable raw material to be converted into boards and other wood products or were the sources of pecans and other nuts that were harvested and shipped to other states and countries for use in holiday pies and for roasting.

Mansura is a Louisiana French town located right on the northern edge of Cajun Country (Avoyelles). , It was first inhabited by the French colonists and later, by the Acadians, after they fled from Nova Scotia (Faragher). The town's original site was settled in the first half of the 19th century by a few French citizens. They found the land to be similar to some areas of central and southern France and likely to be perfect for the new cotton industry (Saucier). Later, the expansion of slavery and the arrival of the Acadians caused the area to experience rapid growth, especially as a farming center. By the beginning of the Civil War, the area boasted some of the largest slave-holding plantations in the state (Census).

When the Civil War ended and the slaves were set free, many fled as far away from their old plantation homes as they could (Warren). Others, either due to physical or economic impairment, fear, nostalgia, or other reasons, remained nearby, often returning to work on the same plantations where they had been enslaved. Over the next century, despite the harsh treatment they suffered under the Black Codes (H. Staff) and the Jim Crow laws (B. H. Staff), the majority of African-Americans remained near their old homes.

By the 1930's, most of the older residents, both black and white, still spoke the Cajun French patois, once so pervasive in the area, as their primary language. The younger folks, especially the young African-American citizens, rarely practiced this second language, thus, causing its continued decline.

Most folks, both black and white, living in the area, share a love for foods such as *cochon de lait* (Roasted milk pig), gumbo, boudin, jambalaya, okra, and sauce piquant, dishes that reflected their French, Cajun, and African traditions. And, of course, all share a love for the abundant areas to hunt and fish nearby, many living on daily diets of rabbits, coons, quails, ducks, perch, garfish, catfish, turtles, and alligators. More recently, the tremendous growth of the crawfish industry has demonstrated to the world how tasty some of the exotic Louisiana foods can be.

FIGURE 2. POSTER FROM MANSURA COCHON DE LAIT FESTIVAL (AD)

Despite these common cultural traditions, Mansura, unfortunately, consists of two worlds that exist culturally and physically close but, in reality, worlds that, racially, socially and politically, remain miles apart.

Part I. Slavery: Where It All Began

FIGURE 3. THE SLAVE TRADE (BIARD)

Slavery, as it was practiced in the southern U.S., was a very difficult situation for the millions of African-American people who endured it. In most cases, it was very intense and up-close for the average African-American. The roughly 4 million, who survived, developed severe emotional and psychological scars that have persisted, and will likely persist, for many generations (Painter).

As a result of poor record keeping, deliberate concealment and a callous lack of regard for the value of maintaining connections to their African past, it is extremely difficult to connect most living African-Americans to their ancestral homes and families in Africa. Sadly, even after considerable research time and effort spent, a typical African-American family tree only begins after the Civil War.

This lack of historical records, coupled with the common views that slaves were less than humans, allowed many misconceptions regarding the intelligence, desire for freedom, courage under fire, and human aspirations of the typical slave. Most slaves were considered dumb, lazy, shiftless and completely lacking in most human qualities such as love, family devotion, self-discipline and the ability to plan for the future.

Thus, slaves were subjected to the harshest treatment at the hands of the Slave Holders, their surrogates and local authorities. Beatings and other forms of torture were common. Only the monetary value of an individual slave prevented them from being murdered more often. In most cases, the rationalization was that these lower species, just like the farm animals, needed hard discipline to force them to perform the most menial tasks.

Sadly, the perpetrators of this horrible institution went unpunished, at least in this world, and died feeling that they had done nothing wrong. In fact, many perversely believed that holding black people in bondage was doing them a great service and that inflicting physical punishment and restricting their movement made them more productive beings.

Chapter 1. The Origins of Slavery in Mansura

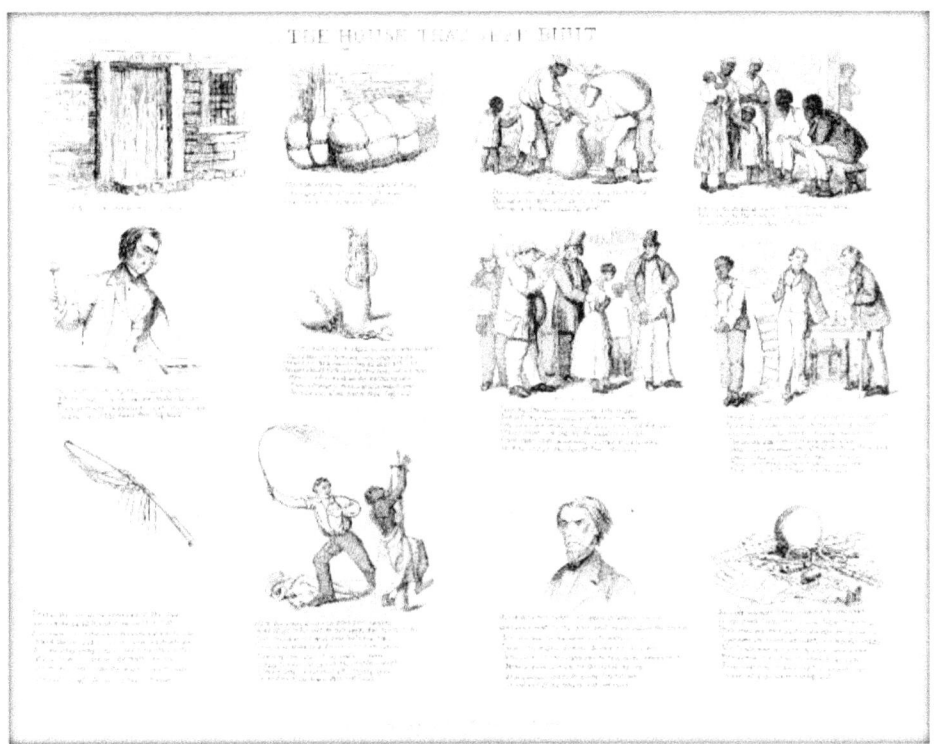

FIGURE 4. THE HOUSE THAT JEFF (JEFFERSON DAVIS) BUILT[1], CIVIL WAR CARTOON (JOHNSON)

Early Slavery: The French and Spaniards - The area that contains the current parish of Avoyelles was first settled by the French explorers beginning in the early 1700's (Mayeux and Decuir). Prior to that time, several indigenous tribes of Native Americans were existent in the area and likely had been there for several centuries.

During the French colonial period in Louisiana from 1699 to 1763, numerous attempts were made to enslave the Native American population, resulting in near complete destruction of their civilizations.

---

[1] Read like nursery rhyme "The House That Jack Built."

The French introduced African slaves to Louisiana in 1710 (Midlo Hall). Eventually, the number of enslaved Africans working to develop the land reached several thousands, with a tremendous loss of life due to disease and inhumane working conditions.

Figure 5 shows residents of the Congo around 1900. This is one of the areas on West Africa (i.e. Senegal, Sierra Leone, Congo and Angola) where many of the slaves arriving in Louisiana were born, lived and were captured.

FIGURE 5. CHURCH GROUP IN BONGANDANGA, DISTRICT OF CONGO, CA. 1900-1915 (UNKNOWN)

The new slaves were first taken to some of the islands in the Caribbeans, where, in many cases, they were "Broken" and forced to accept their enslavement. When they arrived in Louisiana, most still possessed their native culture, including language, religion and political and moral beliefs but with little freedom to practice them.

The enslavement practices by the French began the process of cultural destruction and assimilation of the Africans into the French culture. Some early evidence for this can be seen in the names listed on the early slave ship manifests (Ellis and Halbert) versus the names given to the new slaves. For example, some original African male names were *Namese, Naquay, Cambah, Canga, Gomar, Macosa, Maddee, Momo, Ocara* and *Sabbo*. Some African female names were *Aballa, Cherombo, Colluo, Fata, Hasema, Henna, Hyena, Imbarfoo, Imboeleh, Imbokay, Tumah, Yehley, and Yeowah*.

However, records of slaves being sold in the North America rarely show such African names (See **Figure 6**). Instead, the slaves were listed with names such as Hannah, Rachal, Milo, Jean Baptiste, Charles and Mary (Martin-Quiatte).

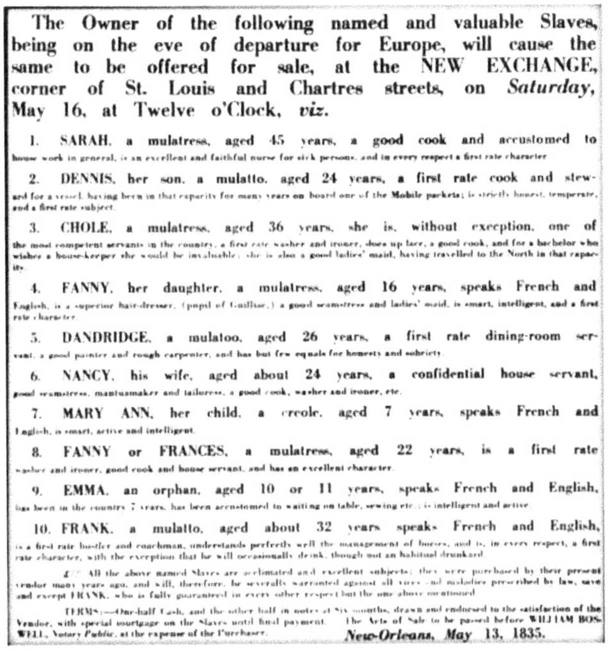

The Owner of the following named and valuable Slaves, being on the eve of departure for Europe, will cause the same to be offered for sale, at the NEW EXCHANGE, corner of St. Louis and Chartres streets, on *Saturday*, May 16, at Twelve o'Clock, *viz.*

1. SARAH, a mulatress, aged 45 years, a good cook and accustomed to house work in general, is an excellent and faithful nurse for sick persons, and in every respect a first rate character.

2. DENNIS, her son, a mulatto, aged 24 years, a first rate cook and steward for a vessel, having been in that capacity for many years on board one of the Mobile packets; is strictly honest, temperate, and a first rate subject.

3. CHOLE, a mulatress, aged 36 years, she is, without exception, one of the most competent servants in the country, a first rate washer and ironer, does up lace, a good cook, and for a bachelor who wishes a house-keeper she would be invaluable; she is also a good ladies' maid, having travelled to the North in that capacity.

4. FANNY, her daughter, a mulatress, aged 16 years, speaks French and English, is a superior hair-dresser, (pupil of Guillioe,) a good seamstress and ladies' maid, is smart, intelligent, and a first rate character.

5. DANDRIDGE, a mulatoo, aged 26 years, a first rate dining-room servant, a good painter and rough carpenter, and has but few equals for honesty and sobriety.

6. NANCY, his wife, aged about 24 years, a confidential house servant, good seamstress, mantuamaker and tailoress, a good cook, washer and ironer, etc.

7. MARY ANN, her child, a creole, aged 7 years, speaks French and English, is smart, active and intelligent.

8. FANNY or FRANCES, a mulatress, aged 22 years, is a first rate washer and ironer, good cook and house servant, and has an excellent character.

9. EMMA, an orphan, aged 10 or 11 years, speaks French and English, has been in the country 7 years, has been accustomed to waiting on table, sewing etc.; is intelligent and active.

10. FRANK, a mulatto, aged about 32 years speaks French and English, is a first rate hostler and coachman, understands perfectly well the management of horses, and is, in every respect, a first rate character, with the exception that he will occasionally drink, though not an habitual drunkard.

All the above named Slaves are acclimated and excellent subjects; they were purchased by their present vendor many years ago, and will, therefore, be severally warranted against all vices and maladies prescribed by law, save and except FRANK, who is fully guaranteed in every other respect but the one above mentioned.

TERMS:—One-half Cash, and the other half in notes at Six months, drawn and endorsed to the satisfaction of the Vendor, with special mortgage on the Slaves until final payment. The Acts of Sale to be passed before WILLIAM BOSWELL, Notary *Public*, at the expense of the Purchaser.

New-Orleans, May 13, 1835.

FIGURE 6. AD FOR NEW ORLEANS SLAVE SALE, 1835 (C. ARTIST)

By the end of the Civil War, most African names and their languages had been wiped out. Only a few indications of the African culture, such as food and traces of religion, remained.

For & in consideration of the sum of one dollar to me in hand paid by Jared Williams Junr the Rect whereof I do hereby acknowledge I have contracted & sold and by these presents do contract & sell and deliver to the said Jared Williams Junr one Negro Woman named Nancy and the increase of her body which said negro woman nancy I do hereby warrant and forever defend by these presents to the said Jared Williams Junr and his heirs Executors administrators and assigns against myself my heirs executors and administrators and all and every other person or persons whatsoever, In Witness whereof I have hereunto set my hand & seal this 27th Day of June in the year of our Lord 1816

Signed & sealed in Presence of Thos L. Williams

Jane E Williams (Seal)

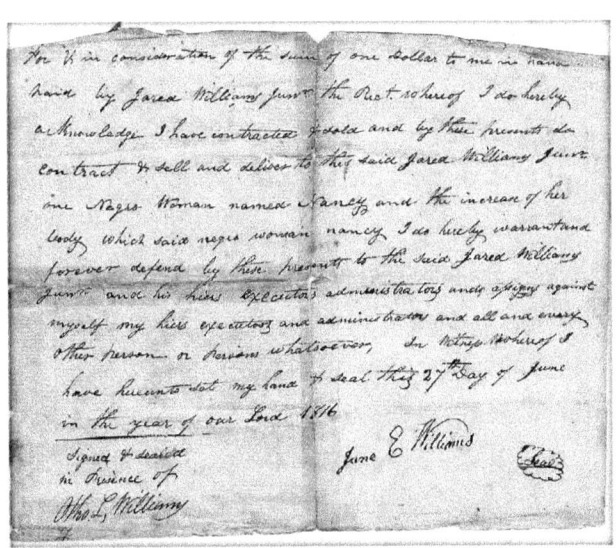

FIGURE 7. 1816 BILL OF SALE FOR A SLAVE WOMAN NAMED "NANCY" (W. C. STAFF)

The French attempted to enforce slavery in Louisiana with an army that was greatly undermanned for the task and little real control of the slaves existed (Midlo Hall). In fact, many slaves ran away and went to live among the Native American tribes, often intermarrying and producing families of so-called "Black Indians" (Katz).

Similarly, the French soldiers, stationed so far from home without female companionship, often took black female slaves as common law wives (Midlo Hall). The children of these relationships were the ancestors of the large mulatto population that still resides throughout the state, especially in the southern part. In one area, known as the Attakapas region, including St. Landry parish, many of these bi-racial descendants of French soldiers were willed land by their white parents making them legal landholders. This entitled them many of the same rights as the white citizens, including suing and testifying in court, free movement without the hated passes, and even the rights to own slaves, which some did (Gates).

Under Spanish rule African slavery in Louisiana surged during the period from 1763 to 1803 (Faber and Chamberlain). During that period, largely due to the newly expanded Louisiana economy, imported slave numbers increased 10-fold to a high of nearly 29,000.

The Spanish government operated differently from the French and allowed slightly more freedom to the slaves. This included more open cultural expressions such as music and language, the ability of abused slaves to file complaints against their Slave Holders and *coartacion* (manumission), where slaves who earned wages from side jobs, could purchase their own freedom. This new atmosphere allowed as many as 2-4 percent of the slave population to become manumitted each year.

Eventually, this led to the development of a significant population of *gen de couleur libres* or Free People of Color (FPC), totaling around 1500, especially in the New Orleans and Attakapas areas. Although mentioned on specific occasions, the general histories of the FPC's, mulattoes, quadroons, etc. are outside the scope of this work.

Over time, the Mansura area remained sparsely populated, although actual numbers are not available. The Avoyelles Post (Louisiana), a Spanish military post, was established around 1780 near the Prehistoric Indian Park on Old River, supposedly to protect the Avoyelles tribe from other nearby enemies.

In 1785, the census of the Avoyelles Post and its surrounding jurisdictional area provided the first documented evidence of the presence of slaves in what is now Avoyelles Parish (Tate and Gremillion). It showed the area to contain 138 Whites, 101 Native Americans and 46 slaves.

U.S. Slavery - It was not until the Louisiana Purchase in 1803 and the new, much stricter control by the U.S. government, that slavery really grew (Slavery in America). Between 1774 and 1804, all of the Northern states had abolished slavery. However, it remained solid throughout the U.S. South. The U.S. Congress abolished the international slave trade in 1808 but did nothing to end the domestic trade and the numbers of slaves in the U.S. tripled to over 4 million by 1860.

During that same period of slavery growth in the U.S., many of the European countries that had originated African slavery were beginning to abandon this practice (Slavery in America). In fact, England, beginning in 1807, and despite it having transported the largest number of slave to the Americas, set up a blockade of the African coast to prevent passage of the slave ships (Lewis-Jones). Notably, the U.S. was one of the few nations refusing to honor the British blockade. By 1833, the British Parliament formally adopted legislation outlawing slavery within the British Empire.

FIGURE 8. 1853 SLAVE TRADER ADVERTISEMENT (TALBOTT)

The development of the cotton gin stimulated conversion of Southern U.S. farming away from sugar and indigo to the more lucrative cotton. Cotton farming was quickly tied to the demand for more slaves and New Orleans soon became one of the main slave trading centers in the country (**See Figures 8 and 9).**

FIGURE 9. 1850S NEW ORLEANS SLAVE MARKET (UNKNOWN)

The high demand for slaves, especially in the southern U.S., created huge increases in the price of an individual slave, as shown in **Figure 8**. To avoid the British blockade, many slave traders resorted to illegal "blockade running" and were willing to risk being arrested by the British navy because the potential monetary rewards were so great. If they happened to be caught with a shipload of illegal human cargo, the "cargo" was simply dumped overboard, thus destroying the evidence (Krikler).

FIGURE 10. ZONG MASSACRE (UNKNOWN)

Slavery in Avoyelles Parish - Mansura's significance to African-American history is, in part, documented in a large collection of church records belonging to St. Paul the Apostle Catholic Church of Mansura (Church). St. Paul's collection includes baptismal and death records for a large number of Catholics, including Blacks, Whites, and Native Americans, dating back to the early 1800s (Church). Those records contain names of the child being baptized, their mother, their Slave Holder and their godparents, as well as their dates of birth and baptism. This, when combined with other records and oral histories, can provide a reasonably good start to identifying African-American ancestors and, possibly their families. In a few cases, the plantation where they were held can be identified.

In addition to the St. Paul records, researchers into African-American genealogy and family history now have access to the United States Census records, public records of transactions involving slaves, slave ship manifests, the Louisiana Brides Book (La Cour) and a number of other family histories focused on Avoyelles Parish residents.

Below are some examples from **Appendix A** of publicly recorded transactions where slaves were purchased, usually in New Orleans, and brought to Avoyelles Parish by some of the local Slave Holders (Saucier), (Notary).

- Three slaves purchased by **Dominique Coco** of Mansura. These included a 20 year-old male named **Baptiste**; a 30 year-old black man purchased from John Brown in New Orleans for $600 on May 24, 1808 and an "Unknown" slave who was listed as being from the Congo;
- An 18 year-old black man named "**Magloire**", born in the "Congo" and who spoke Benue-Congo, was purchased by **Pierre Normand** of Mansura from Louis Esnault in New Orleans for $500 on May 7, 1812;
- Eleven slaves was purchased in a group from Jesse Benton by **Pierre Lemoine** of Mansura. One of these slaves was a 21 year-ole female whose name was **Dixie** and who was described as a "Quadroon"[2]. The others were: **Solomon** (8), **Adam** (21), **Sara** (13), **Charlotte** (21), **Jack** (4), **Petis** (2), **Nancy** (20), **Benny** (4) and Dixie's 2 children, **Jack** and **Charles**;
- Another group of 9 slaves was purchased by **Pierre Lemoine** of Mansura from the widow of George Baron, another local Slave Holder. This group was described as speaking the "Mande" language and coming from "Bamana"[3].

Other public records detail the buying, selling and inheritance of slaves by local farmers as well as the number of slaves held by various Slave Holders (Notary).

---

[2] "Quadroons" were mulattoes whose four grandparents consisted of a minimum of three white and no more than one black persons.
[3] The **Bambara (Bambara**: **Bamana** or Banmana) are a Mandé people living in west Africa, primarily in Mali but also in Guinea, Burkina Faso and Senegal - Wikipedia

By the beginning of the Civil War in 1860, Avoyelles Parish had become home to some of the largest slave-holding plantations in the state with several holding over 100 people in captivity (Blake). Its 7,185 black people were held in captivity by 521 Slave Holders with 33 Slave Holders holding 2,684 people (37% of the total). Prominent among those Slave Holders was **Dominique Coco**, of Mansura, who held 107 black people in captivity (U. C. Staff).

Some of today's most prominent white families in Avoyelles Parish began with their slave holding ancestors. Some of these will be discussed later in this work.

Chapter 2. Living in Slavery

The conditions under which slaves in central Louisiana (and the rest of the South) lived were nothing short of hell, as is so well described by Northrup (Northrup) . In addition to the terrible treatment at the hands of unmerciful and inhuman Slave Holders and their overseers, were the terrible physical conditions. Most slaves had to endure swarms of insects such as gnats, flies, and wasps, and, all the while, avoiding potentially fatal bites from cottonmouth moccasins, rattlesnakes and alligators.

FIGURE 11. WILSON CHINN, BRANDED SLAVE FROM LOUISIANA (KIMBALL)

Homes for slaves in Louisiana, like anywhere else, were not much more than shabbily-constructed, floorless shacks that had little or no furniture other than a place to lie down on the dirt floor or build a fire to cook their meager meals which usually consisted of some sort of corn meal bread eaten with fat back.

FIGURE 12. SLAVE CABINS AT THE AUDUBON STATE HISTORIC SITE IN LOUISIANA (CAR)

An especially interesting set of documents and audiotapes describing the daily lives of slaves in the U.S. are the **WPA Slave Narratives** (Writers), (Yetman). Although hundreds of books and magazine articles were published about the miserable lives of the slaves during the antebellum period of the U.S., most were lost or forgotten following the Civil War and during the first quarter of the 20th century.

As part of his plan to help move the country out of the Great Depression during the 1940s, President Franklin Roosevelt supported the use of hundreds of unemployed writers who were asked to interview as many surviving former slaves as possible. They were able to conduct over 2300 first-person accounts and produce over 500 black and white photographs of former slaves. Their stories give a much more personal view of slavery in the U.S. and will be referenced several times in this work.

Mary Reynolds, a native Louisianan, who was interviewed for the WPA Writers Project when over 100 years old, described her life in great detail (Writers). She claims to have been born during the 1830's on the Kilpatrick plantation near Black River, Louisiana, northeast of Marksville. Several of her comments about her life as a slave are included here as transcribed by the WPA interviewers.

FIGURE 13. MARY REYNOLDS DURING HER WPA INTERVIEW (WRITERS)

In many cases, slaves worked long hours from first light until well past dark doing backbreaking labor while enduring relentless whippings at the hands of their masters, overseers, and public officials such as policemen. Mary said,

> *"The conch shell blowed afore daylight and all hands better git out for roll call or Solomon bust the door down and get them out. It was work hard, git beatin's and half fed. They brung the victuals and water to the fields on a slide pulled by a old mule. Plenty times they was only a half barrel water and it stale and hot, for all us n----rs on the hottes' days. Mostly we ate pickled pork and corn bread and peas and beans and taters. They never was as much as we needed."* - Mary Reynolds (Writers)

She described the brutal work conditions, beatings and physical and psychological torture that have produced a permanent set of emotional and mental scars persisting over several generations.

> *"Slavery was the worst days was ever seed in the world. They was things past tellin', but I got the scars on my old body to show to this day. I seed worse than what happened to me. I seed them put the men and women in the stock with they hands screwed down through holes in the board and they*

feets tied together and they naked behinds to the world. Solomon the [sic] overseer beat them with a big whip and massa look on. The n----rs better not stop in the fields when they hear them yellin'. They cut the flesh most to the bones and some they was when they taken them out of stock and put them on the beds, they never got up again." - Mary Reynolds (Writers)

The death of a slave was of little consequence to the plantation owners except for the financial loss:

"When a n----r died they let his folks come out the fields to see him afore he died. They buried him the same day, take a big plank and bust it with a ax in the middle nough to bend it back, and put the dead n----r in betwixt it. They'd cart them down to the graveyard on the place and not bury them deep nough that buzzards wouldn't come circlin' round. N----rs mourns now, but in them days they wasn't no time for mournin'." - Mary Reynolds (Writers)

FIGURE 14. INSIDE OF A SLAVE CABIN (MRSBETHBARTON)

Free People of Color (FPC) living in Louisiana lived lives not much better than slaves (Midlo Hall). The *Code Noir* (French), originally used by the French military during their occupation of the state of Louisiana, severely restricted their lives and kept them at the mercy of any white person they might encounter. Their homes and diet were also not much better than that of a typical slave.

Chapter 3. Records of Slavery in Avoyelles Parish

As mentioned earlier, public and private records of slave purchases, sales, arrests, baptisms and funerals provide significant historical records on the African-Americans held captive as slaves in and around Mansura. However, it must be pointed out that these records do not represent anywhere near the entire slave population of Avoyelles Parish.

For example, relatively few slaves appear in the local public records for Avoyelles Parish while the U.S. Slave Schedules associated with the census, especially 1850 and 1860, show a much more accurate and larger number (Dollarhide). Unless these slaves were bought, sold or were arrested for some crime, their names do not appear in the public records (Saucier).

The majority of slaves, once brought to a given plantation, spent the rest of their lives there, rarely allowed to leave the property and come into contact with the legal authorities. For those who did, it was usually accompanied by either the Slave Holder, his trusted overseer or other employees, or while carrying a pass signed by the Slave Holder.

Also, the Slave Holder or their overseer were more likely to mete out any punishment for infractions or rule breaking done by the slaves with no involvement by public officials, hence, no public records were ever created. Most slaves chose their "wives" themselves or were paired together for breeding purposes, again with no public records.

The situation for the slaves and Slave Holders appearing in the St. Paul baptismal and burial records were similar to the public records. Once more, relatively few of the actual slaves or Slave Holders were listed (Church). Three possible reasons for this are: (1) not all Slave Holders in Avoyelles were Catholics, (2) not all Catholic Slave Holders were dedicated enough to their religion to make sure that all of their slaves were baptized and (3) most of the larger plantations were located some distance from the church, even as far away as on the Red River, making it difficult to have the slaves baptized unless the priest happened to visit those plantations.

Nevertheless, for those slaves listed in either set of records, the information provided was invaluable.

Public Slave Records – As mentioned earlier, the first records showing slaves in Avoyelles Parish appeared in the 1785 census of the population of the Avoyelles Post while under Spanish control (Tate and Gremillion). Additional records covering the end of the Spanish period, the brief second French colonial period and the first decade of the U.S. showing transactions involving slaves are shown in **Appendix A**.

The 1810 U.S. Census of Avoyelles Parish, Louisiana showed a total of 404 slaves (U. C. Bureau). Only the number of slaves, not defined by name, gender or age group, was shown. The largest Slave Holders in the Parish were: Pierre Lemoine (45 slaves); Alex Plauche' (28 slaves); Madam (?) Holmes (16 slaves); Joseph Joffrion (15 slaves); Alexander Phries (14 slaves) and Francois Bordelon (13 slaves).

The 1820 U.S. census for Avoyelles Parish listed: 782 White Males; 664 White Females; 422 Male Slaves; 360 Female Slaves and 25 Free People of Color (U. C. Bureau). In this case, the slave population was divided into males and females, but no names or ages were given.

In the 1830 U.S. census for Avoyelles Parish, there were 1117 White Males; 997 White Females; 678 Male Slaves; 655 Female Slaves; 21 Male FPC and 14 Female FPC (C. Bureau). Some of the larger Slave Holders operating in or near what is now Mansura were: Pierre Normand & Son (40 slaves); Dominique Coco, Jr. (35 slaves); Francois Bordelon (37 slaves); Lucien Joffrion (28 slaves); Pierre Goudeau (27 slaves) and Francois Tournier (22 slaves).

The Catholic Church -The Catholic Church began to take root in Louisiana during the French and Spanish colonial periods (Fortier and McLoughlin). The Catholic religion was central to their lives (Mayeux and Decuir). For the most part, few actual church buildings or parishes actually existed during that period and the priests generally traveled from settlement to settlement administering to the faithful. It was during the U.S. period that the Catholic Church began to reach some level of stability in Louisiana. St. Paul the Apostle Catholic Church began as sort of a circuit mission, with the priests servicing an area that extended North and South from below Alexandria to North Louisiana and from West to East from Natchitoches to the area around Opelousas. Eventually, the church found permanent residence in Avoyelles Parish near Hydropolis and then in the town of Mansura.

St. Paul's priests were very diligent in providing baptism and funeral services to all Catholics in the area, including the slaves belonging to Catholic slaveholders. These records began around 1824. Since most slaves were not allowed the freedom to travel away from the plantations, even on Sundays, their attendance at mass and participation in the rites of Confirmation, Penance, Communion, or Matrimony rarely occurred.

On many plantations, self-righteous plantation owners often conducted some sort of non-Catholic religious service for the slaves on Sunday. In many cases, the slaves became religious leaders of their own gatherings. This is likely the reason for the eventual rise of non-Catholic religions, such as Baptists and African Methodist Episcopal, as the preferred religions for many ex-slaves in Louisiana (Church).

St. Paul Church Records - The information in the St. Paul Baptism Records (Church) is a listing of the children (and a few adults) who were baptized at what is now called St. Paul the Apostle Catholic Church during the first half of the 19th century. Also included are slaves who were documented to have been baptized at St. Paul's in Mansura between 1831 and 1845 and believed to have lived on plantations in or near the current town of Mansura.

While the public records (e.g. U.S. Census records) only gives the number of slaves on a given plantation or, in some cases, provide the ages and genders of the slaves being documented, the St. Paul records provide the slave children's first names, their mother's (and sometime, father's) first names, the slaves' birthdays and baptism dates and the first names of the slave's godparents.

The following discussion of the Slave Holders, the Slave Mothers and Godparents, is based on the information in the St. Paul records:

- **The Slave Holders** - An example of how the Slave Holders can be studied from the information in the St. Paul's records is shown in **Table 1** below:

SLAVE NAME	BIRTH	MOTHER	SLAVE HOLDER	BAPTISM DATE	GODFATHER	GODMOTHER
Bastien	19 may 1836	Victoire	Felix Marcot	5 mar 1837	Jacques (slave)	Rosette (slave)
Philogene	oct 1837	Seraphine	Felix Marcot	3 dec 1837	Jean Baptiste (slave)	Rosette (slave)
Clarisse	16 apr 1845	Rose	Felix Marcot	7 sep 1845		
Eloise	aug 1837	Josephine	Felix Marcot	3 dec 1837	Jean Pierre (slave)	Louise (slave)

TABLE 1. SLAVES HELD BY FELIX MARCOT (CHURCH)

In **Table 1**, the Slave Holder is **Felix Marcot**, a relatively minor Slave Holder who lived near Mansura and baptized 4 slaves (**Bastien**, **Philogene**, **Clarisse** and **Eloise**) between 1836 and 1845 (L. Bordelon). The slave godparents (**Jacques** and **Rosette**) were being held by Felix Marcot, while **Jean Baptiste** was being held by **Paulin Mayeux**, **Jean Pierre** by **M. Dorseneau** and **Louise** by **Marcelin Bordelon**. Also, **Philogene** and **Eloise** were baptized on the same day. No godparents were listed for **Clarisse**.

Another example of the information that can be obtained is the case of Pierre L'Eglise shown in **Table 2**. Pierre was a very well-known local plantation owner and Slave Holder who, at various times, owned land south of the Red River, in Cocoville and southwest of Moreauville (Robertson). Pierre is listed as the Slave Holder of 8 children being baptized at St. Paul during the 1830's:

SLAVE NAME	BIRTH	MOTHER	SLAVE HOLDER	BAPTISM DATE	GODFATHER	GODMOTHER
Virginie	1836	Rose	Pierre L'Eglise	3 feb 1839	George (slave)	Jule (slave)
Jean	3 jul 1832	Nancy	Pierre L'Eglise	22 dec 1833	Augustine (slave)	Rosette (slave)
Cyrile	nov 1835	Nancy	Pierre L'Eglise	4 mar 1838	Basile (FMC)	Divine (slave)
Octavia	1837	Marie	Pierre L'Eglise	3 feb 1839	Miss (slave)	Elise (slave)
Adolphe	sep 1836	Marie	Pierre L'Eglise	5 mar 1837	Claude (slave)	Josephine (slave)
Kaisy	nov 1838	Marie	Pierre L'Eglise	25 apr 1839	Louis (slave)	
Etienne	jun 1832	Justine	Pierre L'Eglise	15 dec 1833	Augustine (slave)	Artemise (slave)
Donatien	apr 1838	Elisabeth	Pierre L'Eglise	3 feb 1839	Usieque (slave)	Marthe (slave)

TABLE 2. SLAVES HELD BY PIERRE L'EGLISE (CHURCH)

In this case, the slave mothers, **Nancy** and **Marie**, appear 2 and 3 times, respectively, suggesting that they had, at least, that number of children. Of the godparents, 9 were slaves held by Pierre L'Eglise, two (**Claude** and **Josephine**) were slaves held by **Felix Marcot**, one (**Divine**) was held by **George Baron**, one (**Elise**) was held by **Margueritte Radiguez** and one (**Basile**) was a Free Person of Color.

- **The Slave Mothers** – If the information in the St. Paul records is sorted for the slave mothers, some additional information can be found, as in the case of Julien Jules Goudeau, shown in **Table 3**:

SLAVE NAME	BIRTH	MOTHER	SLAVE HOLDER	BAPTISM DATE	GODFATHER	GODMOTHER
Arthemise	24 jul 1833	Marianne	Julien Goudeau	26 oct 1836	Basile (slave)	Severine, FWC
Francois	4 jun 1835	Marianne	Julien Goudeau	25 oct 1836	Coser (FMC)	Clementine (slave)
Theodise	16 dec 1831	Marianne	Julien Goudeau	7 feb 1833	Louis (FMC)	Josephine (slave)
Jules	27 may 1843	Marianne	Julien Godeau	7 may 1845		
Julie	27 may 1843	Marianne	Julien Godeau	7 may 1845		

TABLE 3. SLAVE MOTHERS HELD BY JULIAN GOUDEAU (Church)

It can be seen here that a slave mother by the name of **Marianne** baptized a total of 5 children between 1831 and 1843. Two of the five children were the twins, **Jules** and **Julie**. Also, three of the godparents shown (**Coser, Louis** and **Severine**) were Free People of Color. The three slaves acting as godparents (**Basile, Clementine,** and **Josephine**) were slaves of the Goudeau family.

Another interesting slave mother case is that of **Julie**, shown in **Table 4**. Julie was held captive by **Pierre Michel Goudeau**, the brother of Julien Jules Goudeau:

SLAVE NAME	BIRTH	MOTHER	SLAVE HOLDER	BAPTISM DATE	GODFATHER	GODMOTHER
Xesiovie (sic)	22 apr 1830	Julie	Pierre Goudeau	7 feb 1833	Vignerasse Goudeau	Marceline Decuir
Joachim	25 jan 1834	Julie	Pierre Goudeau	25 oct 1836	Henry (slave)	Pauline (slave)
Jerome	8 May 1828	Julie	Pierre Goudeau	11 Jan 1829	Louis Goudeau, fils	Sophie Aymond
Hortance	2 apr 1832	Julie	Pierre Goudeau	7 feb 1833	Charles Moreau	Claris Godeau
Eugene	1826	Julie	Pierre Goudeau	11 Jan 1829	Valery Moreau	Elise Rabalais
Eloise	2 apr 1836	Julie	Pierre Goudeau	25 oct 1836	Pierre Goudeau	jeune & Claris Goudeau

TABLE 4. JULIE THE SLAVE MOTHER (CHURCH)

Julie appears to have given birth to and baptized at least 6 children over the period from 1826 to 1836. Considering the fact that an average slave was worth about $800, Julie has to have been an asset to the Pierre Goudeau plantation. A possible indication of this is that all but 2 (Henry and Pauline) of her children's godparents were white.

Some other examples, where slave mothers were sorted and grouped together are included below. While it is possible for a given Slave Holder to have had more than one female slave with the same name, it would seem more likely, at least in most cases, that each slave had a unique name, e.g. Celestine, on a given plantation. That being the case, then it becomes possible to link a given slave mother to her children on some of the plantations and consider that group to be a sort of "**Slave Family**". Some examples of Slave Families are as follows:

- **Louise** (Held by Hippolite Couvillion) was listed as the mother of 2 children: **Auguste** (Born 8 Apr. 1828) and **Michel** (Born 6 Sep 1831);
- **Manette** (Held by Francois Tournier) was listed as the mother of 2 children: **Honoroe'** (Born in October, 1832) and **Paulin** (Born 1 Sep 1835);
- **Rosalie** (Held by Jean H. Boyer) was listed as the mother of twin girls: **Victoire** and **Victorine** (Born 28 Oct 1832);
- **Aymee or Ayme** (Held by Laurent Normand) was listed as the mother of 2 children: **Celeste** (Born 1 Mar 1839) and **William** (Born 26 Oct 1832). **See Later for more on Aymee/Ayme**.
- **Paulin or Pauline** (Held by Martin Dufour) was listed as the mother of 2 children: **Clementine** (Born 20 Sep 1835) and **Xavier** (Born in September, 1837);
- **Marie** (Held by Pierre Normand) was listed as the mother of 3 children: **Frederic** (Born 11 Nov 1838), **Marcelin** (Born in 1843), and **Paulin** (Born 3 Aug 1837);
- **Marguerite** (Held by Pierre Normand) was listed as the mother of 2 twin girls: **Julie** and **Julienne** (Born 21 Oct 1836);
- **Felecite'** (Held by Pierre Normand) was listed as the mother of 2 children: **Jean** (Born 11 Aug 1832) and **Ursin** (Born 16 Jan 1838). **(See Book II in this set for more on Felecite' and her descendants)**.

- **The Godparents** – The people listed in the roles of "Godparents" in the St. Paul Records are *a)* additional adults living on the plantations where the children being baptized were being held, *b)* slaves from other nearby plantations, *c)* the Slave Holder, *d)* members of the Slave Holder's family, *e)* other whites living in the area and *f)* a few People of Color.

In the Catholic Church, the godfather (a.k.a. *Paŕan*) and the godmother (a.k.a. *Maŕan*) are considered to have major roles in a child's life. The church's expectation is that, should the parents of the child die or be unable to provide the child with a proper Catholic education and upbringing, then the godparents are obliged to assume those duties. That being the case, the godparents are often considered closer to the child than other relatives.

It is possible that some of the slave godfathers in the St. Paul records could be the actual fathers of the slave child being baptized. There is no evidence to prove this, however, since rarely was the father or other male relatives of a slave identified.

In any case, there is so little information on the slave population that being able to identify one more black man or woman is very important.

- **Free People of Color (FPC's) in Avoyelles Parish -** Despite what many may not realize today, there were quite a number of Free People of Color (FPC's) residing in Avoyelles Parish before the start of the Civil War. In the 1860 census for Avoyelles Parish, there were 5904 Whites, 7185 slaves and 74 FPC's (Blake). In **Chapter 5**, we will go into more details regarding this group of people.

Chapter 4. The Mansura Slave Holders

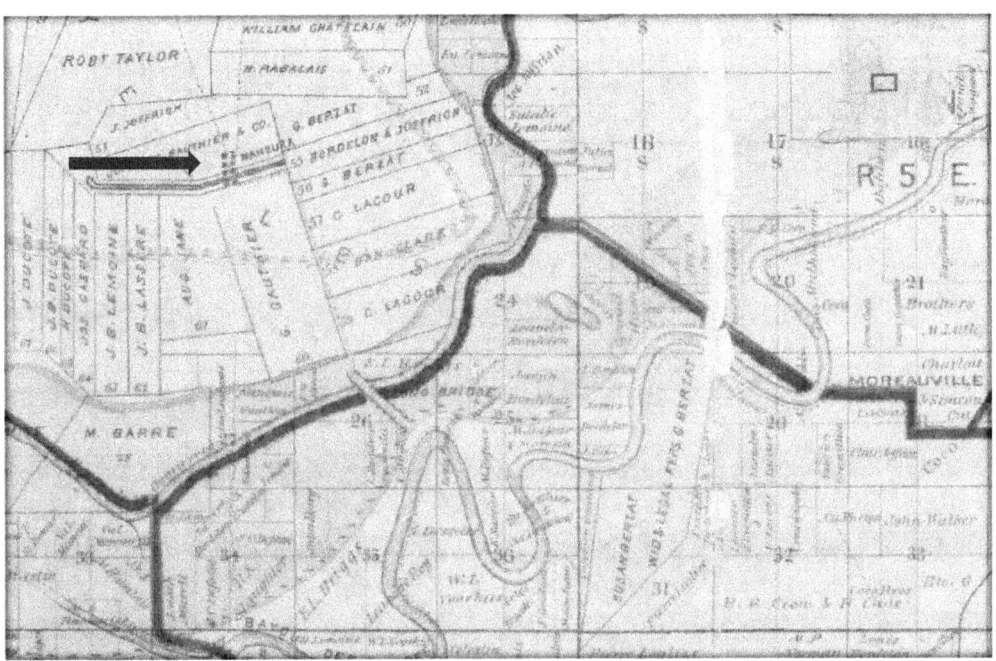

FIGURE 15. PLANTATION MAP OF AREA NEAR MANSURA (ROBERTSON)

In order to understand how this terrible institution known as American Slavery was able to wind itself around the branches of our "free" society and go unchallenged for centuries, it is important to provide a bit more information on some of the more notable Slave Holders who plied their trades in or near the town of Mansura, Louisiana. These were some of the people who considered themselves guardians of liberty and, yet, actively used force to deny liberty to others.

This discussion is especially important since many of the current African-American residents of Mansura and Avoyelles, as well as their relatives residing in other locations, likely had ancestors who were held on the plantations operated by these individuals. Their lives and those of generations to come have been and will continue to be effected by that terrible experience.

The individuals and/or their family members highlighted in this chapter were selected based on 1) Their Total Numbers of Slaves in the U.S. Census; 2) Their Numbers of Slaves Baptized in the St. Paul Baptism Records; 3) The Proximity of Their Plantations or Businesses to the Town of Mansura and 4) The Lasting Impact of Their Family on The African-American Population of Mansura and the Surrounding Area.

The Slave Holders – In 1860, just prior to the start of the Civil War, some of the largest Avoyelles Parish Slave Holders were Samuel Smith (100 slaves), James Callihan (100 slaves), Dominique Coco (107 slaves), Dr. A. Leigh (110 slaves), the Widow of John Glaize (123 slaves), Mrs. Elias Murdock (135 slaves), Hugh Keary (140 slaves), William Pitts (153 slaves) and I.T. Norwood (168 slaves) (Blake). Other than Dominique Coco, the others resided some distance from Mansura, generally in the present-day Bunkie area, and did not appear in the St. Paul Baptism Records, either as children, parents or Slave Holders.

The top 10 Slave Holders baptizing slave children in the St. Paul records were as follows:

- **Pierre Goudeau & Son** - <u>16 Slaves Baptized</u>: Louise, Aglae, Gabriel, Daniel, Adelinore, Philogene, Constance, Xesiovie (sp.?), Joachim, Jerome, Hortance, Eugene, Eloise, Helie, Lucie, Caroline, Alexandre;

- **Pierre Normand & Son** - <u>13 Slaves Baptized</u>: Marcellin (F), Frederic, Julienne, Julie, Jean, Jean, Roselle (ROSESSE (sic), Marinette, Julienne, Fadrian??, Adelaide, Paulin, Ursin;

- **Jean Pierre Ducote** - <u>12 Slaves Baptized</u>: Fanny, Charles, Lezin, Gilbert, Helene, Dorsin, Basile , Adelaide, Victor, Marguerite, Babe, Manette II;

- **Leandre Lacour** - <u>11 Slaves Baptized</u>: Clarisse, Antoine, Augustin, Julia, Narcine, Helena, Henriette, Auguste, Apollinaire, Aigues;

- **Evariste Rabalais** - <u>10 Slaves Baptized</u>: Felicia, Hypolite, Christine, Victorine, Jean, Eugenie, Joachim, Hyppolite, Hubert;

- **Pierre Couvillion** - <u>10 Slaves Baptized</u>: Paulin, Augustin, Pauline, Helene Oren, Virginie, Simon, Valerien, Euproine, Jhloise, Helene, Augustin, Pauline;

- **Lucien Joffrion** - <u>10 Slaves Baptized</u>: Octave, Marie Arseire (sic), Charles, Adelina, Celestine, Honoroine, Simon, Louis, Alfrede, Louis;

- **Louis Bordelon** - <u>8 Slaves Baptized</u>: Sylvainne, Aselina, Helene, Marinette, Ulalie, Manette, Lilvane, Neely;

- **Pierre L'Eglise** - <u>8 Slaves Baptized</u>: Virginie, Jean, Cyrile, Octavia, Adolphe, Kaisy, Etienne, Donatien;

- **Laurent Normand** - <u>7 Slaves Baptized:</u> (Celestin, Claris, Hilaire, Victorine, Marie Louise, Celeste, William).

Some of these Slave Holders and others are discussed below.

The Joffrions

The Joffrion family of Pointe Coupee and, later, Avoyelles Parish were some of the original Slave Holders in the Mansura area. As you will see, many of their slaves were originally from Africa and, in some cases, still held on to their African names. The Joffrions' last plantation was a large one just north of Moreauville on Bayou de Glaise (Robertson). The last group of slaves that they held at that location were probably the ancestors of many current African-American families.

Joseph Joffrion II was born in the Pointe Coupee post in 1753 and married **Marie Francoise Bouchard** in Pointe Coupee in 1773. They became the parents of 12 children: five boys and seven girls. He was an official of the Spanish government during the colonial period and may have served in the Spanish military (GenevaSwis).

In the 1785 Avoyelles Post census (1785 Census Pointe Coupee), Joseph was a 30 year-old man who was listed with his wife, five children and six slaves. Also, separately listed, was his father, 75 years-old **Joseph Joffrion, Sr.**

Joseph II (jr. or fils) appeared in the public records on several occasions with transactions involving slaves. Some examples are:

- On February 12, 1793, he purchased a 25 year-old "Congo Negro" by the name of **Francois** from Andre Dupre for $360 (Martin-Quiatte);
- On August 16, 1810, he purchased a 32 year-old male named **Quaddy** from Richard Gram for $650. The name, "Quaddy" was considered to normally be a female name that was short for **Khadija**, the name of the first wife of Mohamad. It is widely used in Senegambia, especially among the Wolof and Fulbe (Hall).
- On October 21, 1797, he purchased a 40 year-old female from the Guinea Coast named **Berri** from "Joseph of PC Dufief" (?) for $928. The name "**Berri**" was likely the Wolof name, Mberi (Hall).
- On 2/13/1800, there is a listing of the sale and manumission (Freeing) of a two month-old mulatto male slave from one Joffrion to another, although it is not clear who is who. The record strongly implied that the infant was the slave child of one of them but it is not clear which (Hall).
- On 5/6/1817, there is a listing for the manumission of a 39 year-old male slave named **Louis** by Joseph Joffrion, Sr. There was no cost involved and Louis was freed for his *"fidelity and good conduct"* (Hall).
- On 12/5/1820, there was a listing for the manumission of a 65 year-old female slave named **Jeanne**. There was no cost involved and Jeanne was freed for her *"fidelity and good service to his family"* (Hall).

Joseph Joffrion II died in 1827 in Avoyelles Parish and is buried in St. Paul's cemetery (S. P. Staff).

Joseph Joffrion III was believed to be the son of **Joseph Joffrion II** and **Marie Francoise Bouchard**. He was born on November 29, 1795[4]. He married **Die Damie Rabalais** on May 3, 1824 in Avoyelles Parish, Louisiana (Dodd and al..).

During the period from 1838 through 1852, Joseph Joffrion III purchased four parcels of land in Avoyelles Parish (Operations):

- December 8, 1838: 160 acres of land, located about four miles northeast of Moreauville;
- June 25 1848: 80 acres of land, located about four miles northeast of Moreauville;
- October 1, 1852: 74 Acres just east of Mansura, near Grande Ecore;
- October 1, 1852: 80 Acres just east of Mansura, near Grande Ecore.

In the St. Paul Baptismal Records, Joseph Joffrion was listed as the Slave Holder of five slave babies being baptized. In most of these cases, the parent and godparent information is missing:

- **Philogene**, birthdate was unknown but whose mother was **Susanne**. He was baptized on August 5, 1845 but his godparents were not listed;
- **Aurelise**, who was born sometime in 1848 and whose mother was **Nellie**. There are no records of her baptism date or godparents;
- **Edolph**, who had no further information listed;
- **Antoine**, who had no further information listed;
- **Adrienne**, who was born sometime in 1841, but had no additional information listed.

Joseph Joffrion III also appeared in at least one public record involving slave transactions (Martin-Quiatte):

- On December 26, 1808, he sold a group of five slaves, including a 25 year-old slave named **Antoine** and a 23 year-old light-skinned slave named **Sam**, to his father, "Joseph Joffrion *pere*" for $2000.

In the 1840 U.S. census, Joseph appears as a white male, age 40-49 (Likely 45). In his household, he had one white female, age 20-29 (His wife?); one white male, age 10-14; one white female, age under five; 12 male slaves and 14 female slaves (U. C. Bureau).

---

[4] There is some confusion regarding who his father was since there were two or more Joseph Joffrions in the area during that same period. In fact, Joseph Joffrion II had a younger brother also named Joseph Joffrion.

In the 1850 U.S. census, Joseph Joffrion was listed as a 48 year-old farmer, living between Leon Drouin and Francois Tassin, near Mansura (1850 U.S. Census for Avoyelles Parish, Louisiana). One census house beyond Francois Tassin lived **Father Hiacinthe Tumsing**, a Catholic priest. Joseph listed his 1850 property value at $18,500. Living with him was his 40 year-old wife, now called, **Donnie**, an 18 year-old male named **Eloi**, an 11 year-old male named **Evariste**, a seven year-old female named **Celestine**, a three year-old male named **Joseph**, and a recently-married couple, **Joseph** and **Coralie Chatelain**.

In the 1860 U.S. census, Joseph and Damie Joffrion were living near Mansura (U. C. Bureau). Living next to them were both their married sons, Eloi and Evariste. The value of their property was listed as $59,000. He was listed as holding 42 slaves captive on his plantation while his son, Eloi, held five slaves and his son Evariste was holding two slaves (U. C. Bureau).

The Normand and Coco Families

The Normand and Coco families, because of their eventual merging as a result of the marriage of Valery Coco and Clara Normand (See Below), could be considered to have had the greatest and longest lasting effects on African-Americans in the immediate Mansura area.

The Normands

The Normand family first came to the area around Avoyelles Parish during the 18th century, about the time of the American Revolution (Sorrels). They, just as most early French settlers, were Roman Catholics and supported the establishment and growth of the church in the new world.

Their acceptance and continued use of African people as slaves to farm their land seems so paradoxical since the French Revolution was occurring around that same time and freedom from tyranny and oppression was such an important part of that revolution.

In any case, by the early 1800's, the Normands were well documented Slave Holders (U. C. Bureau). A narrative describing the death of Laurent Normand, Jr. (See Below) suggested that brutality towards slaves was not a stranger to them (Hyacinth).

An additional aspect of the relationship of the Normands to the slaves seems to have been more intimate in nature. Several sources, while not completely verifiable, mention the nightly sexual dalliances of the Normand men inside the slave cabins (M. J. Normand), (Herbert_Holmes_1). Some proposed results of these relationships are as follows:

- Several mulatto persons, found living in the vicinity of Cocoville after emancipation, bore the surname, Normand (Herbert_Holmes_1).
- Many of these same people appear to have chosen to marry members of families who were of similar skin color, resulting in additional generations of mulattoes. Rumors still persist about those who managed to move to other areas, e.g. New Orleans, and engaged in *passé blanc* (Passing for White).
- Others, who chose to marry people darker than themselves, ended up with children and grandchildren who were also much lighter in skin color than their darker parents. This likely accounts for some of the lighter skin features found in some families in the Mansura-Cocoville area.

Jean Pierre Normand (a.k.a. Jean Normand) (1742 - 1824) and his wife, **Marguerite Vicknair** (1750 - 1826), "came to Avoyelles and settled on the Red River, having obtained a grant of land there, which later became known as "Normand's Landing", then "Gorton's Landing," and then "Barbin's Landing." (Saucier), (M. Normand). This was the first important landing in Avoyelles Parish and the river traffic was vital to the growth of the Parish throughout the 19th century.

Their children were as follows (CJ):

- **Francoise Normand Dupuy** (1767 - 1848)
- **Justine Normand Dupuy** (1769 - 1855)
- **Pierre Normand** (1774 - 1846)
- **Laurent Normand** (1780 - 1842)
- **Jean Baptiste Manuel Normand** (1791 - 1803)

"Jean Normand" was listed in the 1810 U.S. Census for Avoyelles Parish (U. C. Bureau). His family only included himself (Male, Over 45) and his wife (Female, 26-44). He was listed as holding ten black people as slaves.

He died on October 20, 1824 and is buried in St. Paul the Apostle Cemetery near Mansura. Marguerite Normand died on October 16, 1826 and is also buried in St. Paul's Cemetery (S. P. Staff).

Pierre Normand, Sr., Jean Pierre and Marguerite Normand's son, was born on December 22, 1774 (C. C. Staff). He married **Irene Marie Joffrion** (1782 – 1827) (U.S. and International Marriage Records).

In the 1810 U.S. Census, "Pierre Normand" (Male, 26-44) and his wife (Female, 26-44) were listed as residents of Avoyelles Parish (U. C. Bureau). They also had the following children: one male and one female (10-15) and one male (16-25). They had no slaves listed.

There are 2 public records showing slave ownership by Pierre Normand, Sr.:

- **Magloire** - Purchased on May 17, 1812 from Louis Esnault (Hall). Magloire was described as being an 18 year-old, born in the "Congo", and spoke "Benue-Congo".
- **Jacob** - Purchased on December 22, 1817 from Marguerite Wienaire (Hall). Jacob was described as a 30-year old who was born in Africa.

In the St. Paul Baptismal records, Pierre Normand I was shown baptizing six slave children:

- **Fadrian**?? (No birth or other baptism information);
- **Frederic** (Born - November, 1838); Mother - **Marie**; Godfather - **Frederic** (Slave held by Pierre Normand; Godmother - **Felicite'** (Slave held by Pierre Normand);
- **Julie** (Born October 21, 1836); Mother - **Margueritte**; Godfather - **Francois** (Slave held by Pierre Normand); Godmother - **Durciene** (Slave held by Pierre Normand);
- **Julienne** (Born 1837); No other baptism information;
- **Julienne** (Born October 21, 1836); Mother - **Margueritte**; Godfather - **Antoine** (Slave held by Pierre Normand); Godmother - **Marie Elisabeth** (Slave held by Pierre Normand);
- **Marcellin** (Female, Born in 1843); Mother - **Marie**; No other baptism information.

An additional slave, **Adelaide** (Born August 25, 1845), whose mother was **Louise**, was baptized on October 1, 1845. In this case, Pierre Normand was listed as "deceased". No additional baptism information was given.

Pierre Normand Sr. died in 1846 and is buried in St. Paul the Apostle Cemetery in Mansura, Louisiana (Ducote).

Pierre Belizaire Normand (a.k.a. Pierre Normand, Jr.), Pierre Normand, Sr.'s son, was born in Avoyelles Parish, Louisiana on March 3, 1799 and married **Lucille Lemoine** at St. Paul the Apostle Catholic Church in Mansura, Louisiana on June 28, 1825 (McAllenR14). Pierre and Lucille had five children: **Pierre III**, **Claire**, **Clarisse**, **Clara**[5] and **Alcide** (U. C. Bureau).

---

[5] Clara Normand, Pierre's daughter, was 15 years old when she married 23 years old Valery Coco on September 12, 1848. The couple was residing with Pierre and his family in 1850.

In the 1830 census (U. C. Bureau), Pierre, now listed as "Pierre Normand, Jr." lived just north of Moreauville[6]. His household consisted of one white male, aged 30-39 (Pierre?); one white female, aged 15-19 (His wife?) and one white female, aged 50-59 (His mother?). At that time, he was holding 40 black people in captivity, which included 19 males and 21 females.

In the St. Paul Baptismal records, Pierre Normand, Jr. was listed as the holder of six slaves who were being baptized between 1837 and 1838 (Church):

- **Jean*** (Born - August 11, 1832); Mother - **Felicite'***; Godfather - **Octave**; Godmother - **Seraphine**;
- **Jean** (Born - June 1833; **Father - Francois**; Godfather - **Sylvain**; Godmother - **Salie**;
- **Marinette** (Born, March 16, 1838); Mother - **Azelie**; Godfather - **Wiliston**; Godmother - **Marie**;
- **Roselle** (Born, November 15, 1832); Mother - **Emelie**; Godfather - **Williston**; Godmother - **Marie**;
- **Paulin** (Born 3 Aug, 1837); Mother – **Marie**; Godparents were white: Joseph Lafond, Lucile Lemoine);
- **Ursin*** (Born 16 Jan, 1838); Mother - **Felicite'***; Godfather – **Paulin** (Slave held by Pierre Normand, Jr.); Godmother – **Marie** (Slave held by Pierre Normand, Jr.).

More discussion about Jean, Ursin and Felicite' will occur in Book II of this set

On June 25, 1848, Pierre Normand, Jr. purchased 80 acres of land between Boutte de Bayou and Bayou DeGlaise, about 3 miles from Mansura (Management).

In the 1850 U.S. Census, Pierre Normand, Jr. was listed as the holder of 22 slaves (U. C. Bureau). This included 12 males and 10 females.

In the 1860 U.S. Census, Pierre Normand, Jr. was listed as the holder of 20 slaves (1860 U.S. Federal Census - Slave Schedules). This included 14 males and six females.

In 1870, Pierre, now widowed and 70 years old, was shown living with his daughter, Clara Coco and her husband, Valery Coco, near Mansura (U. C. Bureau). He died that same year.

Jean Laurent Normand, Sr. (a.k.a. Gaspard Normand), the brother of Pierre Normand, Sr., was born in St. John the Baptist Parish, Louisiana in 1780 (Shellystafford). His parents were Jean Pierre Normand and Marguerite Vicknair. His wife was **Gertrude Couvillion** and they had 4 daughters: **Lea**, **Celine**, **Margaret**, and **Marianne**; and three sons: **Laurent, Jr.**, **Barthelemy** and **Prudent** (LindaNall66).

---

[6] Based on his neighbors shown in the Library of Congress map of Avoyelles Parish and their proximity to him in the 1830 census.

In the 1810 U.S. Census, Laurent Normand, Sr. was shown holding five slaves in captivity (U. C. Bureau).

The Louisiana Slave Records show the purchase of a slave named **Harry** by Laurent Normand on July 16, 1818 from Baptiste Moclaux (Hall). Harry was described as 10 years-old and purchased as part of a group of four slaves for $3000.

Although the census and St. Paul records do not distinguish Laurent Sr. from Laurent Jr., Laurent Jr. was born in 1816 (See Below), making it likely that most, or all, of the slave baptisms and census records listed during the 1820's and 1830's, were those of Laurent Normand, Sr. Thus, in the St. Paul Baptism records, Laurent Normand, Sr. was shown to have baptized seven slaves from 1832 to 1839 (Church):

- **William** (Born October 26, 1832); Mother - **Ayme**; Godfather - **Joseph** (Free Man of Color); Godmother - **Louise** (Slave held by the widow of P. Couvillion);
- **Celeste** (Born March 1, 1839); Mother – **Aymee**; Godparents (white) - Neuville Gremillion & Lea Normand);
- **Marie Louise** (Born in March, 1832); Mother – **Constance**; Godfather – **Francois** (Slave held by Laurent Normand); Godmother - **Ursule** (Slave held by Laurent Normand);
- **Victorine** (Born in May, 1837; Mother – **Melie**; Godfather – **Jim** (Slave held by Hippolite Mayeux); Godmother - **Victoire** (Slave held by Vve. Pierre Bordelon);
- **Hilaire** (Born in October 1833; Mother – **Meline**; Godfather –**Gabriel** (Slave held by Laurent Normand); Godmother - **Artemise** (Slave held by Laurent Normand);
- **Claris** (Born October 15, 1838); Mother – **Patsy**; Godparents (white) - George Baron & Lea Normand;
- **Celestin** (Born March 3, 1839); Mother – **Sylvie**; Godfather -**Pierre Labiche** (FMC); Godmother -**Athemise** (Slave held by Laurent Normand).

The 1840 census for Avoyelles Parish showed a person named "L. Normand, Sr." who was identified as a male, age 60-69 (U. C. Bureau). Living in his household was a female, age 40-49, and a female, age 10-14. He was holding 28 slaves in captivity.

Laurent Normand, Sr. died on October 1, 1842 and is buried in St. Paul the Apostle Cemetery in Cocoville (S. P. Staff).

Jean Laurent Normand, Jr. (U. C. Bureau) was born in Avoyelles Parish around 1816. His parents were Laurent Normand Sr. and Gertrude Couvillion. He married **Eliza Bordelon**, at St. Paul the Apostle Catholic Church in Cocoville on July 30, 1829 (Dodd and al.).

On May 1, 1849, Laurent Normand, Jr. purchased 80 acres of land south of Lake Pearl in Avoyelles Parish (Office). At the time of his death in 1860, his plantation was in Cocoville, in the vicinity of St. Paul's Cemetery (See Below).

In the 1850 U.S. census, Laurent (40) and Eliza (36) were listed with their four daughters: **Helene** (18), **Florida** (14), **Helena** (7), and **Lorens** (6) and three sons: **Orphila** (10), **Leon** (3) and **Louis** (0) (U. C. Bureau).

The U.S. census for 1850 showed Laurent holding 25 slaves (U. C. Bureau): 14 females (ages two to 45 years old) and 11 males (ages six months to 36 years old). He was said to be holding around 60 black people as slaves at the time of his death in 1860 (Hyacinth). His estate was valued at over $50,000.

Laurent's violent death, in 1860, at the hands of two slaves, **Spencer** and **Daniel**, being held on his plantation, was described in a letter written by **Mother Mary Hyacinth**, an Ursaline nun, living at the Presentation Convent in Cocoville (Hyacinth), and, recently, dramatized in a short account by Mark J. Normand (M. J. Normand).

Mother Mary speculated that Laurent's mistreatment of the slaves and his nightly excursions to the slave cabins could have been a factor in their rising up against him:

> *"Mr. Normand was highly respected; he was a genteel person, but he was strict with his slaves, so severe...to the point of barbarity at times. He had sixty or eighty slaves, old and young ones, large and small. The slaves lived in small cabins not far from the master's house. Mr. Normand used to visit his slaves before going to bed. He was coming back from this visit when all of a sudden two assassins jumped him, and hit him over the head, one with a pick-axe and the other with a hatchet, cutting his head open and scattering his brains and blood."* He was buried *"in the Church cemetery just down the Cocoville road from the Normand plantation"*. - Mother Mary Hyacinth

According to the account by Mark J. Normand, following Laurent's death, 23 of the slaves were kept by his widow while the rest were given to family or sold to 13 different buyers.

The fates of the slaves were also described by Mother Mary:

> *"They handcuffed and jailed the criminals. They imprisoned them in Alexandria. On February 2, they were judged. Spencer and Daniel were sentenced to be hanged. Richard received thirty-nine lashes in public. On the third of the month at 11 o'clock they passed here, tied and bound, to show the authorities where the body was hidden. Father Janeau heard their confessions that morning and baptized Spencer. Daniel had been baptized in his childhood. Spencer was twenty or twenty-two years old; Daniel was twenty-six. Father Janeau and Father Rebours left them only at the moment*

their souls seemed to be in the presence of their Sovereign Judge. They were in good dispositions, they said before dying".

The Coco Family

The Coco's became one of the preeminent families in Avoyelles Parish, largely as a result of their large farming enterprise made possible through their use of slave labor during the 18th and 19th centuries and sharecropping during the 20th. Their family homes, still located on L'Eglise Street in Mansura, are reminders of their past prominence. The area still known as "Cocoville" and a Mansura street called "Coco Street" serve as further evidence of their influential past.

FIGURE 16. DESFOSSE' HOUSE, LOCATED ON L'EGLISE STREET IN MANSURA (PRIER, DESFOSSE' HOUSE)

By the middle of the twentieth century, the Coco family, under the leadership of Edward Coco, operated a new-style plantation using a variation of the share-cropping methodology (See below). There, a number of black families resided and worked the Coco land in a sort of fiefdom, where the workers exchanged their manual labor in return for food and housing for their families. This land, lying north of Coco Street in Mansura, stretched from L'Eglise Street to the swampland to the east and remained in operation until well into the 1960's.

The Coco's were also involved in other business and political activities. For example, the DRUCO lumber company, still located on L'Eglise Street, was started as a joint business owned by Claver

Drouin along with Edward Coco's two sons, Lysso and Merlin Coco. Lysso Coco also served two terms as mayor of Mansura during the mid-1940s (Mayeux and Decuir).

Dominique Coco, Sr., the Coco family patriarch, was one of the earliest Slave Holders in the area, purchasing significant numbers of slaves from the start of the 1800's. He and, later, his children continued the practice of slavery up to the Civil War. In the 1860 U.S. Census, the Coco family members held a combined total of nearly 200 slaves in captivity in the Mansura area (See below).

Dominique Coco, Sr. was likely born in Nice, Italy around 1750 (Committee). He appears to have been born with the surname, Baldany, but used the name, Coco, as his actual name. He is believed to have landed in Charleston, South Carolina in 1777, possible accompanying General Marquis de Lafayette, and traveled to Louisiana.

He married **Elizabeth Rabalais** on August 10, 1784 in Pointe Coupee Parish, Louisiana, using the surname, Coco (Tate and Gremillion). Dominique Sr. and Elizabeth were the parents of **Dominique Coco Jr.** and **Joseph Coco I**.

Dominique Coco, Sr. was a very prominent citizen of Avoyelles Parish and was listed as one of the first "Avoyellean of the Year" (Committee). He is believed to have been the builder of the Desfosse' House, which remains standing on L'Eglise Street in Mansura, adjacent to the city hall. The house sits on land that he acquired as a land grant and which was eventually owned by J. Joffrion and Gauthier and Co. and later redistributed (Mayeux and Decuir).

Dominique Coco, Sr. died in Pointe Coupee Parish around 1790.

Dominique Coco, Jr. was born in Pointe Coupe Parish, LA on May 14, 1785 (Bordelon). He was the son of **Dominique Coco, Sr.** and **Elizabeth Rabalais**. He married **Zoe Marie Juneau** on January 22, 1803; **Carolyn Bordelon** on November 5, 1824; and **Melazie Le Doux** on June 10, 1851.

In 1820, Dominique stated his home as "islands south of the Red river" (U. C. Bureau). However, he was a prolific land purchaser throughout the east-central part of the parish (Recorders):

- On November 16, 1835, he purchased 81 acres of land just south of Bayou de Glaise, west of Long Bridge, Louisiana;
- On October 1, 1845, he purchased 160 acres of land just south of the town of Moreauville, Louisiana; and three parcels of land totaling 320 acres, three miles further south;
- On June 28, 1849, jointly with Leon Gauthier, Dominique purchased 160 acres of land located just north of Moreauville;

42

- On June 28, 1849, jointly with Celemene Lacour, Dominique purchased 160 acres of land located immediately to the west of the land purchased jointly with Leon Gauthier.

In the 1830 census, Dominique Jr. was listed as the head of household for a family with 10 free white persons and 35 slaves (U. C. Bureau).

In the 1850 census (U. C. Bureau), he was listed as a farmer whose real estate was valued at $75, 000. He was the sole parent and had five sons residing with him: **Ferdinand** (28), **Adolph** (24), **Alphonse** (21), **Anatoly** (15), and **Philogene** (9); and one daughter, **Eugenie** (12). Also residing in their household was a 30 year-old mulatto female named **Elsey**.

Three other sons, **Lucien Dominique Coco** and twins, **Valery** and **Joseph D. Coco**, were not listed in the 1850 census:

- **Lucien Dominique Coco** married **Julienne Goudeau,** the daughter of **Julien (Jules) Goudeau** (See below) in 1852 (patsybaker19);
- **Valery Coco** had married **Clara Normand**, the daughter of **Pierre Normand**, in 1848 (Recorder);
- **Joseph D. Coco** had married **Pauline Mayeux** in 1846 (pinkladyrider59).

Dominique Coco, Jr. began his activities as a prolific slave purchaser as early as 1805 and became one of the largest Slave Holders in Louisiana (Blake), listing 13 slaves in the 1820 census, 35 slaves in the 1830 census and 107 slaves, living in 20 cabins, in the 1860 U.S. census. That year, Dominique (75) and Melazie (48) Coco listed their estate as having a value of $185,000, a huge fortune for that time (U. C. Bureau).

As shown below, he purchased a number of both individual slaves as well as slave mothers with as many as three children (Hall):

- **Jeffrey** - 30 year-old male, purchased on May 24, 1808 from John Brown for $600;
- **Nero** - 24 year-old male, purchased April 17, 1815 from Guillaume Gauthier for $600;
- **George** - 26 year-old male, purchased on May 28, 1819 from Henry Brown of Missouri Territory for $750;
- **Henry** - 15 year-old male, purchased on May 12, 1819 from Isabella Rabalais (deceased master) for $1130;
- **"Unnamed Slave"** - Adult, purchased on 17 December 1805 from "Golier" for $600;
- **Julie** - A five year-old female, purchased in slave group along with mom and three boys, on March 24, 1814 from Joseph Coco (deceased master) for $940;
- **Julie** - A four year-old female, purchased in a slave group made up of mom, three boys and one girl, on September 1, 1814 from Phillipe Duplechain for $1000;
- **"Unnamed Infant"** - A three month-old, purchased along with mother on May 5, 1819 from Augustin Junott for $1350;

- **Cadet** - A three year-old male mulatto, purchased in a slave group made up of mom and three boys on March 12, 1814 from Joseph Coco (deceased master) for $940;
- **Jean Louis** - Unknown Age, purchased as part of slave group made up of mom, two boys and one girl, on September 1, 1814 from Phillippe Duplechain for $1000;
- **Jean Louis** - A two year-old male, purchased as part of a slave group made up of mom and three boys, on March 24, 1814 from Joseph Coco (deceased master) for $940.

In the St. Paul Baptismal Records (Church), Dominique Coco, Jr. is listed as baptizing only three slave children:

- **Isadore**, who was born on November 4, 1835 and whose mother was **Felicite'**. He was baptized on October 21, 1836 and his godparents were **Julien**, a slave held by Lucien Coco, and **Eugenie**, a slave held by "Rousseau".
- **Elizabeth**, who was born in November, 1837 and whose mother was **Caroline**. She was baptized on December 5, 1838 and her godparents were **Willis**, a slave held by Prudent Normand, and **Susanne**, a slave held by Dominique Coco.
- **Henri**, who was born sometime in 1802 and whose baptism date or godparents were not listed. Henri died on December 2, 1850 (Ducote). He could be the same person as Henry, the slave listed above, who was purchased from Isabelle Rabalais in 1819.

Dominique Coco, Jr. died on September 12, 1864 in Cocoville, LA and is buried in St. Paul the Apostle Cemetery in Cocoville (Bordelon).

Joseph Dominique Coco was born on March 1, 1827, a twin of **Valery Coco** (Sturgell). His parents were **Dominique Coco, Jr.** and **Carolyn Bordelon.** He married **Marie Pauline Mayeux** (1831 -1870) on May 26, 1846 (J. R. Dodd).

In the 1850 census (U. C. Bureau), Joseph and Pauline had an 8-month old baby boy, **Paulin**, living with them. Also listed with them were three white males: **Henry Saucier** (17), **E. Fritz** (32) and **Nicholas Saucier** (43); and four mulatto male bricklayers: **Prosper** (28), **Pierre Hernandez** (30), **Delhoste** (25) and **Joseph** (24).

In the 1860 U.S. census (U. C. Bureau), Joseph and Pauline were listed with five children: **Paulin** (11), **Aurelia** (9), **Aurelien** (7), **Dominique** (5), and **Oscar** (3). They likely were living on his land, about three miles east of Boutte de Bayou, near Mansura (Robertson). They were shown as holding 12 slaves: nine males and three females and the value of their real estate was $22,000.

In 1870, Joseph (43) and Pauline (39) were living near Moreauville (U. C. Bureau). Living with them were the following children: **Aurelia** (18), **D. Camille** (15), **Oscar** (13), **Victor** (8), **Rosa** (6), **Josephine** (4), and **Adele E.** (1).

Joseph died on July 2, 1872 and is buried in Sacred Heart Cemetery in Moreauville, Louisiana (Sturgell).

Lucien Dominique Coco was born on February 12, 1812 in Avoyelles Parish (Bordelon). He was the son of **Dominique Coco, Jr**. and **Zoe Juneau** (See above). He married **Julienne Goudeau** on September 9, 1852 (Ancestry.com) and became the father of five children (**Emma**, **Lestan**, **Albert**, **Jules**, and **Elodie**).

In the 1850 U.S. census, Lucien Coco was shown as holding 80 black people in captivity (U. S. Bureau). In the 1860 U.S. census, he was holding 58 Blacks in captivity, who lived in 10 cabins (U. C. Bureau). His plantation was over 1000 acres in size and valued at about $100,000, making him one of the largest, and richest, Slave Holders in the parish.

In the 1870 U.S. census, Lucien and Julienne were farmers, living near Mansura (U. C. Bureau). The value of their property was $20,000. Living with them were three young females: **Emma** (15), **Eliza** (11) and **Elodie** (2); and three young males: **Louis** (13), **Albers** (9) and **Jules** (5).

Lucien Coco died on September 22, 1879 in Mansura, LA and is buried in St. Paul the Apostle Cemetery in Mansura (Bordelon). An excerpt from his obituary reveals the paradoxical view of his family or friends toward a person whose whole life and fortune depended on those whom he and his family held in bondage (Editor):

> *"Frugal, temperate, energetic he amassed a large fortune which he handled judiciously. The cold exterior of Lucien D. Coco was not a correct reflex of his warm heart, and his death will disclose that his acts of assistance and charity were numerous."*

Valery Coco was born on March 1, 1827 (Bordelon, Valery Coco). He was the 4th son of **Dominique Coco, Jr**. and **Carolyn Bordelon Coco**. He married **Clara Normand**, the daughter of Pierre Normand, on September 12, 1848 (J. R. Dodd). She was 14 and he was 21 at the time.

In the 1850 U.S. census, Valery and Clara were shown as living with her father, Pierre Normand (U. C. Bureau). Valery was described as a farmer whose real estate was valued at $2000. He was listed as holding three slaves (Taker).

In the 1860 U.S. census, Valery Coco was listed as holding 10 slaves, ranging in ages from 9 months to 40 years old (U. C. Bureau).

In the 1870 U.S. census, Valery (43) and Clara (37) were listed as farmers living in Avoyelles Parish (Takers). Living with them were Clara's father, *(Pierre)* **Belezaire Normand** (70), as well as Valery's brother, **Philogene Coco** (29) and his wife, **Eugenie** (25). Also present was a one year old boy, **Horace Coco**, an 11 year-old boy named **Woodless Heron**, a 12 year-old girl named **Emilie Bordelon** and a 15 year-old black boy named **John Washington**.

In the 1880 census, Valery (53) and Clara (45) were farmers, living in the town of Mansura, Louisiana (1. C. Takers). Living with them were his niece, **Adele Coco** (11), his nephew, **Camile Coco** (26), a farm overseer, **Francois Morris** (15) and a black female servant, **Mary Banks** (60).

Valery died in Mansura, Louisiana in June, 1899 and is buried in St. Paul the Apostle Catholic Cemetery (Bordelon, Valery Coco).

In the 1900 U.S. Census, widowed Clara Coco was shown living in Mansura with her brother, **Alcide Normand** and his wife, **Zoe** (1. U. Census). Also living in the house was her great-nephew, **Edward Coco** (24)[7] and great-niece, **Mercedes Coco** (19), as well as three black servants: sisters **Aurelia** (12) and **Sophie Lavalais** (10), and **Clarisse Augustine** (60).

Sophie Lavalais eventually married **Dennis Batiste** and resided in Grande Bayou. She attended Our Lady of Prompt Succor Church until her death. Aurelia spent her entire life on the Coco farm as a domestic servant.

Clara Coco showed up for the last time in the 1910 census where she was living in Mansura with Mercedes Coco and a black maid named **Laura Rock** (1. C. Takers).

Edward Coco, along with his wife, Emma, became the parents of **Ashton, Lysso, Lawrence, Merlin** and **Bernadine Coco** (1. C. Takers). He eventually became the head of what has been called the "Coco Plantation" (See Below) by many of the black citizens of Mansura who lived there during most of the first half of the 20th century.

The Roy Family

The Roy family of Mansura became a powerful force in the local government and businesses of the town from the last half of the 19th century to the end of the 20th century (Mayeux and Decuir). Roys served

---

[7] Edward was the son of Aurelian Dominique Coco, whose father was Joseph Dominique Coco, Valery Coco's twin brother.

in practically all important government positions including Mayor, Chief-of-police, Fire Chief, Postmaster and Police Juror (Mayeux and Decuir).

In addition to their political roles, Roy family members were involved in a number of other activities. For example, three of the town's physicians were Roys (Thomas A., Kirby and Elliot), the movie theater was operated by Ben Roy and the first nursing home, Rio Sol, was established by members of the Roy family.

Tesca Roy was a prominent farmer who operated a large sharecropper operation in the vicinity of Grande Ecore that employed, and was home to, several black families. Although the Roys were minor Slave Holders by most standards, they played a more significant role in the lives of many black residents of Mansura as a result of their farm practices and their treatment of black people during the early to mid-twentieth century (See Later).

Some of the key Roy ancestors are described below.

Joseph Marie Roy, Sr. (Meeler) was born in St. Valier, Bellechasse, Quebec, Canada on June 28, 1729. His parents were **Jean Noel Roy** and **Angelique Lacasse**, both of Quebec province. He married **Julie Bizet Vicque** in Pointe Coupee Parish, Louisiana on June 19, 1776 and they had 11 children (**Unknown Male Child, Joseph II, Simon, Eugenie, Marie, Godefroy, Elise, Julie, Helene, Jean Baptiste** and **Constance**).

Joseph Marie Roy II was born in Pointe Coupee Parish, Louisiana on June 28, 1781 (Meeler). His parents were **Joseph Marie Roy, Sr.** and **Julie Bizet (Bissette) Vicque**. He married **Marie Ann Bordelon** in 1798 in Avoyelles Parish, Louisiana.

In the 1810 U.S. census (U. C. Bureau), Joseph Roy's family consisted of one white male (Joseph?) and one white female (Julie?) both ages 26 - 44; three white males and one white female under 10; one white female age 10 - 15; and two slaves.

In the 1840 U.S. census (U. C. Bureau), Joseph Roy's family consisted of one white male, age 50- 59 (Joseph?); one white female, age 40 - 49 (Julie?); two white females, ages 20 - 29; and three white males, ages 5 - 9. Also, seven slaves were listed.

From family tree records (Meeler), Joseph II and Marie's children consisted of : **Emelie** (1800-1851), **Joseph Marie III** (1802-1833), **Severine** (1804-1870), **Francois** (1807-1861), **Leandre** (1809-1854), **Josephine** (1816-1850), **Villeneuve** (1817-1880), **Ameline** (1819-1880), **Marie "Azilia"** (1822-), **Adelaide** (1824-1920), and **Adele** (1829-1918).

Of Joseph and Marie's offspring, only Francois and his son, Leandre Francois, held significant numbers of slaves.

Joseph Marie Roy III died on August 2, 1845 in Avoyelles Parish.

Francois Roy was born in 1807 in Avoyelles Parish (Meeler). His parents were **Joseph Marie Roy** II and **Marie Ann Bordelon**. He married **Mary Ducote** on August 30. 1824 in Avoyelles Parish.

In the 1850 U.S. Census (U. C. Bureau), Francois and Mary were listed along with their eight children: **Leandre** (23), **Jean Bte.** (17), **Leonard** (12), **Azelie** (10), **Francois** (8), **Vitaline** (6), **Felice** (4), **Celine** (2), and **Prudence** (1).

In the St. Paul baptism records (Church), there are three slaves being baptized who were held by Francois Roy:

- *Isabelle* (Born 15 Aug 1844); her mother was not listed;
- *Louisa* (Born April, 1839); her mother was **Babe'** and her godmother was a slave named *Marguerite* (Held by Jacques Roy);
- *Marie* (Born 15 Jul 1853); her mother was a slave named **Louise**.

On January 1, 1849, Francois Roy purchased 2 parcels of land in Avoyelles Parish:

- A 35.4-acre parcel about 4 miles west of Mansura (Laughlin);
- A 47-acre parcel just to the north and adjourning his other land (Laughlin).

On May 15, 1852, he purchased an additional 30 acre parcel of land adjourning his other properties (Terry). Thus, he, eventually, owned over 100 acres of land between Mansura and Hessmer.

In the 1860 U.S. Census, Francois Roy was listed as the holder of 19 slaves: 7 females and 12 males (U. C. Bureau).

Francois Roy died November 26, 1861 and is buried in St. Paul the Apostle Cemetery in Mansura.

Leandre Francois Roy (douetk), (Bordelon), Francois' son, was born on August 26, 1827 in Avoyelles Parish, LA. He married **Victorine Adeline Cailleteau** on June 12, 1851. He lived most of his life in Avoyelles where he was described as a prominent Mansura merchant. He died on November 12, 1878 in Mansura and is buried in St. Paul the Apostle Cemetery. Their children were:

- **Francoise** Lodoiska - (1852 - 1937)
- **Oscar Ovide** - 1858 - 1860)
- **Marie Estelle** - (1861 - 1863)
- **Pascalis Dasylva** - (1856 - 1893)
- **Lewis Pierre** - (1864 - 1956)
- **Thomas Alcide** - (1867 - 1923)
- **Robert Tesca** - (1869 - 1962)
- **Victor Leandre** - (1871 - 1968)
- **Josephine Inez** - (1874 - 1956)

Leandre Roy held 2 males slaves in the 1850 U.S. Census, making him the only child of Francois Roy shown to have held slaves. There are no records showing him holding slaves in 1860.

Leandre's son, **Robert Tesca** (a.k.a. Tesca), mentioned above, became a prominent local farmer. **Lewis Pierre Roy** became a well-known Marksville businessman and politician.

Other Local Slave Holders

As mentioned earlier, there were many Slave Holders in the Mansura area in the period leading up to the Civil War. Most individuals or families were not economically able to pay the substantial costs to purchase a slave ($500 - $1500, in some cases) and rarely held more than a few black people in captivity. Since much of the wealth and political power accumulated in the pre-Civil War South was based on slavery, few of their family names reached the level of prominence as the Normands, Cocos or Roys.

Nevertheless, some of these Slave Holders need mentioning since they held significant numbers of slaves captive in or near the town of Mansura or because they left behind family records that could allow some level of identification of individual slaves or their families.

Two such families are those headed by **Leandre Lacour** and **Julian Jules Goudeau**.

Leandre Lacour I held a significant number of slave parents in captivity whose babies were baptized at St. Paul's. Also, his plantation on Bayou des Glaise was in relatively close proximity to Mansura (Robertson), making it very likely that the black people he held captive were ancestors of some current black residents of Mansura, Moreauville and the local area.

He was born on November 10, 1799 in Avoyelles Parish, Louisiana. His parents were **Cyprien Lacour** and **Genevieve Joffrion**. He married **Victoire Berza** on April 24, 1821. They became the parents of 9 children between 1822 and 1845: **Leandre II**, **Sosthene**, **Jean Marie Brett**, **Celeste**, **Lea Susan**, **Adolph**, **Alzire**, **Joseph**, and **Numa** (Luttrell).

Leandre Lacour I was listed as a Slave Holder, baptizing 11 slaves at St. Paul's over the period from 1823 to 1850 (Church). These are listed below[8]:

- **Aigues** (No additional birth or baptism information given); Died September 3, 1850;
- **Antoine** (Born July 15, 1823; Baptized March 10, 1825); Mother - **Perline**; Godfather - Leandre Lacour, fils; Godmother - Magdalaine Gillard; Died December 27, 1852;
- **Apollinaire** (Born 1823; No additional birth or baptism information given); Died October 5, 1851;
- **Auguste** (Born October 28, 1823; Baptized October 10, 1825); Mother - **Golde**; Godfather - Silvaire Baillio; Godmother - Madalaine Gillard;
- **Augustin** (Born October 28, 1823; Baptized March 10, 1825); Godfather - Joseph Gillard, fils; Godmother - Margaritte Lacour);
- **Clarisse** (Born January, 1828; Baptized March 10, 1825); Mother - **Rita** (?); Godfather - Appolonaire Baillio; Godmother - Cecile Lacour);
- **Henriette** (Born June 28, 1825; Baptized March 10, 1825); Mother - **Golde**; Godfather - Gervail Baillio; Godmother - Helene Vallery;
- **Helena** (Born January 1, 1844; Baptized March 23, 1845); Mother - **Helene**; Godparents Unknown;
- **Julia** (Born October 30, 1844; Baptized March 23, 1845); Mother - **Julie**; No additional information given;
- **Narcine** (Born February, 1850); Mother - **Henriette**; No additional information given;
- **Isadore** (Born July 1827; Baptized May 18, 1828); Mother - **Oldag;** Godfather - Leandre Lacour II; Godmother - Magdalaine Lacour.

In the 1830 U.S. Census, Leandre Lacour was shown to be living in Avoyelles Parish (U. C. Bureau). Living with him was one white female, age 20-29 (Victoire?); two white males, under five; one white female, under five; and one white male, age 5-9. Also present were four slaves: two females and two males.

In 1840 (U. C. Bureau), Leandre Lacour's household included nine "Total Free White Persons" and 11 slaves: five males and six females.

---

[8] In some cases, the name of the mother and the dates of birth or of godparents of the babies being baptized were not listed

In 1850 (U. C. Bureau), Leandre and Victoire were living on a farm in Avoyelles along with their single children (Lea, Adolph, Alzire, and Numa) as well as their married son (Sosthene), his wife (Eliza), and their child (Ferrier). Also present was an additional family consisting of F. Wm., Clementine Lacour and a child named Emma. Leandre Lacour II was not present since he had married Felonise Lacour on July 16, 1844. That year, Leandre and Victoire were holding 20 slaves in captivity, consisting of 9 males and 11 females.

Leandre Lacour died in July, 1856 near Bayou De Glaise in Avoyelles Parish, Louisiana (Luttrell).

Julien Jules Goudeau I - Julien Jules Goudeau I was born in Bayou Rouge Prairie, Avoyelles Parish, Louisiana on August 8, 1805 (Moreau). His parents were **Pierre Michel Goudeau II** and **Eugenie Goudeau**. He married **Marceline Decuir** on January 8, 1828 at St. Paul the Apostle Catholic Church in Mansura. He and Marceline appeared to have lived near the area currently called Goudeau, east of Evergreen.

Although they did not live as near to Mansura as some of the other Slave Holders described in this book, he and Marceline held very close ties to Mansura because **Lucien Dominique Coco** (See Above) married their daughter, **Julienne Goudeau,** in 1852 (patsybaker19).

Julien and Marceline had 10 children: **Julien II**, **Julienne**, **Virginie**, **Elodie**, **Marceline**, **Angela**, **Amade'e**, **Marcellin**, **Pierre**, and **Emile**.

The most important reason for including Julien Goudeau and his family in this work is because their family records include a document dated 1858 (near the end of slavery) that actually names two slave families, including the husband and wife, as well as their children (Gremillion). A second document, listing his former slaves by age, name, skin color, and (sic) estimated monetary value, followed the first (Gremillion) .

Documents such as these, where slaves were actually named, are extremely rare and could provide critical links between people who were held in captivity during the slavery period and their current descendants.

In the St. Paul Baptismal records, Julien Goudeau was listed as the Slave Holder of the following black children being baptized (Church):

- **Theodise** - (Born December 16, 1831, Baptized February 7, 1833); Mother: **Marianne;** Godfather: **Louis** (FMC); Godmother: **Josephine** (Slave);

- **Arthemise** - (Born July 24, 1833, Baptized October 26, 1836); Mother: **Marianne;** Godfather: **Basile** (Slave); Godmother: **Severine** (FWC);
- **Lisa** - (Born 1834, Baptized October 25, 1836); Mother: **Eugenie;** Her godparents were white (Vignerasse Goudeau and Celine Goudeau);
- **Francois** - (Born June 4, 1835, Baptized October 25, 1836); Mother: **Marianne;** Godfather: **Coser** (FMC); Godmother: **Clementine** (Slave);
- **Jules** (Twin with Julie) - Born May 27, 1843, Baptized May 7, 1845); Mother: **Marianne** ; No Godparent Information;
- **Julie** (Twin with Jules) - (Born May 27, 1843, Baptized May 7, 1845); Mother: **Marianne**; No Godparent Information;
- **Divine** - (Unknown Birthdate); Mother: **Clarisse**; Godfather: **Julien** (Slave); Godmother: **Charlotte** (Slave).

In the 1850 United States Census, Julien Goudeau was listed as holding 52 black people as slaves on his plantation (U. C. Bureau).

Julien died in Avoyelles on September 25, 1852. In 1858, five years after his death, a decision was made to disburse his estate, since, in addition to his surviving widow, Marceline, there remained four minor children: Amede', Marcelin, Pierre' and Emile. Prior to any decision, a Property Inventory was authorized to define what assets constituted the Goudeau estate.

A "Family" meeting was held in which several uncles and other relatives of the minor children participated, along with Julien's widow, Marceline (Gremillion). The decision was made to allow Marceline to retain a certain plantation of 580 acres, on which she resided, along with the following slaves:

- **Henry** and **Marianne** along with their 2 children: **Roseline** and **Carmelite**;
- **Jessy** and **Rosemonde** and their 3 children: **Edmond**, **Jessy**, and **Octave**;
- **Bazile, Francois, Clarise, Clementine, Philomene, Henriette**, and **Martin**.

In addition to the above slaves, the widow Goudeau was allowed to retain:

> *"also the following stock mules and horses, ten in number; a lot of cattle - oxen - carts - wagons - a gang of hogs, blacksmith's tools and farming utensils as can be seen by reference to the Inventory taken by me, Recorder, on the date of today."*

The Property Inventory mentioned above is unique since it included specific information regarding the slave population on the Goudeau plantations (Gremillion). Those slaves mentioned in that inventory are listed below:

- **Cola**, Negro man, 65 years, value $25.00;

- **Charles**, Negro man, about 53 years, value $600.00;
- **Matt**, Negro man, about 43 years, value $800.00;
- **Little Henry**, Negro man, about 29 years, value $1,000.00;
- **Charles Mateille**, Negro man, about 32 years, value $900.00;
- *Francois**, Negro man, about 21 years, value $1,000.00;
- **Faublas**, mulatto boy, about 17 years, value $600.00;
- **Adolphe**, Negro boy, about 17 years, value $600.00;
- *Jules**, Negro boy, about 13 years, value $500.00;
- **Thomas**, mulatto boy, about 10 years, value $500.00;
- **Little Charles**, Negro boy, about 11 years, value $350.00;
- **Charles Rey**, mulatto boy, about 5 years, value $400.00;
- **Jane**, Negro woman, about 43 years, value $400.00;
- *Theomise**, Negro woman, about 27 years, value $600.00;
- **Adilimore**, mulatto woman, about 32 years, and her three children, viz; **Homise,** 9 years old; **Simion**, 7 years old; and **Edward,** 3 years old. Total value was $1,500.00;
- **Gustine**, Negro woman, about 20 years, and her two children, viz; **Florestine**, a girl aged 3 years, and **John** aged about one month, value $1,000.00;
- **Nancy**, Negro woman, about 45 years, and her two children, **Louise** aged about 5 years, and **Ellen** aged about 3 years, value $800.00;
- **Eulalie**, Negro woman, about 31 years and her four children, **Elizabeth** aged 9 years, **Roy** aged 5 years, **Caroline** aged 3 years, and **Mary Avon** aged 2 months, $1,800.00;
- **Mary**, mulatto woman aged about 25 years, and her two children, **Alphonse** aged 6 years, and **Simmia** aged about 3 years, value $1,500.00;
- *Julie**, Negro girl, about 13 years, value $550.00;
- **Little Mary**, Negro girl, about 13 years, value $600.00;
- **Margueritte**, Negro girl, about 12 years, value $450.00;
- **Elizabeth**, mulatto girl, about 11 years, valued $400.00;
- **Sophie**, Negro girl, about 11 years, value $450.00;
- **Bazile**, Negro man, about 39 years, value $800.00;
- **Old Henry**, Negro man, about 55 years, value $250.00;
- **Martin**, Negro man, about 39 years, value $1,200.00;
- *Francois* Magloire*, Negro man, about 20 years, value $1,000.00;
- **Jessy**, mulatto man, about 30 years, value $800.00;
- **Rosemonde**, Negro woman, about 29 years, and her three children, **Edmond** aged about 9 years, **Jessy** aged about 6 years, **Octave** aged about 9 months, value $1,500.00;
- **Clarisse**, Negro woman, about 54 years, value $350.00;
- **Clemintine**, mulatto woman, about 34 years, value $600.00;
- **Harriet**, Negro woman, about 35 years, value $600.00;
- **Marienne**, Negro woman, about 40 years, and her two children, **Roseline** aged 9 years, and **Carmelite** aged about 7 years, value $1,000.00;
- **Louis**, mulatto boy, about 17 years, value $700.00;
- **Falma**, mulatto boy, about 14 years, value $600.00;

- **John Baptiste**, Negro boy, about 15 years, value $600.00;
- **Little Bazile**, Negro boy, about 11 years, value $600.00;
- **Philomima**, mulatto girl, about 14 years, value $600.00.

It is important to note that some of the slaves shown being baptized in the St. Paul Baptismal Registry by Julian Goudeau (i.e. Francois, Jules, Theomise, Julie.) were also listed in the 1858 property inventory (*In Italics*). Since, from the St. Paul Records, we already know the birthdates and mothers of these baptized persons, this combined information now makes it easier to further identify some of these individuals by searching for them in the U.S. Census records for 1870 and 1880.

Also, since many of these people likely lived well into the 20th century, using some level of diligence, it should be possible to identify many of them as ancestors of African-Americans living today.

Chapter 5. Free People of Color and Mulattoes

FIGURE 17. WELL DRESSED MULATTO WOMAN, CA. 1855 (MOISSENNET)

In this chapter, we will briefly discuss some of the background information on the Free People of Color (FPC) in Avoyelles Parish prior to the Civil War (U. C. Bureau). We will also briefly touch on the mulattoes in the Mansura area in the 1st half of the 20th century.

While there were relatively few FPCs, some of their surnames still persist and their descendants can trace their heritage back to them. A thorough study of that group of people is beyond the scope of this work.

The term **Free People of Color** (Gens de Couleur Libres) originally referred to persons of mixed African and European descent who were not enslaved (Laver). The term was especially used in the

French colonies, including Louisiana and settlements on Caribbean islands, such as Santo Domingo, Guadeloupe, and Martinique. Over time, it included all non-whites who happened to be free, although the majority of this group remained of mixed race decent.

In Louisiana, primarily New Orleans, the children of mixed French and African decent, now called **Creoles**, flourished. By 1840, fully 20% of the city's population was comprised of these French speaking creoles. **Quadroons** (Voltz), those who were at least 75% white, were highly popular among the white male aristocrats and the **Quadroon Balls** were held to allow these men to meet and select some of the Quadroon women to be their concubines. It was common for the children of these relationships, a.k.a. **Placage**, to be sent to the best schools and to inherit considerable wealth from their white fathers.

By the 1850s, free people of color owned more than $2 million worth of property, mostly in the **Faubourgs Treme** and **Marigny** neighborhoods of old New Orleans (Elie) . By 1855, nearly 85% of black Creoles were classified as doctors, clerks, teachers and skilled workers. They also thrived in trades like carpentry, masonry and cigar-making. Some even owned slaves

Outside of New Orleans, however, the story of Black-White relationships was not so glamorous. In many cases, the concubine was forced into the relationship by a violent and lust-driven Slave Holder who was willing to inflict as much torture as he felt was needed to force her to give in. Clearly, this resulted in hostility toward the slave female by the Slave Holder's wife, destruction of slave marriages, distrust of the slave concubine by the other slaves and hostility toward the Slave Holder.

The relationship between the Slave Holder and his wife was generally strained, at best. In many cases, her inability to stop the relationship between her husband and his slave mistress led to open hostility toward him and his slave mistress, public embarrassment and, in some cases, her own depression, illness and death. Mary Reynolds (Writers):

> *"Once massa goes to Baton Rouge and brung back a yaller girl dressed in fine style. She was a seamster n----r. He builds her a house way from the quarters and she done fine sewin' for the whites. us n----rs knowed the doctor took a black woman quick as he did a white and took any on his place he wanted, and he took them often. But mostly the chillun born on the place looked like n----rs. Aunt Cheyney allus say four of hers were massas, but he didn't give them no mind. But this yaller gal breeds so fast and gits a mess of white young'uns. She larnt them fine manners and combs out they hair."*

According to Mary Reynolds, there was always a tense relationship between the Slave Holder's legitimate children and those he fathered with slave women he held captive.

> *"Onct two of them goes down the hill to the doll house where the Kilpatrick chillun am playin'. They wants to go in the dollhouse and one the Kilpatrick boys say, That's for white chillun.' They say, "We ain't no n----rs, cause we got the same daddy you has, and he comes to see us near every day and fotches us clothes and things from town.' They is fussin' and Missy Kilpatrick is listenin' out her*

chamber window. She heard them white n----rs say, He is our daddy and we call him daddy when he comes to our house to see our mama."

The Slave Holder's wife, although not happy with his sexual involvement with the female slave being held on his plantation, seemed powerless to do anything about it. She seemed easily swayed by his gifts and promises.

"When massa come home that evenin' his wife hardly say nothin' to him, and he ask her what the matter and she tells him, Since you asks me, I'm studyin' in my mind bout them white young'uns of that yaller n----r wench from Baton Rouge. He say, Now, honey, I fotches that gal jus' for you, cause she a fine seamster.' She say, It look kind of funny they got the same kind of hair and eyes as my chillun and they got a nose looks like yours.' He say, Honey, you jus' payin' tention to talk of li'l chillun that ain't got no mind to what they say.' She say, Over in Mississippi I got a home and plenty with my daddy and I got that in my mind."

"Well, she didn't never leave and massa bought her a fine new span of surrey hosses. But she don't never have no more chillun and she ain't so cordial with the massa. Margaret, that yellow gal, has more white young'uns, but they don't never go down the hill no more to the big house."

The 1860 United States Census collected the following information on all free people in the country, including Whites, Native Americans (Indians), Asians, Hispanics and FPC's: Name; Age; Gender; Color[9]; Birthplace; Occupation; Value of real estate they owned; whether married, single or widowed; deaf, dumb, blind or insane; a pauper or a convict; whether able to read or speak English and whether the person attended school within the previous year.

That year a new designation for skin color, **yellow**, was also added to the official "Colors" of White, Black or Mulatto, presumably to describe those of Asian descent. Interesting, that color was randomly used by the census takers to describe some people who might normally have been called mulattoes.

After the Civil War and the new U.S. census forms were instituted, the word, **mulatto**, was specified as the official U.S. government designation of any African American with a skin color that resembled Europeans. Eventually, the term mulatto was dropped and substituted with the words Black or Colored.

----

[9] It not clear if "Color" referred to skin color or nationality. For example, "Yellow" could refer to mulattoes, people of Asian descent or to those whose skin jU.S.t happened to be yellow in hue. In the current discussion, it is the latter that seems to be the case.

APPENDIX B lists the FPC's who were registered in the 1860 U.S. Census for Avoyelles Parish. It lists the following by color: four Blacks (B); 46 Mulattoes (M); four Indians (I) and 23 Yellow (Y).

Whole families of FPC's were usually shown living together. In some cases, it appears that several FPCs in a given area were living together, perhaps in some sort of bunk house.

In many cases, the FPC only had single names, just as most slaves did. In other cases, they had full names, including a last name. The reader will likely recognize some familiar last names, such as "**Laveley**", now spelled "**Lavalais**", "**Bontemps**", now spelled "**Bonton**", while "**Dauzat**" and "**Laurent**" are still spelled the same way.

Most FPC's lived on or near slave plantations and generally performed jobs and had lives that were not much different from the slaves themselves. In some cases, the FPC's were skilled craftsmen such as blacksmiths, carpenters, brick masons, etc.

The St. Paul Baptism Records (Church) lists 13 FPC's who appeared as the **Godparents** of slave children being baptized. These are listed below, along with their godchild, the child's mother, the year of the baptism and their Slave Holder, if known:

- **Basile** - Godchild: Cyrile; Mother: Nancy; Baptism Year: 1838; Slave Holder: Pierre L'Eglise
- **Severine** - Godchild: Arthemse; Mother: Marianne; Baptism Year:1836; Slave Holder: Julien Goudeau;
- **Sidonise** - Godchild: Benjamin; Mother: Rachal; Baptism Year: 1830; Slave Holder: A. Biosset
- **Coser** - Godchild: Francois; Mother: Marianne; Baptism Year: 1836; Slave Holder: Julien Goudeau;
- **Francois** - Godchild: Rosaline; Mother: Josephine; Baptism Year: 1837; Slave Holder: Unknown;
- **Joseph** - Godchild: William; Mother: Ayme; Baptism Year: 1833; Slave Holder: Laurent Normand;
- **Julien Berzat** - Godchild: Julien Rosalie; Mother: Zenon Boyer; Baptism Year:; Slave Holder: Unknown;
- **Justin** - Godchild: Helie; Mother: Eulalie; Baptism Year: 1836; Slave Holder: Pierre Goudeau;
- **Ayme** - Godchild: Helie; Mother: Eulalie; Baptism Year: 1836; Slave Holder: Pierre Goudeau;
- **Louis** - Godchild: Lucie; Mother: Celeste; Baptism Year: 1836; Slave Holder: Pierre Goudeau;
- **Louis** - Godchild: Theodise; Mother: Marianne; Baptism Year: 1833; Slave Holder: Julien Goudeau;
- **Pierre Labiche** - Godchild: Celestin; Mother: Sylvie; Baptism Year: 1839; Slave Holder: Laurent Normand;
- **Stonocine** (sp.?) - Godchild: Honoroe; Mother: Manette; Baptism Year: 1832; Slave Holder: Francois Tournier.

Pre-Civil War family histories of FPCs who had surnames are much easier to define than for Blacks who were held in slavery and had no published surnames, hence, no family history. An example is that for **Joseph Laurent**, whose life is documented from his birth in 1817 to his death in 1870:

> **Joseph Laurent** was a mulatto who was born about 1817 to unknown parents. He married Marie Louise Berzat, also a mulatto, in Avoyelles Parish on December 9, 1835 (J. R. Dodd).
>
> Joseph and Marie had 8 children in the 1850 U.S. census: **Louis** (13), **Joseph II** (10), **Silvin** (8), **Josephine** (6), **Euphenie** (4), **Laurent** (2) and **Angela** (1) (L. Bordelon). He was described as a carpenter even though he and his family lived in an area where there were mostly white farmers.
>
> The 1860 U.S. Census only lists Joseph (41), Marie (38), Joseph II (25) and Sylvandre (23) (Cockrone).
>
> Joseph Laurent died on September 11, 1870 (Coronor).

Had Joseph Laurent been a former slave with no surname, his life story would have begun with the 1870 census.

In the 1910 United States Census for Mansura and the surrounding area (Lemoine), there were several families living near each other whose members were described as mulattoes. They all appeared to be living north of Mansura along the Grande Bayou and Marksville roads. These included the following surnames: **Bontemps, Reynaud, Demouy, Berger, Coco, Prevot, William, Deshotel, Berzat, Laurent, Lehman, Normand,** and **Prunell**.

Other local mulatto families living outside the above area had the following surnames: **Thomas, Lavalais, St. Romain, Mairie, Francois, Francisco** and **Rogers**.

While many of the surnames of the Grande Bayou mulattoes persisted into the 1960's, today, many of them are gone. Some have moved away while others have passed on. In addition, those individuals still with those surnames no longer have predominant European features and have assumed more African cultural styles.

Part II. The Civil War - The Gates of Hell

FIGURE 18. HISTORICAL MARKER ON L'EGLISE STREET IN MANSURA[10]

The American Civil War began on April 12, 1861 with the attack on the United States garrison quartered at Fort Sumpter, South Carolina and ended on May 9, 1865 with the surrender of Confederate General Robert E. Lee at Appomattox Courthouse in Virginia.

The war was initially fought over state's rights but quickly changed to slavery once the economic value of that institution to the South was recognized and the influence of the Northern antislavery movement gained traction.

The two adversaries in the war were the Union (i.e., the North, the United States government) and the Rebels (i.e., the South, the Confederacy). A number of significant historical figures evolved as a result of their roles in the war and the anti-slavery movement: Abraham Lincoln, Jefferson Davis, Ulysses Grant, Robert E. Lee, George McClelland, Stonewall Jackson, Harriet Tubman, Sojourner Truth, Frederick Douglas, John Wilkes Booth and many others.

The war was easily the most vicious and costliest in terms of human lives, with the 750,000 deaths exceeding the combined death total for World Wars I and II combined.

---

[10] Historical Sign Located on L'Eglise Street in Mansura

At the end of the war, the Confederacy had collapsed, the South's financial and political infrastructure was in disarray, and slavery was abolished.

The emotional damage and its resulting anger and hatred has remained a large part of American life, even after over 150 years.

Chapter 6. A Prelude to War

For the enslaved Blacks in the United States seeking freedom from tyranny, the Civil War did not begin with John Brown's raid on Harper's Ferry (Banks) or with the Confederate attack on Fort Sumter (Hatcher). Rather, it began well before the American Revolution and continued throughout the 19th and 20th centuries.

Unlike the stories told in the history books about slavery that have been taught for over 200 years, slaves were not ignorant, weak-minded beasts of burden who just happened to have the appearance of a white man or woman. Slaves were not happy or "Gay". Slaves never thought themselves better off as enslaved Christian instead of as free heathens.

In reality, slaves were never content in their imprisonment and persisted in every way possible to free themselves from those who held them against their will. In most cases, the resistance of the slaves to their imprisonment took the form of simple acts such as sabotage or arson, poorly per-formed work, faked illness or running away (H. C. Staff). In some cases, however, violence was used.

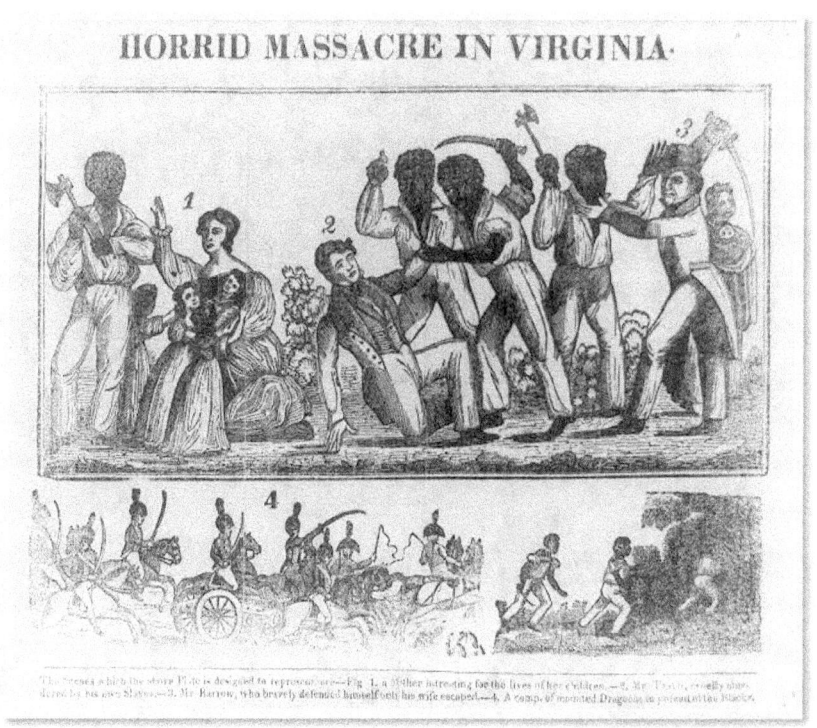

FIGURE 19. WOOD CARVED SCENES FROM NAT TURNER REBELLION, CA. 1831 (UNKNOWN)

Early Attempts at Freedom - The Civil Right Movement of the 20th century was generally non-violent. However, in earlier centuries, the numerous attempts by enslaved Blacks to gain their freedom were far from non-violent (H. L. Gates). It is estimated that there were between 33 and over 200 slave revolts in both the American colonies and the United States beginning as early as 1739. As a result of these attempts at freedom, hundreds of slaves, as well as white men, women and children, were killed. In most cases, the rebellions were crushed and the black participants were put to death in some of the harshest ways, i.e. shooting, hanging, burning, boiling, quartering, beheading and skinning.

While these violent slave revolts created fear and hostility, the **American Abolitionist** movement was generally non-violent and appealed to the country's sense of humanity and fairness (Press). Based on the religious beliefs of churches such as the Quakers, the Abolitionists used moral and religious propaganda to further their cause of freedom for the slaves.

The "Back to Africa Movement" was an early attempt to free Blacks from slavery by removing them from this country and setting them free in a sparsely populated area of West Africa (Harper). This movement began with the formation of the **American Colonialization Society** in 1817. The leaders of this movement, unfortunately, embraced the concept of Blacks as inferior beings who needed to be back in their primitive native land in order to survive, versus living in a complex world owned by superior whites. For example, an 1854 Pennsylvania newspaper editorial stated:

> "*We think we have a proper estimate of the character of the negro, and our feelings towards the race are of the most kindly character. We would elevate them, but not at the expense of the white man. We have no idea of sinking our own race, in order to raise up the inferior African. This country belongs to the white man, and not to the negro, and that, in our estimation, is the purest philanthropy, which seeks to place upon the shores of Africa again, those whom cupidity has stolen from their native soil.*"

A few emancipated slaves were actually sent to Haiti in 1863 with the support of Abraham Lincoln and financing from the U.S. Congress. This venture was a disaster and the colonists were wiped out. In the end, most leaders of the abolitionists rejected the American Colonialization Society's ideas and plans.

The most effective antislavery efforts began with the establishment of the newspaper, **The Liberator**, by **William Lloyd Garrison** in 1831 and his role in the formation of the **New England Anti-Slavery Society** in 1832 (B. Staff). The ensuing flood of books, pamphlets, newspapers and petitions greatly increased the awareness of a Northern population previously indifferent to slavery. Abolitionists (H. Staff) such as **Harriet Beecher Stowe**, **Sojourner Truth** and **Frederick Douglas**, gained fame and helped increase the anti-slavery fervor while the **Underground Railroad** and the activities of **Harriet Tubman** helped slaves find their way to freedom.

The election of Abraham Lincoln, with strong anti-slavery support, and **John Brown's Raid on Harper's Ferry** were two of the key events that set in motion the country's slide towards war.

Pre-Civil War Slave Rebellions in Louisiana - During the two decades before the Civil War began, the white population in the South became very nervous and worried about possible slave rebellions. This was fueled by the news of the many slave rebellions in the U.S. (H. L. Gates).

For Avoyelles whites, an earlier, albeit aborted, 1795 slave uprising in nearby Pointe Coupe Parish was a strong indicator of what could occur and how holding so many people against their will and under the harshest circumstances could cost them their lives (Holmes), (S. R. Staff).   In this case, a large number of slaves, centered on the plantation of **Julien Poydras**, along with slaves from several other nearby plantations and a few whites, planned an elaborate uprising where they would set fire to the Poydras plantation and seize the stored arms and ammunition. When other local Whites showed up to help put out the fire, they would slaughter them, along with the creoles who sided with the Whites. The plot was discovered and those involved arrested.

After a trial on May 4, 1795,

> *"Fifty-seven slaves and three local whites were convicted. By June 2, twenty-three slaves were hung, their heads cut off and nailed on the posts at several places along the Mississippi River from New Orleans to Pointe Coupee. Thirty-one slaves were sentences to floggings and to hard labor in Spanish fortresses in Mexico, Florida, Puerto Rico, and Cuba. All three whites were deported, and two of them were sentences to six years of forced labor in Havana."*

The Pointe Coupee Parish Slave Uprising clearly had a strong emotional impact on the Whites in Avoyelles Parish for the following reasons:

- Many of the Whites living in the future Avoyelles Parish area at the time of the 1795 uprising had moved there from Pointe Coupee and probably still had family members living there (See Above). These included Dominique Coco, Jr.; Joseph Joffrion, II; Joseph Marie Roy II and Colin Cyprien Lacour (Father of Leandre Lacour);
- Several slaves, who testified in the trial of the people involved in the uprising, were identified as being held by Whites who had the same surnames as residents of Avoyelles, e.g. Goudeau and Lacour (Holmes). This is further evidence that these Pointe Coupee Slave Holders were relatives of the white Avoyelles residents, making the slave uprising in Pointe Coupee even more personal to them.

While it is possible that there were other disturbances by local slaves prior to the start of the Civil War, the event that likely created the most tension and fear among the white population of Avoyelles Parish was the 1860 murder of Cocoville plantation owner and Slave Holder, Laurent Normand (See Above). Despite the belief that Normand's murder was the result of his involvement with fe-male slaves (M. J. Normand), the fact that local slaves had the audacity and boldness to plan, attack and murder a well-respected, white Avoyelles Parish Slave Holder was simply beyond belief.

White Reprisals - The news of Laurent Normand's murder likely spread great fear and distrust of the slaves among the local white population and the image of the docile, god-fearing and mindless beast of burden was gone forever. Now, the Whites realized, any slave could be hiding a hostile plan and had the courage and desperation to implement it.

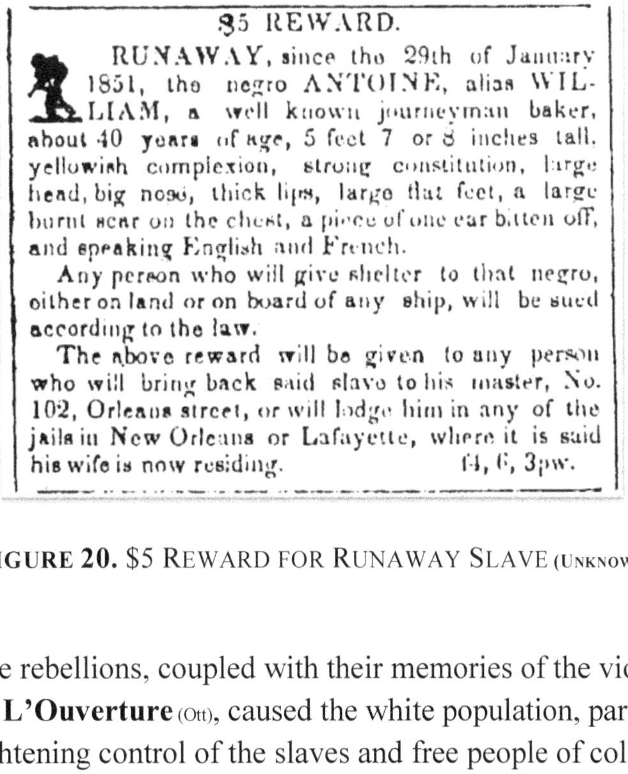

> **$5 REWARD.**
>
> RUNAWAY, since the 29th of January 1851, the negro ANTOINE, alias WIL-LIAM, a well known journeyman baker, about 40 years of age, 5 feet 7 or 8 inches tall, yellowish complexion, strong constitution, large head, big nose, thick lips, large flat feet, a large burnt scar on the chest, a piece of one ear bitten off, and speaking English and French.
>
> Any person who will give shelter to that negro, either on land or on board of any ship, will be sued according to the law.
>
> The above reward will be given to any person who will bring back said slave to his master, No. 102, Orleans street, or will lodge him in any of the jails in New Orleans or Lafayette, where it is said his wife is now residing.   f4, 6, 3pw.

FIGURE 20. $5 REWARD FOR RUNAWAY SLAVE (UNKNOWN)

News of these U.S. slave rebellions, coupled with their memories of the violent 1791 Haitian revolution led by **Toussaint L'Ouverture** (Ott), caused the white population, particularly in the South, to begin systematically tightening control of the slaves and free people of color (Thomas). Now, passes to travel outside the plantations became much more difficult to acquire and could be challenged by any white person. Also, groups of white men began patrolling the roads and bayous at night looking for slaves traveling without passes. Rules forbidding any type of assembly by slaves, without a white person being present, became the norm. Penalties for violating these rules often ranged from beatings, imprisonment, being sent to more isolated and harsher work environments and death. Any non-work related contact between slaves and Free People of Color became highly restricted.

Chapter 7. The Civil War in Louisiana

Louisiana, along with the other Southern states, voted to secede from the United States in early 1861 and joined the Confederacy a few months later. All members of the Confederacy committed to provide the war effort with money, goods and services and, especially, manpower in the form of men willing to fight to defend their way of life. (Sacher), (C.-W. Staff)

By the time the war was over, over 2,750,000 Union and about 1,250,000 Confederate soldiers and sailors had participated in the war. Of these, the Union suffered 360,000 deaths due to combat and disease, while the Confederate suffered about 258,000 deaths from the same causes. Nearly 180,000 black troops fought in the war, nearly all on the Union side, losing about 36,000 to combat, disease, accidents and a few military executions (Davis).

As many as 60,000 white men from Louisiana joined or were conscripted into the Confederate military. From that number, there were casualties totaling 3,444 dead or wounded and another 868 from disease. The state contributed about 5000 white men to the Union armies, of which 945 died from all causes.

Louisiana Blacks, many, after running away from plantations during the Union Army's occupation of the southern part of the state, enlisted in large numbers during 1864 and 1865. By the end of the war, over 24,500 black soldiers and sailors from Louisiana, the largest number of any state, had served in the Union military (Gladstone). The actual numbers dying from battle-inflicted wounds or other causes remains unknown.

Fear and Uneasiness Back Home - Once the war started, the vast majority of able-bodied white men in Louisiana left their homes and joined the Confederate forces doing battle in other states. They apparently assumed that the war would be short-lived and they would soon be returning home, victoriously. That was not the case and many of those who managed to return home were gone for the whole course of the war.

As a result of the departure of the men, not much manpower was available back home to protect their families and homes except the relatively weak local police authorities, supported by the women, children and elderly. Those left behind soon realized that they were now living in a world where they were vastly outnumbered by the slaves with little ability to defend themselves.

As time and the war dragged on, the growing fear and anxiety among the Whites in Louisiana rose to the level of hysteria and began to manifest itself in many ways. Some examples were (Rodriguez):

- Local planters and political officials brought their fears of possible slave rebellions and the resulting bloodbaths to the leaders of the state and of the Confederacy, including Jefferson Davis, its president;
- Some Southern governors began to hold back on their troop commitments to the Confederacy in order to provide sufficient safeguards against a slave rebellion back home;
- Local white officials and civilians resorted to tactics where any slave considered a possible conspirator might be arrested, beaten and, often, put to death;
- Most parish governments passed or enhanced the existing slave laws to: prevent slaves from leaving the plantation without a pass, assembling anywhere without white supervision, gambling, drinking alcohol, owning or possessing a horse, etc. (Ripley);
- The "Parish Patrols", formed in each parish from men ages 15-50, became much more active, both day and night: watching for unauthorized slave movement; canvassing slave cabins for anyone who might be absent; and acting as a sort of home militia.
- Any white person who might be a stranger to the area was considered to be a possible slave sympathizer and was often ordered to leave under veiled threats to their lives;
- Free people of color found themselves being arrested and imprisoned on trumped-up charges to prevent them from associating with the slaves. It was feared that they might provide the knowledge and leadership the slaves needed to have a successful rebellion.

There is ample evidence to demonstrate that there were, indeed, several planned slave rebellions throughout Louisiana and Mississippi during the Civil War (Rodriguez). For example,

- In May, 1861, a Tensas Parish planter, hiding under the floor of a slave cabin, heard several slaves plotting to join up with five abolitionists and begin a revolt on July 4, 1861. The plot was crushed.
- In June of 1861, mass hysteria gripped the area around the coastal parish of St. Mary when rumors spread of an impending abolitionist invasion and slave uprising. There were numerous report of gatherings of slaves in bayous through the area. Several slaves were arrested and six were hung. Others received life sentences at hard labor [sic].
- A group of slaves in Concordia Parish was discovered plotting a revolt during the summer of 1861. A "Planter's Court" tried the conspirators and sentenced 10 to death by hanging. Before their sentence, each was allowed to "confess" and the planters were astounded by the level of thought and planning the slaves had put into their conspiracy as well as their lack of remorse and their passionate hatred for whites.
- As the Union troops took control of New Orleans in April of 1862, slaves all over the area began to engage in work stoppages, open threats against white masters, or running away.

Black Louisianans in the Civil War: The Louisiana Native Guard- At the beginning of the war, the Union's strategy was to capture the Mississippi River and split the Confederacy in two. This began in early 1862 with the capture of New Orleans, which remained in Union hands throughout the war (W. Staff). For the rest of the war, most of the Union military's action in Louisiana consisted of small skirmishes, foraging for food and other supplies, building bridges and roads, and managing runaway slaves. Although the numbers of runaway slaves following the Union was overwhelming, the idea of enlisting them in combat service was slow in coming.

Many local slaves, believing that the Union's military had come to rescue them from slavery, quickly began escaping from their plantations and flooding into New Orleans. The Union military commander, **General Benjamin Franklin Butler**, responsible for maintaining order in the city, soon realized that his forces were being overwhelmed by the mass of refugees fleeing the plantations in the region. His initial response was to attempt to return the escaped slaves to their plantations. He stated in a letter,

> *"Be sure that I shall treat the negro [sic] with as much tenderness as possible but I assure you it is impossible to free him here and now without a San Domingo. A single whistle from me would cause every white man's throat to be cut in this city. Accumulated hate has been piled up here between master and servant, until it is fearful....there is no doubt that an insurrection is only prevented by our bayonets."*

A more antislavery-leaning subordinate of Butler, **General John Wolcott Phelps**, took a different approach to controlling the former slaves. He proposed that the Blacks be organized into military units and be provided educational opportunities. Butler reacted very angrily to Phelps plan and caused Phelps' resignation.

However, Butler, under pressure from the U.S. government, abolitionists and the slaves themselves, reluctantly began to accept Phelps' idea and, eventually, allowed the formation of a black militia, called the **Native Guard** (Berry), made up of freedmen from New Orleans. Within 2 weeks, the Native Guard has grown to over 1800 black men and by the end of 1862, Butler had 3 infantry brigades and 2 batteries of heavy artillery made up of mostly former slaves. He had also appointed 66 black men, mostly Free Men of Color, as lieutenants and captains.

Unfortunately, Butler's willingness to allow Blacks to become soldiers did not extend to combat roles. Not only was there prevailing doubt among most of the Union's military and political leaders about the courage of black soldiers in combat situations, the whole idea of armed black men doing battle with white men, irrespective of the sides during the war, was totally intolerable to most Whites, both Union and Confederate. This all changed later once the Union army began to suffer staggering losses on the battlefield coupled with difficulties in providing replacements.

Nevertheless, General Phelps' ideas remained a cornerstone of the Union's process for managing the huge crowds of runaway slaves and, ultimately, led to the legitimate inclusion of Blacks in the U.S. military. The siege of Port Hudson, Louisiana was a turning point in the whole concept of how Blacks might participate in the military.

The Siege of Port Hudson - By the summer of 1862, the Union military had seized control of New Orleans, Baton Rouge and Memphis, effectively giving itself control of both the lower and upper sections of the Mississippi river (Hewitt). This prevented the Confederates from conducting any type of trade with some of the European countries seeking their products, mostly cotton.

One glaring flaw in the Union strategy was the lack of control of the Red River, a vital supply line from the Western Confederate states to the southeast. Both sides recognized the strategic importance of this river and sough to gain its control.

The Confederates, under **General John Breckenridge**, hurriedly selected a perfect location for the defense of the mouth of the Red River near the town of Port Hudson, just north of Baton Rouge and about 50 miles south of the mouth of the Red River. There, they constructed a heavily-fortified military fort on an 80-foot high bluff overlooking a sharp bend in the Mississippi by the spring of 1863. Their 20 huge guns overlooking the river now posed a threat to any Union vessel attempting to travel the Mississippi.

After a spectacular, although failed, attempt to run seven Union ships past the new Confederate fortification by Union **Admiral David Farragut** in March 14, 1863, the Union army leaders decided to launch ground attacks, thus, initiating the siege of Port Hudson.

FIGURE 21. UNION FLEET PASSING POST HUDSON (HAMILTON)

The battle and siege of Port Hudson occurred between May 22 and July 9 of 1863. It began with an unsuccessful Union ground assault on the Confederate stronghold there. This was followed by several further failed attempts to capture the fort by the Union army that resulted in large losses while the Confederate losses were much smaller. When the Union commander, General Nathaniel P. Banks, recognized his army's inability to capture the fort, a protracted siege began.

During the siege, black troops, who comprised the **1st Louisiana Native Guard** (T. L. Jones), (Berry) distinguished themselves through their battlefield skills and courage (Hewitt).

FIGURE 22. LOUISIANA NATIVE GUARD DISEMBARKING AT FORT MCCOMB (O. S. ARTIST)

Although unprepared for battle, on May 27, 1863, a unit of the 1st Louisiana Guard was suddenly assigned the task of attacking the Confederate stronghold over a narrow pontoon bridge and under extremely heavy fire from rifles, field artillery and coastal guns. Nevertheless, under the leadership of **Captain Andre Cailloux**, a free black citizen of New Orleans, who gave orders in both English and French, the black troops moved forward without flinching. Unfortunately, when Captain Cailloux was killed and the troops suffered heavy casualties, the attack was called off.

FIGURE 23. FUNERAL OF CAPTAIN ANDRE CAILLOUX, 1ST LOUISIANA NATIVE GUARD (ARTIST)

The Native Guard suffered 167 casualties in that battle. Sadly, their dead were left to rot on the battle field when the Union commanders claimed that Confederate snipers prevented them from retrieving the bodies.

While the Native Guard's attack was repulsed without inflicting any casualties on the Confederate defenders, it was their demonstrated courage during a hopeless situation that so impressed the white commanders. Their battle field bravery received wide notoriety, especially in Northern newspapers.

FIGURE 24. SOLDIERS OF THE NATIVE GUARD REGIMENTS AT PORT HUDSON (HARPER'S WEEKLY NEWSPAPER)

The testimony of the white Union soldiers who witnessed the black troop involvement at Port Hudson, and the resulting positive press eventually led to the acceptance of black troops in the Union military. The renewed trust in their courage under fire resulted in the eventual inclusion of over 180,000 black troops to the Union ranks by the end of the Civil War.

Once the war was over, however, the exploits of the black soldiers and sailors were soon forgotten and their involvement in future wars was marginalized.

FIGURE 25. MAP SHOWING INVOLVEMENT OF BLACK TROOPS IN CIVIL WAR BATTLES (KENMAYER)

The Civil War in Avoyelles Parish – In 1864, a decision was made by the U.S. War Department to have General Nathaniel Banks, the commander of the Union army occupying New Orleans, move a large force of Union soldiers from New Orleans north to capture Shreveport (W. Staff, Red River Campaign).

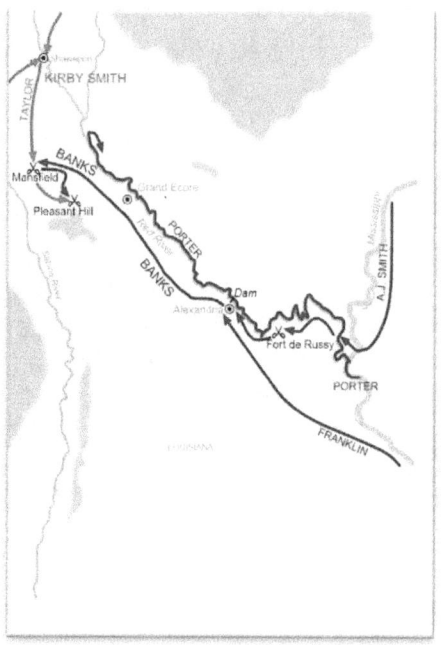

FIGURE 26. RED RIVER CAMPAIGN MARCH-MAY 1864 (UNKNOWN)

The Union forces used a two-pronged attack, traveling from the Mississippi River north of Baton Rouge and up the Red River via boats. The rest of the Union forces traveled overland from New Orleans by way of south Louisiana. Both groups used Alexandria as a stopping point.

FIGURE 27. BAILEY'S DAM IN ALEXANDRIA DURING RED RIVER CAMPAIGN (LESLIE)

This "**Red River Campaign**" turned out to be a military failure despite having engaged over 40,000 men and suffering nearly 10,000 casualties. Confusion and poor leadership by the Union's general staff led to them being unable to effectively challenge the strong and determined Confederate force guarding the northern part of Louisiana.

However, as the large Union army moved through south Louisiana and then up past Alexandria and Natchitoches, on the way to Shreveport, large numbers of slaves began to run away from the plantations all along the way. In many cases, as many as 300 slaves ran away each day, hoping to follow the Union Army to freedom.

The Union army pressed many of these ex-slaves into service, foraging for food, chopping trees for firewood, building bridges and clearing underbrush. In many cases, the ex-slaves participated in the raiding and demolition of plantations along the way. What they left behind was many plantations that were abandoned, destroyed, or left in the hands of newly liberated former slaves.

The Battles of Fort DeRussy and Mansura (contributors) - General Banks' army, while passing through Avoyelles Parish (See **Figure 26**), captured **Fort DeRussy** on the Red River near Marksville, on March 14, 1864 as it traveled north toward Shreveport. Parts of that same Union Army participated in the brief skirmish called the **Battle of Mansura** on May 16, 1864 as it retreated back towards the Mississippi River (contributors, Battle of Mansura).

- **Battle of Fort DeRussy** - Fort DeRussy was located four miles north of Marksville, Louisiana. In 1864, it was a Confederate stronghold, manned by 350 troops and well-fortified. Its primary responsibility was to defend the lower Red River Valley in Louisiana and prevent the passage of any Union ships, especially the ironclads. Their position was also reinforced by tons of debris that was submerged in the river to prevent ships, including the Union vessels participating in the Red River Campaign, from passing through.

   On the evening of March 14, a Union force of about 10,000 men, led by Union **General A. J. Smith**, charged the fort and the battle was over and the Confederates surrendered in 20 minutes. In all, the Union lost 48 men killed or wounded and 2 missing. The Confederates suffered 2 killed, 5 wounded and 317 captured. This opened the Red River route to Shreveport for a part of General Bank's army.

- **Battle of Mansura -** On May 16, 1864, Union Forces, retreating from the Red River Campaign and traveling to Simmesport, encountered a small force of Confederates with artillery massed on the prairie just north of Mansura. The Union forces began to set up a flank attack, causing the Confederates to retreat into the town itself. It's not clear if there were any losses on either side.

The Union forces, though under constant harassment by the smaller Confederate garrison, continued its march to Simmesport, where it crossed the Atchafalaya River and continued on to engage the Confederates in other battles.

Freedom!! - The passage of the Union army was certainly greeted as a ticket to freedom for many of the slaves being held on the various plantations around Mansura. In all likelihood, just as when Banks' army traveled elsewhere throughout Southern and Western Louisiana, large numbers of slaves took this opportunity to escape their bondage. This idea is supported by a story that has been verbally carried down from that fateful day within the Augustine, Berzat and McGlory families of Mansura[11]:

> *In early 1864, on the day that the Union Army was approaching Mansura, word quickly spread among the slaves. On one particular plantation, a 34 year old female slave named Josephine had the daily task of braiding her white female captors' hair. Her four year old daughter, Victorine, was the "pet" of the plantation owner's daughter, and would have, likely, grown up to be the girl's personal slave.*
>
> *Suddenly, the plantation bells started ringing and the slaves began shouting that freedom had come and everyone started running from the plantation, hoping to catch up with the Union Army.*
>
> *As Josephine ran past the plantation house, her white female Slave Holder was sitting on her front porch. She yelled at Josephine to stop and demanded that she come back and braid her hair, as was her duty. Josephine, it is said, stopped, raised up the back part of her skirt, told the mistress to "kiss", picked up Victorine and continued running.*
>
> *Josephine was Josephine Luc who eventually married Jean Baptiste Berzat and her daughter was Victorine Berzat. Josephine had seven other children including Heloise, Luke, and Antarnette Berzat.*

Black Avoyelleans in the Union Army – While records are scarce, there are a few scattered ones showing that Mansura Blacks did serve among the approximately 180,000 black troops who were eventually enlisted in the Union Army and Navy and fought for their own freedom.

---

[11] This story is attributed to Josephine Luc, great-great-grandmother of Mary Bernell Augustine Prier. Josephine was held in captivity near Mansura.

FIGURE 28. BLACK UNION SOLDIER DURING THE CIVIL WAR (OLDERSHAW)

The United States Colored Troops (USCT) were regiments in the United States Army composed of African-American (colored) soldiers, most of whom were former slaves (C. W. Staff). These black troops came from numerous states, both North and South. The state of Louisiana was home to the largest number, about 25,000. By the end of the war in April, 1865, the 175 USCT regiments constituted about one-tenth the manpower of the Union Army.

A number of black [and mulatto] men from Marksville, Mansura, and the surrounding area served in the USCT. Some are listed below. Many were recruited into infantry units such as the 49th and 50th Regiments as well as the 10th Colored Heavy Artillery. Several of them showed their point of enlistment as being at "DeGlaze, Louisiana", which was likely on Bayou Deglaise near Moreauville.

It should also be noted that the enlistments dates of those men listed below occurred in April 1864. This is during the period, from March 1864 to May 1864, which happens to be between the Battle of Fort DeRussy and the Battle of Mansura. This is the timeframe when the Union army was present in Avoyelles Parish and likely manned an encampment on Bayou Deglaise.

As mentioned above, as the Union army passed by, hundreds of slaves fled the plantations each day. This strongly suggests that the black troops, listed below, were recent runaways from Mansura-area plantations, who joined the Union Army to fight for their freedom and that of their families.

- **Jean Baptiste Berzat** served in Company E, 46th Regiment of the United States Colored Infantry under the alias, **John Grimes** (Database). This information is contained in a 1901 application for Civil War Pension by his widow, **Josephine Berzat**. Jean Baptiste and Josephine's decedents include **Heloise**, **Luke**, and **Antarnette Berzat** of Mansura.

- **Louis Oliver** (Administration) and his future wife, **Marie Charlot,** appear to have served in the Union Army as volunteers in the 50th U.S. Colored Infantry (Affairs). They were married on May 9, 1868 and became farmers in the Grande Bayou area of Mansura (H. f. Staff). They had six children listed in the 1880 census: **Jerome**, **Oliver**, **Ernestine**, **Estelle**, **Angelica**, and **Flavie** (I. A. Taker). In the 1900 census, their family included three additional children: **Edward**, **Leonce**, and **Eunice** (I. U. Census).

- **Joseph Magloire** served in Company C, U.S. Colored Troops 73rd Infantry Regiment during the Civil War under the alias, Joseph Margass (JosMagPen). His widow, **Celestine Magloire,** filed for his pension on June 15, 1900. His descendants include most of the McGlorys in Avoyelles Parish, including **Helen**, **Victoria** and **Lula McGlory** of Mansura.

- **Pierre Sampson** was born in Avoyelles Parish around 1842 (JacqAug1870). His father was **Benjamin Sampson** and his mother was **Rachal-Melice**[12]. He enlisted in the 49th United States Colored Infantry under the alias, **Pierre Washington**, in April, 1864 at Fort DeRussy and was discharged in 1865 (Daggett).

After the war, Pierre returned to Mansura and, with his wife, **Mary Ann**, continued farming as he had before the war. They had six children: **William**, **Horace**, **Leon**, **Wilson**, **Sidonia** and **Angela**. His decedents include several members of the Sampson family of Mansura.

Some of the other black men from Mansura who risked their lives for freedom for themselves and for their brethren held in slavery are listed below (Archives):

Name	Home Town/POB	Rank	Enlistment	Discharge
Isador Riason,	Mansura, LA	Private	Jan 1864	Jan 1866
Celestin Normand,	Mansura, LA	Private	Apr 1864	Jan 1866
Francois Normand,	Mansura, LA	Volunteer	Apr 1864	Dec 1865
Scott Normand,	Mansura, LA	Private	Apr 1864	Mar 1866
Gustave Celestin,	Mansura, LA	Private	Apr 1864	Oct 1865
Moise Rabalais,	Mansura, LA	Private	Apr 1864	Jan 1866
Robert Rogers,	Mansura, LA	Sailor	Apr 1864	May 1865
Johnson Wright	France	N/A	N/A	N/A

[12] Some records listed Ben's wife as "Rachal" while others, as "Melice".

Many of these men from Avoyelles Parish served in the Union army during the siege of Vicksburg and, likely, in later campaigns as the Union army closed in on the Confederate military.

Once the war was over, these men returned home and became farmers as they were before the war, except, now as **free** farmers. **Johnson Wright**, who was born in France, worked as a servant in the home of **Adeline Roy**, widow of the late **Leandre Roy**, of Mansura, in 1880 (See Later).

A History of Heroism - The heroic exploits of the American black soldiers and sailors in warfare continued over the next century. For example, the stories of the **Buffalo Soldiers** during the Indian Wars are legendary (Dobak). Their key role, as one of the leading attacking units during the so-called charge up **Cuba's San Juan Hill** by **Teddy Roosevelt and his Rough Riders** during the Spanish-American War, remains distorted.

FIGURE 29. BUFFALO SOLDIERS WHO HELPED FREE CUBA (UNKNOWN)

Similarly, black troops played important roles in World War I and II, where units such as the **Harlem Hell Fighters**, the **Red Ball Express** and the **Tuskegee Airmen** became legendary (See Later).

In most cases, the U.S. military refused to engage black troops in combat until the supply of white troops began to diminish or when the causalities of war began to get out of control. Then the black troops were rushed in at the last moments, often with less than adequate training, but still managed to play pivotal roles.

The involvement of black troops from Louisiana in the siege of Port Hudson, was a major turning point in changing the perception that Blacks lacked the courage and discipline in battle to provide adequate military service to their country. Vicksburg's ultimate surrender led to the surrender of the Confederate garrison at Port Hudson and the complete control of the Mississippi and Red Rivers by the Union. By then, the final collapse of the Confederate military was just a matter of time.

Part III. Post War Turmoil

FIGURE 30. EMANCIPATION (KING & BAIRD)

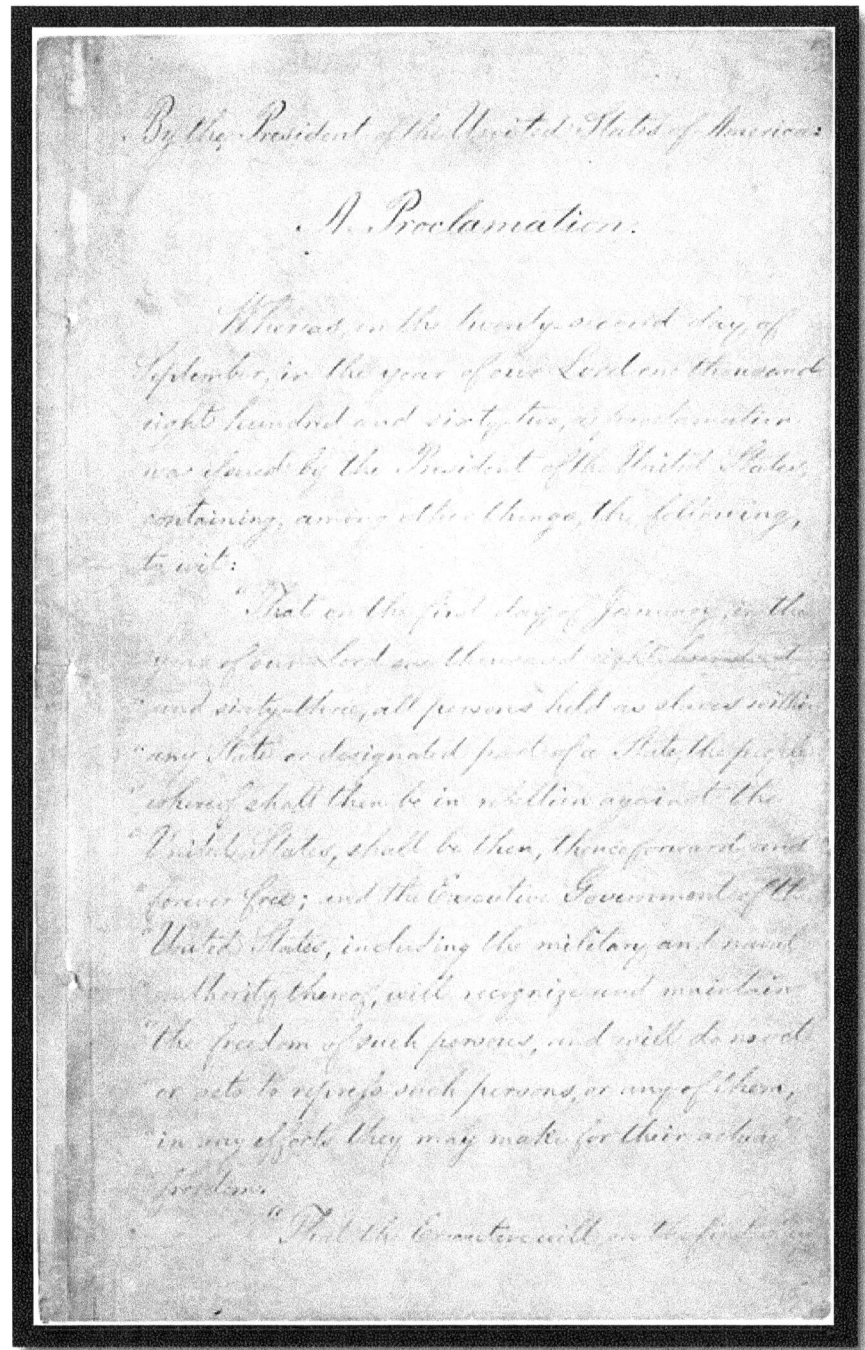

FIGURE 31. THE EMANCIPATION PROCLAMATION

President Abraham Lincoln, via his executive order and constitutional powers as commander-in-chief, issued the Emancipation Proclamation on January 1, 1863, less than a year after the commencement of Civil War hostilities. The order was only directed at those states and parts of states in rebellion against the United States as well as all areas under the control of the United States government. It only affected slaves in 10 states due to its limited reach. However, since most of the slaves were being held in states in rebellion, the status of over three of the four million slaves held in bondage were immediately changed from slave to free.

The Proclamation also allowed the freed slaves to become paid members of the U.S. military and ordered the military to protect the freedom of the former slaves. It did not compensate the Slave Holders for their financial losses, did not outlaw slavery, and former slaves did not become citizens as a result.

As a result of its limited reach, many slaves continued to be held in bondage long after the Proclamation was issued. For example, the Union Army had only a small number of troops in Texas during the war. As a result, it was not able to enforce the Emancipation Proclamation until near the end of the war. Finally, on June 19, 1865, a contingent of Union soldiers, led by **Major General Gordon Granger**, arrived at Galveston, Texas announcing that the war was over and that the **slaves had been freed two and a half years earlier**. The **Juneteenth Celebration** is a memorial to that event.

Once the war had ended, the now disenfranchised South watched powerless as the **13th** (Freedom to all slaves), **14th** (Protected the rights of former slaves) and **15th** (Provided voter protection for all) **Amendments** were passed granting the former slaves the same constitutional rights as the former Slave Holders.

Unfortunately, the Post-Civil War period (a.k.a. **Reconstruction**) was nothing less than a roller coaster ride for the former slaves in the South. First came freedom and newly-acquired civil rights, including involvement in state legislatures, local government, land ownership and education. This was soon followed by a reign of terror where former slaves were terrorized, imprisoned, and often killed by marauding bands of white thugs who were often aided by local law enforcement officials.

State governments, once returned to the control of hostile white citizens, quickly began passing and enforcing extremely restrictive **Jim Crow** laws that included the curtailment of the voting rights that the U.S. constitution appeared to guarantee to all citizens, including all former slaves. The Jim Crow laws remained in effect until the 1970's.

Chapter 8. Southern Backlash

Once the Civil War had ended, returning Louisiana Whites found their world totally upside down (Du Bois), (Vincent). Not only had they been defeated by the Union military, but most of their homes were destroyed, many friends and family were either dead, missing, or badly maimed; the state was under martial law; most Whites had lost the right to vote; and the state itself was being required to pledge allegiance to the U.S. in order to gain re-admittance to the union.

To add insult to injury, the slaves had been freed and now were walking around as they pleased. Many ex-slaves were perceived as uppity and disrespectful to Whites, vagrants and feeble-minded. Also, with the help of the northern Republican "**Carpetbaggers**", many local and state offices were occupied by Blacks, including Avoyelles Parish where **Alexandre Noguez** and **Pierre Magloire** served as sheriff in 1870 and 1872, respectively:

> *"**Alexandre Noguez** was the first black sheriff of Avoyelles Parish. He was elected December 26, 1870. Sheriff Noguez also served as coroner, which was customary at the time. On April 3rd, 1875, Noguez was elected Registrar of Voters, and in 1879 he served as one of the representatives for Avoyelles in the state legislature. Noguez was formerly a brick mason. Alexander Noguez married Feb 10, 1869 Marie LeDoux. Marie LeDoux was probably a member of the mullato branch of the LeDoux family of Pointe Coupee. Witnesses to their marriage were Alfred H. Bordelon, Louis D. Laurent, and Pierre Magloire. **Pierre Magloire** was the second black sheriff of Avoyelles, succeeding Alexander Noguez."-* (Ashur772)

The anger of the Whites in Louisiana led them to begin a true reign of terror against the newly-freed Blacks and their supporters. Their attacks came in two forms, **Political Extremism** and **Racial Violence**.

Political Extremism (Du Bois) - After the death of Abraham Lincoln, **Andrew Johnson**, his successor and a strong State's Rights believer, quickly moved to release the Southern states from the restrictions that had been imposed at the end of the war. He also allowed them to regain control of their states and get back the right to vote.

Once the Whites had regained control of the states in 1865-66, they began to pass a set of laws meant to control the movement, voting, work and everyday lives of Blacks. The "**Black Codes**" (Dethloff), as they were called, placed severe restrictions on black Americans that were very similar to those used during slavery, that, despite the fact that slavery was over. These new state laws so angered the Republican-led U.S. Congress that it passed the **Civil Rights Act of 1866**, the **Fourteenth Amendment** and the **Second Freedmen's Bureau Bill**.

After the election of 1866, Congress passed the **Reconstructions Acts**, placing the South under military rule. In 1877, after a very controversial Louisiana state and U.S. presidential election, the so-called "**Compromise of 1877**" removed the military occupation of the South and, without U.S. government oversight, the "Jim Crow" era began.

Racial Violence against Blacks began as soon as the Whites started returning home from the war (Dauphine). Much of it was spearheaded by organized groups of former Confederate soldiers, calling themselves the **White League**, the **White Camellias** or "**White Caps**" as some Blacks called them. These paramilitary groups of violent racists existed for the following purposes: (1) "reclaim control of the state government" and (2) provide "protection of the white race against the increasing encroachment of the negroes". Their violent attacks against former slaves and their Republican supporters quickly spread throughout the state of Louisiana, especially in the northern part and the areas around New Orleans and Opelousas.

The **Freedman's Bureau** (See Below) maintained records of these attacks and whether the perpetrators were ever brought to justice (H. Staff, Freedmen's Bureau). A summary of the violence perpetrated on freedmen during the period from March 1867 to November 1868 is contained in a report from the Louisiana Freedmen's Bureau staff to a leader of the organization in Washington, Brigadier General Samuel Thomas (L. F. Staff):

> *"General,*
> *In accordance with instructions contained in communication from War Dept. Bureau Ref. Freedmen and Abandoned Lands, Washington D. C. of January 24th, 1867, I have the honor to submit the following report of the number of murders and outrages committed in this state since the organizing of the Bureau to February 20th, 1867 in which Freedmen have been victims or parties as reported to this office by the Agents of the Bureau.*
> *The following statement will show the number of outrages or victims in the aggregate, a detailed history of each case being given in succeeding pages of the report.*
> *Freedmen killed by whites 70*
> *Freedmen supposed to have been killed at Riot in addition to those reported 10*
> *Freedmen murdered - no clue to perpetrators 6*
> *Freedmen shot at, whipped, stabbed, beaten &c 210*
> *Freedmen supposed to have been wounded at Riot in addition to those reported 20*
> *Freedmen murdered by Freedmen 2*
> *Whites murdered by Freedmen 1*
> *In no instance in any of the foregoing cases has a white man been punished for killing or ill treating a freedman. In some few cases the guilty parties are in jail awaiting trial but the majority have either been justified by a Coroner's Jury, acquitted or admitted to bail in sums varying from $300 to $1,000 and in one instance $3,000.*
> *On the other hand, of the three freedmen charged with murder, two have been convicted and hung. There can be no doubt but that in some of the North Western Parishes of this state many murders and outrages have been committed which will never be brought to right and it is thought the aggregate number of murders given above would be more than doubled had all the cases been reported to the Agents of the Bureau."*

Three especially violent clashes were the so-called **New Orleans Massacre,** the **Opelousas Massacre** and the **Colfax Massacre**:

- **The New Orleans Massacre** (Hollandsworth), on July 30, 1866, was a spontaneous street battle in which whites attacked black parade marchers outside the Mechanics Institute in New Orleans.

  The Radical Republicans, mostly Blacks and liberal Whites, in Louisiana had called for a new Constitutional Convention to block the state legislature's enactment of the Black Codes and to allow black men the right to vote. White Democrats considered the reconvened convention to be illegal and believed it to be an attempt by Republicans to increase their political power in the state.

  While it remains unclear who committed the first act of violence, it is known that the black marchers were largely unprepared while the whites were. The violence culminated with a group of Blacks being trapped and savagely beaten. In all, casualties were estimated at 38 killed and 46 wounded, most of them Blacks.

FIGURE 32. NEW ORLEANS MASSACRE (T. R. DAVIS)

- The **Opelousas Massacre** (Tunnell) took place on September 28, 1868 in Opelousas, St. Landry Parish, Louisiana. It actually began in the town of **Washington, Louisiana** when some Opelousas Blacks attempted to join the mostly white Democratic organization there. In responses, a group of Opelousas white supremacists, known as the **Seymour Knights**, an arm of the **Knights of the White Camellia**, rushed to Washington to force the Blacks to leave the organization. Significant violence ensued.

  Emerson Bently, a white, Ohio-born school teacher and newspaper publisher was attacked and beaten in his classroom because of his coverage of the violence that the Seymour Knights had used on the Blacks in Washington. When Bently vanished and escaped to Ohio, the Opelousas Blacks, believing that he had been killed, decided to consider vengeance.

Hearing these rumors, the Seymour Knights mobilized thousands of their supporters from throughout the state, preparing for the long-expected "Race War". Both sides assembled in Opelousas and were heavily armed. The battle that began on September 28 soon turned into a massacre due to the overwhelming numbers of Whites versus the Blacks.

In the end, many Blacks were shot and killed or surrendered and then executed. Others, who escaped into the swamps were hunted down and killed on sight. Twelve leaders of the black Republicans surrendered and were executed the next day. There are no exact numbers for those Blacks who were killed that day but estimates put the death toll at 150.

- The **Colfax Massacre**, or *Colfax Riot*, took place on Easter Sunday, April 13, 1873, in Colfax, the seat of **Grant Parish, Louisiana** (Stolp-Smith). It was, without doubt, one of the worse incident of racial violence in post-Civil War America.

It was the result of a confrontation between opposing political forces of liberal white and black Republicans versus white Democrats. As was the case in the New Orleans riot, white Democrats, armed with rifles and a small cannon, attacked Republican freedmen and state militia (also black) trying to control the Grant Parish courthouse in Colfax.

While white Republican officeholders were not attacked, most of the casualties were freedmen, over 50 of whom were killed later that night after being held as prisoners for several hours. Three whites and as many as 150 Blacks were killed. Between 15-20 were shot on the banks of the river and none of their bodies were ever found.

FIGURE 33. THE LOUISIANA MURDERS—GATHERING THE DEAD AND WOUNDED (H. W. STAFF)

Most important of all, when some of the captured white perpetrators appealed their convictions to the U.S. Supreme Court, the court ruled that the 14th Amendment only protected people (i.e. Freedmen) against the actions of state governments, not individuals.

This made it illegal for the government to enforce protection against the various paramilitary groups such as the White League forming around the state. This gave them freedom to intimidate and suppress black voters, eventually leading to the white Democratic Party gaining control of the state, which they retained until the mid-1960s.

Two examples of this violence that occurred in Avoyelles Parish and cited by the Freedman's Bureau are as follows (L. F. Staff):

- *"August 31st, 1866 - Lieut. W. S. Collins, Marksville, states William Wells (white) committed a most murderous and unprovoked assault with a knife on Lewis Wilson (freedman). Arrested, held to bail on $250. Not being able to procure it, bail was reduced to $200. Accused was then allowed to go (on a pledge of his employer) to get security. At last accounts he was at liberty without bail. At this same court a freedman was committed to jail on some trifling offense being unable to procure $500 bail".*

- *"October 2nd, 1866 - Lieut. A. S. Collins, Marksville, reports Simeon Bordelon, freedman, was taken from his house at night by some 15 or 20 white men, tied, gagged, taken to the woods and whipped because he would not pay a debt he had already paid, and which was contracted while he was a slave. The whites say he was insolvent and cursed somebody. The Grand Jury after some little opposition allowed him to enter his complaint and eight of the guilty parties were* ~~*arrested*~~ *indicted but have never been arrested. Bordelon was then accused of stealing a knife and fork but owing informality in indictment was* ~~*(discharged)*~~ *quashed on Feb. 10th, 1867. Agent reports up to this time none of the parties have been arrested by the Civil Authorities nor will they be".*

An example not recorded, but carried forward in family oral history is as follows[13]:

> *A black family living inside the city of Mansura around 1890, on some especially desirable property, was attacked by members of the White League and forced to flee from their home in the middle of the night. The father was threatened with death if he didn't abandon his home. He fled with 2 of his daughters to Mississippi, never to return. His wife, after hiding in the fields for several days with her other children, eventually returned to live with relatives where she remained until her death.*

This type of extreme violence, perpetrated against Blacks throughout Louisiana and the rest of the South, persisted until well into the 1930s with hundreds of lynchings, beatings, and general intimidation.

---

[13] McGlory Family Oral History: This family was headed by Gervais Arnat Magloire and his wife, Victorine Berzat. The two children taken to Mississippi were Helen and Victoria. Helen was the mother of Laura Augustine while Victoria was the wife of Eddie Hollis of Mansura. The two children left behind were Lula, who married Willie Walter and her brother, Joseph.

Chapter 9. Revival of the Black Family

Reconstruction & the Freedman's Bureau (1865 – 1880) (Du Bois) - The end of the Civil War found the South in shambles. For the newly-freed Blacks, however, this was a new and wondrous world, filled with opportunities that had been denied them before.

To obtain a chance at these new opportunities required overcoming some serious challenges. At the top of the list was (1) Avoiding the hatred and violence directed at them by hostile Whites; (2) Obtaining new Identities; (3) Legitimizing their families (4) Getting a formal education and (5) Finding means to shelter and feed their families.

Unfortunately, by 1880, the U.S. government had decided to place the fate of the freedmen in the hands of hostile state and local white-controlled governments in the South. The institution of the Jim Crow laws changed everything and made it much more difficult for Blacks to overcome any of these challenges.

The Freedman's Bureau served as a major source of needed assistance to the newly freed slaves and their supporters.

Disrupting Families - Since slaves had no basic rights, their marriages had no legal standing and did not serve as barriers to prevent a "husband", "wife" or child from being sold. The terrible heartache and sorrow caused by the sale of a family member is still a part of the emotional history of most African-Americans.

In most cases, slave families were broken apart as a result of one or more of the following reasons: (1) the selling of individuals or small groups of slaves, (2) individual slaves running away and seeking freedom in the North and (3) the chaos of the war, where hundreds of thousands of slaves ran away, many vowing never to return to the plantations. The majority of slaves, however, chose not to leave the security of the plantations on their own, further adding to the family divisions (Project).

The slave marriages, although performed by plantation owners, were considered sacred and binding by the slaves themselves. Their commitment and devotion to their family units were just as strong as any and the loss of members of slave families was just as hurting and devastating as to anyone else. The following comments by Mary Reynolds were taken from the WPA Slaves Narratives now held in the Library of Congress (Project):

> *"After while I taken a notion to marry and massa and missy marries us same as all the n----rs. They stands inside the house with a broom held crosswise of the door and we stands outside. Missy puts a li'l wreath on my head they kept there and we steps over the broom into the house. Now,*

that's all they was to the marryin'. After freedom I gits married and has it put in the book by a preacher." - Mary Reynolds, Former Slave for WPA Writer's Project. (Fort)

Well before the end of the war, members of slave families, separated as described above, sought, desperately, to locate their missing loved ones (H. A. Williams). Despite having very limited freedom, knowledge of local and national geography and resources, they tried every method possible, including sending letters and messages through the grapevine, traveling to plantations believed to have their family member in bondage and even running away to try and locate them.

Once the war was over, the tasks of reuniting the former slaves to their families, assigning them surnames and legalizing their marriages fell to the Freedmen's Bureau.

The Freedmen's Bureau (H. Staff, Freedmen's Bureau) - In 1864, President Lincoln, perceiving that there would be a serious problem with so many former slaves trying to survive in a free country, signed legislation into law creating the Freedman's Bureau, officially named **The U.S. Bureau of Refugees, Freedmen, and Abandoned Lands**. It was established to provide immediate assistance to over 4 million newly-freed former slaves as well as poor whites in the form of food, housing and medical aid, schools and legal assistance.

FIGURE 34. THE FREEDMAN'S BUREAU (WAUD)

Despite being constantly at the mercy of Washington politics, attacks by angry Southerners and a pro-Southern president (Andrew Johnson) and a lack of proper funding and staffing, the Freedman's Bureau managed to operate for 7 years. During its existence, it was able to feed millions of people (both black and white), build hundreds of schools for Blacks in the South, establish several black colleges, build hospitals and provide medical care, help Blacks legalize their marriages and locate lost relatives.

New Identities - Former slaves had complete names for the first time in the 1870 U.S. Census (U. C. Takers). Now, for the first time, we get to see actual former slaves and their families, with each person listed by name, age, gender and occupation. More importantly, most people now possessed a **last name**.

Also called a surname or family name, a last name is not just an issue of identity. It also implies that this person has a family who can not only support them in times of need, but can also assume some level of responsibility for that person's assets or act on their behalf should they die or become incapable of managing themselves. A last name is what a person leaves behind as their legacy.

This was a truly remarkable change from 5 years earlier when most black slaves only had a single "**Slave Name**", e.g. Ajax, Francois, Claire, Clementine, Sampson, etc. (Church) Often, those were names given to the slaves by their white Slave Holder or members of the Slave Holders' families. In many cases, the slave names represented some white relative of the Slave Holder, some white public official or literary figure, or a biblical personality.

Having no last name implied that the slave had no family or family ties, could not own any assets or pass any on to their relatives and, basically, could be sold or given away, without attachments, as easily as one might sell a horse or other farm animal.

The process of acquiring a last name was generally part of the whole process where slave families that had been broken apart, were once more reunited (H. A. Williams). There does not appear to have been a specific moment in time when all slaves got to change and accept a permanent surname. On the contrary, slaves appeared to acquire surnames as follows:
* Many had already taken surnames, even before emancipation, as is shown in the enlistment records of slaves joining the Union army (Daggett);
* Some used surnames of former Slave Holders, although few retained those names (Blake);
* Some declared new surnames when participating in legal activities, e.g. census, marriage, etc. (H. A. Williams);
* Some never added a surname (Ducote).

Real Marriages - Once families were physically reunited, the Freedman's Bureau, churches and benevolent societies, the U.S. Military, and others worked to help them become legally united in marriage, thus providing a foundation for their family structures.

In Avoyelles Parish, and specifically in Mansura, numerous new marriages were recorded by both civil and religious authorities between 1865 and 1880 (Court), (La Cour). Often, the new brides and grooms already had large families that were acquired during slavery. It is not clear, however, whether or not they were all living together before the war or were united in the roughly 5 years following the end of the war. Nevertheless, several new marriages included the legitimizing of existing children.

Many of these new marriages are recorded in the Louisiana Brides Book (La Cour). Others can be located in St. Paul's Catholic Church records and the Louisiana Department of Vital Records[14].

Some examples of these post-slavery marriages are shown in the listing below:

FIGURE 35. MANSURA POST-CIVIL WAR MARRIAGES

Bride	Groom	Marriage Date	Claimed Children	Source
Rosalie Gustin	William James	30 SEP 1866	Jean Pierre, Celestine, Jean Bpte., Lucille, Augustine, Rosalie, Pauline	St. Paul Baptismal Records
Ludy Johnson	Avis Augustine	10 MAY 1866	None Listed	St. Paul Baptismal Records
Josephine Luc	Jean Bte. Berzat	5 Sep 1869	Victorine, Victor, Jean Bte., Mary Delphine	St. Paul Baptismal Records
Celestine Gabriel	Joseph Magloire	23 FEB 1871	Gervais, Eliska, Alicia, Aristide, Ludger	St. Paul Baptismal Records
Roseline Gabriel	Jacques Dupas	13 DEC 1870	Charles, Angele, Irma, Rose, Laurenza, Julien	St. Paul Baptismal Records
Therese Lemoine	Ursin Augustine	6 May 1867	Sylvest , Perry, Josephine, Hermaine, Silas	1870 U.S. Census; LA Marriages 1718-1925

1870 and 1880 U.S. Censuses - The U.S. Census records, from 1870 and 1880, provide additional information on the newly-defined black family structures in the Mansura area. Here we can see, for the first time, the names of families that exist today. While the formats used varied each time the census was taken, the basic information is usually present (Name, age, gender, race, where born, etc.). In some of the later censuses, additional information, such as where parents were born, occupation, etc. was included.

In the 1880 census, some of the local Avoyelles census takers elected to include only initials for the first names of the people being counted. This makes tracking individuals somewhat difficult. Also,

---

[14] LA Office of Vital Records Department of Health & Hospitals | P. O. Box 629 | Baton Rouge, LA 70821-0629; *628 N. 4th Street | Baton Rouge, LA 70802*

the 1890 U.S. census was mostly destroyed in a fire, destroying some of the most valuable information.

Here are some general observations regarding the 1870 and 1880 U.S. Censuses as they applied to Avoyelles Parish and to Mansura:

- Mansura was not listed separately, likely since it had only become incorporated in 1860 and Marksville remained the focal point for the local censuses. However, knowledge of familiar family names allows one to identify the general location of a particular family. Also, proximity to some of the larger white families, who rarely moved due to their land ownership, provides some additional information as to the actual location of black families.

- Most adult black males who were head of households are listed as "farm laborers" while their white counterparts are listed as "farmers". The black heads of household's wives are listed as "keeping house". Most other adult black males or females were listed as "farm laborers", with a few working as domestic servants. Most children were listed as being "at home".

- Many of the black family names appearing in the 1870 Avoyelles Parish census do not appear in later censuses (i.e. 1880, etc.), suggesting that many of the Blacks listed either were living there temporarily, later changed their family names or died during that decade. Some examples of these "lost" black family names are: GABRIEL, LUC, LEMOINE, PACE, PIERROT, SCOTT, HECTOR, WILLIS, BECTEL, and GASPARD. What became of these family names is a question requiring further research.

On the other hand, many of the family names still in existence in and around Mansura and Avoyelles were present in the 1870 U.S. Census. Some of these are: ALEXANDER, AUGUSTINE, BERZAT, BENJAMIN, BROWN, CELESTINE, DUPAS, FOX, FRANCISCO, FRANCOIS, JACKSON, LAVALLAIS, LEE, LEWIS, MCGLORY, PRIER, OLIVER, SAMPSON, St. ROMAIN, THOMAS, WASHINGTON and WILLIAMS.

- Most people, both black and white, spoke French, many exclusively. Since most Blacks lacked formal education and spoke French, when they provided names and other information to the census takers, it was usually up to the census takers to determine how to spell their name. As a result, many names changed both in spelling and pronunciation from one census to the next.

- The somewhat controversial issue of whether many Blacks assumed the surnames of their former Slave Holders is debatable (Blake). There were a few such cases, for example, Normands. However, most black families acquired unique names. One general observation is that the surnames of the white citizens were mostly French, e.g. Gremillion, Joffrion, L'Eglise, Lemoine, etc., while those of the Blacks were mostly English, e.g. James, Johnson, Sampson, Washington, etc.

- A significant percent of the black families are listed as "MULATTOES". It is not clear what the criteria for defining someone as "mulatto" may have been at the time. One might guess that it was likely based on arbitrary decisions made by the census takers. In many cases, someone described as a mulatto in one census was often described as black in another census. Some of the families described as mulattoes were: BERZAT, FRANCOIS, GASPARD, GUILLOT, LAURENT, MAGLOIRE, NORMAND and THOMAS.

In **Book II** of this set, we will take a detailed look at some specific African American families in Mansura. Those families were selected based on their sizes in the 1870 and 1880 U.S. censuses for Avoyelles Parish.

Chapter 10. Post-Civil War Mansura -
Black Religions

FIGURE 36. AFRICAN AMERICAN SPEAKER BEFORE AN AUDIENCE (ORIGINAL)

The practice of religion has, and remains, an integral part of the lives of African Americans (Levin). It began in Africa long before the arrival of the Europeans and Asians. It has transcended through the ages despite the arrival and departure of tribal and ethnic warfare, various invasive forms of government, slavery and the forced movement of millions of people from the African continent to the Americas.

Today, African-American religions are practiced with a wide range of expectations that include traditional salvation in the afterlife, health and peace in this life and the acquisition of wealth and power by some religious leaders. Despite the various forms that African-American religion practices can take, there is a fundamental undertone that works to unite most practitioners into a strong, cohesive and persistent ethno-political force that always manages to exert its presence when threatened.

Religion in Africa before Slavery

Religion in Africa before Slavery - Before the Europeans came to Africa and enslaved millions of people, religious practice was an integral part of most African daily lives (Ehret). The main difference between the African religions and the European-Middle Eastern-Eastern religions was their structure. While those non-African religions generally were centralized and run by some central figure (e.g. Pope, Bishop, etc.) who governed the religion from some distant religious capital (e.g. Rome, Mecca, etc.), the African religions were generally local in their organizational structure, often led by a village religious figure, e.g. shaman, who may or may not have reported to the village chief.

The non-African religions, through their leadership hierarchy, exercised more control of the main teachings and operations of their religions. They, thereby, provided more consistent messages, clearer definition of the spiritual deities, and more active proselytizing of non-believers.

The African religions, on the other hand, were much more tied to local and family history or culture (Britannica). Often, one village could be found practicing a form of religion that was completely different from that practiced in a village nearby. Those specific religions, however, may have been practiced in each of those villages for hundreds of years.

While the non-African religions tended to worship a single, all-powerful, celestial deity (e.g. God, Allah, Yahweh, etc.), the African religions, called Animism by some, generally served numerous gods and deities[15]. Those were believed to be tied to earthbound objects or phenomena such as lightning, thunder, sunshine, rivers, etc. Those African religious beliefs and practices can be linked to tribal culture as much as to religion.

Not all Africans practiced Animism or worshiped those local deities, however. Although both Christianity and Islam have recently made significant progress in converting Africans, especially those near the Sahara desert (Lugo), there is little evidence that more than a few hundred Muslims were captured and transported to the Americas as slaves (H.-N. Contributors).

Slave Religions on Coming to Louisiana

Slave Religions on Coming to Louisiana (Hall) - Most Blacks, brought to mainly Catholic Louisiana during the French and Spanish colonial periods (17th and 18th centuries) as slaves, came either directly from Africa, from islands in the Caribbean, or from some of the main slave trading centers located in New Orleans, Virginia, or Maryland (Jones).

---

[15] Animism is the worldview that non-human entities such as animals, plants and inanimate objects, possess a spiritual presence.

FIGURE 37. SLAVES BAPTIZED IN A MONROVIAN CONGREGATION (U. ARTIST)

Generally, these first generation slaves still retained their original religious beliefs, i.e. Animism: the worship of nature-based deities, etc. In some cases, the new slaves, especially those who came to North America via the Catholic Caribbean islands, included adherents to the Voodoo religion.

As part of their "civilizing" process, all slaves were forced to abandon their native languages, customs, and religions and replace them with those practiced by the European Slave Holders. By their 3rd generation in slavery, few Blacks still practiced their African languages, customs or religious practices[16].

However, most slaves still held deep beliefs in the existence of a higher power and sought ways to express their faith and beliefs. As a result, black people were always willing to actively participate in any established religion, when allowed. In many cases, some of their original religious rituals, such as rhythmic singing and dancing, hand-waving, shouting, drum-playing, etc. were modified and included in the way former Africans practiced the new Christian religions. The "Old Negro Spirituals", still sung in most U.S. churches, are examples of how the African style was added to the European musical styles, creating a completely new genre.

St. Paul the Apostle Catholic Church (Mayeux and Decuir) - As mentioned earlier, the Catholic Church in Louisiana, represented in this work by St. Paul the Apostle Catholic Church, was the earliest and longest operating religious organization in the Mansura area. St. Paul began in an area called Hydropolis, between Mansura and Marksville, Louisiana in 1796 under the name of Our Lady of Mount Carmel. After much chaos and confusion, multiple priest changes, and attempts at

---

[16] In the Mansura area, most slaves were nominally considered to be Roman Catholics.

establishing a permanent building, the church, now known as St. Paul the Apostle, was founded in 1845. It was moved to Mansura in 1871 when a new church building was finally built.

From the earliest days in Avoyelles Parish, St. Paul attempted to provide some type of religious experience for all of the people in the area for which it was assigned. For the white members, this meant that they could freely enjoy the services that the church provided, including all of the sacraments (i.e. Baptism, Confirmation, Holy Eucharist, Penance, Extreme Unction, Holy Orders, and Matrimony). White members could travel to mass on Sunday and other days on which it was offered. They could baptize their children and allow them the opportunities to attend religious education, become confirmed, receive communion, and be married in the church. Those who wished it, could become priests or nuns. At death, the sacrament of Extreme Unction was administered and a Catholic burial provided.

For Blacks held in slavery, being a member of the Catholic Church in the Mansura area meant that they could be baptized, if their Slave Holders allowed it, and buried, either with or without a Catholic service[17]. Attendance at mass was rarely allowed except for those slaves who might live near the church and could accompany their Slave Holders to the services. Records of those slave baptisms (Church) and burials (S. P. Staff) are important sources of ancestral information for the descendants of slaves in the Mansura area.

Once the Civil War was over, former slaves who remained Catholics were allowed to attend services but their involvement was restricted. For example, at St. Paul, provisions were made to allow those Blacks who attended mass to sit in a few "Reserved" pews at the back of the building. Blacks were forced to enter and exit via side doors to minimize their direct contact with the white parishioners (Saucier). Black families could "Buy" a pew and no one else was allowed to sit in them without permission[18]. These practices persisted until about 1938 when Our Lady of Prompt Succor Catholic Church was established for the black Catholics of Mansura.

Our Lady of Prompt Succor Catholic Church (Pastor) - Our Lady of Prompt Succor was established in 1937 and dedicated in 1938. The church was built with a $5000 donation provided by Dr. James Sullivan of Boston, Massachusetts, through the efforts of Father Nothofer, pastor of St. Paul the Apostle Catholic Church in Mansura.

---

[17] Oral history among black community in Mansura
[18] The parents or older children attended "Early Mass" and the younger children attended the "Second" or "Children's" mass and sat in the family's pew. If no family member attended mass that day, then their pew became open to anyone else.

FIGURE 38. OUR LADY OF PROMPT SUCCOR CHURCH

The dedication of the new church, in May of 1938, was attended by Bishop Desmond, head of the Alexandria Diocese, numerous priests and nuns from Alexandria and the area local to Mansura, as well as a large number of Catholic parishioners, both black and white, from the area.

FIGURE 39. DEDICATION OF OUR LADY OF PROMPT SUCCOR CHURCH, MAY 1938

Following the dedication, the church remained under the leadership of Father Thomas Wren and other priests, who were pastors of Holy Ghost Catholic Church, an all-black church, located in Marksville, Louisiana.

Finally, in 1944, Our Lady of Prompt Succor Church became an independent entity and was assigned its own pastor, Father Frances G. Walsh.

Black Protestant Churches - Protestant religious organizations began to appear in Avoyelles Parish near the end of the Civil War and demonstrated significant growth once the war was over and some semblance of normalcy had returned to the area (Saucier).

Most historical accounts of slavery claim that, although the slaves were generally not allowed to leave the plantations on Sunday, the Slave Holder or his delegate, would have the slaves gather and take part in some type of religious service (Northrup). These were informal gatherings, often held out in the open, with the Slave Holder acting as a sort of lay minister. Slaves were allowed to speak or preach during these services and the singing of spirituals was a key part.

Thus, it is likely that these "Sunday Meetings" were the birthplace of the many forms of Protestant worship that exist within the black community today. In the Mansura area, the Baptist churches were the first to be established, followed by the St. Paul Lutheran Church.

Little Zion Baptist Church[19] - Located on Old LA Highway 1, Long Bridge, LA, was founded in 1869 in a cotton gin in Long Bridge, Louisiana. The pioneering founders were Reverend Miles Johnson and Reverend Elder Dorsey of Lettsworth, Louisiana. In 1880, land was purchased from the Avoyelles Parish School Board for the construction of a church and school.

FIGURE 40. LITTLE ZION BAPTIST CHURCH, LONG BRIDGE, LA

During the early 1900's the church was under the leadership of Reverends Eli Johnson, R.L. Lee, Steve J. Williams, J.C. Stafford, and Elie Williams. The church historians assert that:

> *"There wasn't much fashion, but much devoutness. There wasn't much light, but the Bible gave light for the way. There was very little warmth except for maybe one stove, but there was, deep in their hearts, the warmth of God's love and the love they had for each other."*

---

[19] Information and picture from Church Anniversary Program provided courtesy of Marilyn Pierre.

Reverend Willie L. Blackman (a.k.a., William Blackman) assumed the leadership of Little Zion in 1913 and remained pastor for nearly forty years. During this time, the church grew and he was instrumental in acquiring additional land for further expansion.

Rev. W. L Blackman

FIGURE 41. REVEREND WILLIAM L. BLACKMAN

Little Zion remains a strong part of the African-American community in the Long bridge, Moreauville and Mansura area.

Old Jerusalem Baptist Church[20] - Located on Petite Cote Road, Mansura, Old Jerusalem was founded in 1919 by a group of people who had formally worshipped with members of Peacock Baptist Church of Donaldsonville, Louisiana. The initial pastor was Reverend William Blackman (a.k.a. Willie L. Blackman). Although the church had no lights, running water, or indoor plumbing, a "*good time in The Lord*" was had by everyone whenever they met".

---

[20] Information and pictures from church bulletin provided courtesy of Pilgerine Blackman

FIGURE 42. OLD JERUSALEM BAPTIST CHURCH

Some of the original church leaders were:

- **Gospel Preachers** - Elder William Blackman, Reverend Clifton Johnson, Reverend Benson Lavalais, Reverend Horace Simmons, Reverend Howard Simmons and Reverend Prudent Guillory;
- **Deacons** - Brother Mose Talley and Brother Willie Walter;
- **Church Secretaries** - Sisters Lucinda Jacobs, Ella Talley, Sarah Harris, Dorothy Murray and Elise Guillory;
- **Church Mothers** - Sisters Betsy Carter, Matilda McKinley, Dora Brooks, Corrine R. Prier and Dora Deshoutelle.

FIGURE 43. REVEREND GUILLORY AND CHURCH LEADERS

St. Paul Lutheran Church[21] - The church, located on LA Highway 107 in Cocoville, Louisiana, was the inspiration of a bird trapper named Henry Thomas, who was exploring the varied species of birds known to be found in Avoyelles Parish. He discovered that the community had no Lutheran church to attend and no school to send their children to. He convinced his pastor and church to look into it.

FIGURE 44. ST. PAUL LUTHERAN CHURCH

On March 10, 1889, the Lutheran Church Synod held the first church service for the French-speaking Creole community in the home of Scott Normand[22]. A church building, consisting of a 30 X 40 foot chapel, built by the men of the community, was completed at the end of March, 1899.

Calvin Peter Thompson was a member of the first confirmation class on Palm Sunday, 1900. In 1910, Calvin married Edna Thomas, the niece of the bird trapper, while they both attended Immanuel Lutheran College in New Orleans. St. Paul's Lutheran Church, which remains functional today, was a center of black education and culture from 1899 until the depression era, and also served as the meeting site of the community's first NAACP chapter, chaired by Rev. Calvin Thompson in the 1930's.

That little community church holds the record in the Lutheran Church-Missouri Synod for sending the largest number of boys from one congregation into the Lutheran Ministry. St. Paul had a total of 12 boys who attended Lutheran Seminaries to become Lutheran ministers. Furthermore, members

---

[21] St. Paul information provided by Ladricca Price, granddaughter of Rev. Calvin Peter Thompson
[22] The uncle of Dr. Rev. Calvin Peter Thompson, who took over the church/school in 1925, until his death in 1974

of the Thompson family are credited with founding over 25 start-up Lutheran churches throughout the United States.

FIGURE 45. REV. CALVIN PETER THOMPSON (Eakins)

Reverend Thompson received considerable acclaim for his spiritual, educational, and civil rights leadership. His work was noted in several publications, including a published poem and a film, sponsored by historian, Dr. Sue Eakins, who received financial support from LSU. The film noted that:

> *"During the development of black cultural and political consciousness in the mid-20th century, especially in the rural regions of central Louisiana, the church played a major role. The story of one man, the Rev. Calvin Peter Thompson, as he became a leading force in the black struggle, offers a critical assessment of this development. As an educator and clergyman, Thompson overcame social and economic hardship to provide a model for succeeding generations of black Americans."* (Whitehead)

Reverend Thompson penned his autobiography in 1972 and in 1973, was awarded an honorary doctorate degree by the Concordia University in New Orleans to commemorate his life's dedication to religion and education.

St. Paul's Lutheran Church was added to the National Register of Historic Places in 1990[23].

The church has been and remains a fundamental part of the lives of most African-Americans, originating in Africa and going through a transformation from the native Animism religions to the more structured Christian faiths.

---

[23] National Register Information System". *National Register of Historic Places*. National Park Service. 2010-07-09.

Following the end of slavery, the church grew as a foundation of the African-American community in Mansura and the surrounding area, supporting many needs including spiritual, political, educational and communal.

In more recent years, the array of religions in the Mansura area has grown from the basic Baptist, Catholic and Lutheran to now include Assemblies of God, Church of Jesus Christ of Latter-day Saints, Methodists, Jehovah Witness and other Non-denominational churches.

Chapter 11. Post-Civil War Mansura - Black Education

Immediately after the end of the Civil War in Avoyelles parish, the Freedman's schools were an immediate success, springing up all over the parish (Du Bois). At first, just as throughout the South, about a third of the teachers in black schools were local Whites, most of whom were very happy to find any type of employment. Eventually, as more educated black teachers could be acquired, the teaching staffs changed to mostly Blacks.

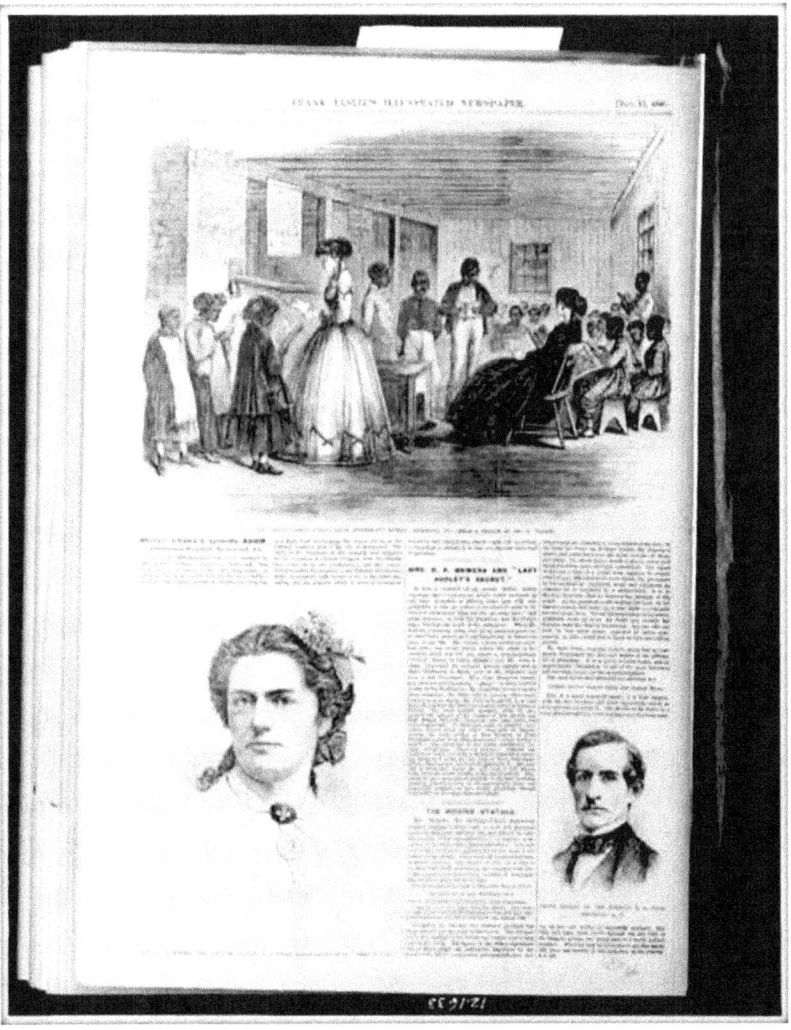

FIGURE 46. THE MISSES COOKS SCHOOL (TAYLOR)

The education of black citizens in Louisiana began in 1869 with a Republican-supported state law making it a requirement that all state schools accept all boys and girl between the ages of 6 and 21. Black and white students attended the same schools until 1876, when the Democrats regained control of the state government.

Schools for Blacks faced severe funding problems once the Freedman's Bureau was dismantled in 1872. However, thanks to an inspired and motivated black population, working with the help of several Northern benevolent societies, and a small amount of support from the state, the schools for Blacks in Avoyelles were able to survive.

By 1899, there were 22 schools for Blacks in Avoyelles Parish with a total enrollment of nearly 1700 (Saucier). The public schools operated under the control of the Avoyelles Parish School Board and reported through a supervisor of schools. Almost all of these schools were one-room buildings and the average session was 3 months. One teacher per school was typical.

By 1915, the total black student enrollment in Avoyelles Parish was 795 boys and 917 girls. There were 14 teachers employed. One held a diploma from Straight University, one from New Orleans University and one from Leland University. In addition, two men and 10 women held 3rd Grade Certificates. The average salaries for black teachers was $30 per month for men and $28 per month for women.

In the Mansura area, the schools for Blacks tended to be housed in the local black churches, including ones at Jerusalem Baptist Church in the Petit Cote and Little Zion Baptist Church in Long Bridge, LA.

There was no documented Catholic school education for Blacks in Mansura until the establishment of the Mansura Colored Convent School in 1910. Until then, black Catholic children appeared to have attended the black public schools.

Little Zion Baptist Church School - Little Zion was one of the first organizations to establish a school for Blacks in the area. The school, which was built in about 1880, acted as a key site for black education for several generations. The classes were held inside a building that was separate from the church building. By the 1936-1937 school year, there were 60 students and 1 teacher (Saucier).

A number of prominent members of the black community served as teachers at Little Zion, including:

- **John B. Lafargue,** who was born a slave near Mansura, taught school in Avoyelles and, later, founded Peabody High School in Alexandria (Saucier);

- **Sarah Mayo**, a graduate of Straight University, who taught at Little Zion School during the 1880's and, later, married John B. Lafargue (Saucier);
- **Mary Jane Blackman,** the wife of Reverend William L. Blackman;
- **Beatrice Blackman,** the wife of Reverend Pilcher Blackman.

Mansura Colored Convent School[24] - The Mansura Colored Convent School was established around 1910 (Laird). The school was housed inside of a two-roomed building located near the T&P railroad track, right behind St. Paul's Catholic Church. During its first 34 years of existence, the school was staffed by black parishioners under the direction of St. Paul's church. Although few records exist that identify them by name, one teacher, who many people still remember from the 1930's, was **Dolfrey Berzat**, who was referred to as "Professor Berzat". Another teacher was **Lula McGlory Walter**.

The original school operated for 6 months a year and went to grade 4. The children walked to school and were required to bring their own lunches in the beginning. Eventually, a small building was provided as a cafeteria where meals were prepared and served. The meals, generally government-surplus beans, included large pieces of cornbread and a square of butter to either add to the beans or spread on the cornbread[25].

When the new Our Lady of Prompt Succor Church was completed in 1937, $500 remained of the original $5000 donated for the new church. Permission was given to use the money to construct an additional classroom at the back of the school, bringing it to 3 classrooms and up to the 8th grade. The school was renamed **Our Lady of Prompt Succor Elementary** after the new church was established in the early 1940's. Eventually, a Gym and an additional classroom were added. The school operated until the construction of the new Cardinal Cushing Elementary School in 1960.

Old Jerusalem Baptist Church School - The school, located at the Old Jerusalem Baptist Church on the Petite Cote Road, was established the early 1900's[26]. The school sessions were held inside the church itself. As with the other schools, there was only one teacher and the children were distributed in groups within the church by grade levels. In the 1937-38 school year, there were 44 students enrolled in grades 1-7.

---

[24] This information is from Our Lady of Prompt Succor Church brochures and local oral history.
[25] Information provided by Leanna Sampson from her memories of her attendance at the school.
[26] This author's father, Oliver Prier, fondly told stories of his time spent at the Jerusalem school around 1910. He described how he had to walk to school through the fields from his home in the Gremillion Cotes, between Mansura and Hessmer. His lunch was typically a piece of homemade bread (Hoecake) and syrup, carried to school in a syrup can.

Some of the teachers who were employed there include: **Mary Jane Blackman** and **Celina Batiste.**

Despite its relatively long distance from town, most black children from Mansura, who attended school during the early 1900's, attended Old Jerusalem Baptiste Church School. The typical means of transportation to and from school was walking.

St. Paul Lutheran School - In 1925, Rev. Calvin Thompson and his wife, Edna, opened the first school that would educate children all the way up to 8th grade (Whitehead). Reverend and Mrs. Thompson sent their own children away to school to complete high school and at least 2 years of college. Afterwards, they sent them to manage and teach "satellite" schools in communities such as Cottonport, Hickory Hill, Lafargue, etc., until a public high school was finally built in the late 1930's.

During the depression years, Pastor Thompson and his wife wrote and were awarded a grant for a community canning factory. Mrs. Thompson taught members of the local community how to preserve vegetables and fruit from their crops and gardens, saving them from starvation.

Part IV. The Dawn of a New Century

FIGURE 47. FREEDMEN VOTING IN NEW ORLEANS, 1867 (UNKNOWN)

Two Snakes

"Slavery wus a bad thing en' freedom, of de kin' we got wid nothin' to live on wus bad. Two snakes full of pisen. One lying wid his head pintin' north, de other wid his head pintin' south. Dere names wus slavery an' freedom. De snake called slavery lay wid his head pinted south and de snake called freedom lay wid his head pinted north. Both bit de nigger, an' dey wus both bad." - Patst Mitchener, Former Slave in North Carolina (Mitchner)

"We're just killing a few negroes that we've waited too damn long about leaving for the buzzards. That's not news" - Newspaper Quote by a White Southerner (Raper)

Despite having to live their lives in a world full of danger where being black made you a target of hostile Whites who were more than willing to beat you, arrest you, terrorize you and your family, chase you off your land and murder you, most African-Americans were able to survive the horror that persisted from the end of the Civil War to well past the middle of the 20th century.

In order to survive it was necessary for an African-American to learn how to always avoid eye with any white person, never speak first when addressing a white person, to never disagree or talk back to a white person, always say "Mister, Madam, Yes Sir, Yes Ma'am, etc." when speaking to a white person and, always, step off the sidewalk when meeting a white person.

The African-American citizens were able to develop a rich culture outside the view of the average white person by living in communities well away from those occupied by the Whites. They were able to develop churches, schools and strong social ties as well. Although few were able to progress in school beyond the rudimentary levels, it was enough to allow them to instill in their children the notion that there was more to life than what they saw around them.

In some cases, external events such as wars, floods, and other natural disasters forced major changes in the lives of African-Americans. In many cases, these were changes that opened the doors to better lives for the children, grandchildren and great-grand-children of slaves.

Chapter 12 - Surviving in the Reign of Terror

Once the slaves were freed, the harsh reality, that freedom also meant self-survival, soon set in. There were two forces at work. One was the newly-freed Blacks desperately seeking to gain their economic independence via land ownership and personal freedom. The second was the white farmers seeking to re-establish control of the labor forces that had, so long, been accessible to them, usually in the form of slave-labor gangs.

The attitude of the whole country seemed set on dehumanizing and ridiculing black people in every way possible, especially in commercial advertisement and in entertainment. Some examples are shown below (Turner):

"40 Acres and a Mule" - Following his march through Georgia, **General William T. Sherman** established a false expectation among former slaves. He awarded some of them small parcels of land, i.e. 40 acres, on the islands and coastal regions of Georgia, and a few hundred mules that were no longer needed in battles.

Although still talked about by many Blacks as something that was due them, Sherman's "40 Acres and a Mule" policy was soon debunked by President Andrew Johnson in the summer of 1865. He ordered all land under federal control to be returned to its former owner (H. Staff). In the following years, Blacks soon found themselves struggling to find work, housing and basic needs to support their families.

Following the end of the Northern occupation of the South after the bloody Civil War and the return of the control of state governments to the Democrats, the country entered a period of relative peace (Du Bois). This was an extremely odd type of peace for the black citizens, especially in the South.

There were no major wars occurring on American soil, other than the "Indian Wars" out west. However, for the average black person, it was a daily battle to survive in a world where violence in the form of lynchings, beatings, false imprisonment and general deprivation of basic civil rights was the norm.

Often, the members of the state and local governments, who were elected to provide justice and protection from harm to all citizens, were, in fact, officials during the day and racial terrorists by night. These individuals provided no level of protection to black citizens and, in most cases, sought only to find means to terrorize the black population.

This resulted in various means of injustice being perpetrated on Blacks and a few unfortunate Whites. This ranged from sentences by "Kangaroo Courts" that resulted in false imprisonment of Blacks or illegal eviction from their land to executions based on little or no evidence of a crime having been committed by them. Often, mob rule was the process used, leading to outright lynchings.

From 1882-1968, 4,743 reported lynchings occurred in the United States (Finley). Of those people who were lynched, 3,446 were black, accounting for 72.7% of the people lynched. The three most common reasons given as "justification" for the lynchings of Blacks were: Homicide (40.8%), Rape (19.2%) and attempted Rape (6.1%). Many of the 1297 Whites lynched were for "crimes" such as helping the Blacks, being anti-lynching or even for domestic crimes.

In the state of Louisiana, there were 333 reported lynchings of Blacks between 1882 and 1936 (Finley).

It remains unclear why, in the eyes of Whites, **black lives did not matter**. They viewed the execution or lynching as a sort of purging of the population to rid themselves of undesirables. The public executions and lynchings were most often huge public events, attended by large crowds. Many brought their children and picnic baskets for an event filled with much frivolity. Cheers rang out when the victims were executed and, in many cases, members of the crowd took pieces of their clothing and even body parts home as souvenirs.

FIGURE 48. THE LYNCHING OF HENRY SMITH (MERTINS)

Government-Supported Racism - The institutionalized racism, the so-called Jim Crow era, began when, "in 1890, in spite of its 16 black members, the Louisiana General Assembly passed a law to prevent black and white people from riding together on railroads. *Plessy v. Ferguson*, a case challenging the law, reached the U.S. Supreme Court in 1896. Upholding the law, the court said that public facilities for blacks and whites could be "separate but equal." Soon, throughout the South, they had to be separate (Du Bois).

FIGURE 49. PLESSY V. FERGUSON MARKER[27]

Two years later, the Supreme Court seemed to seal the fate of black Americans when it upheld a Mississippi law designed to deny black men the vote. Given the green light, Southern states began to limit the voting right to those who owned property or could read well, to those whose grandfathers had been able to vote, to those with "good character", and to those who paid poll taxes. In 1896, Louisiana had 130,334 registered black voters. Eight years later, only 1,342, or 1 percent, could pass the state's new rules (Foundation).

FIGURE 50. JIM CROW WATER FOUNTAIN, CA. 1938 (VACHON)

---

[27] Photo of the front of Plessy v. Ferguson marker in New Orleans, Louisiana, U.S.A. written by historian Keith Weldon Medley for placement by the Crescent City Peace Alliance and placed on the corner of Press Street and Railroad Yards Feb. 12, 2009

One of the most important events of this time period that appeared to suggest that Blacks were satisfied with their status in both the legal and social structure was the so-called "**Atlanta Compromise**" (Harlan). In a speech at the Cotton States and International Exposition in Atlanta, Georgia, on September 18, 1895, Booker T. Washington, a black educator, declared that vocational education was much more beneficial to Blacks than higher or professional education, political rights, or social acceptance. He felt that this was the appropriate path to economic independence. His assertion that "In all things that are purely social we can be as separate as the fingers, yet one as the hand in all things essential to mutual progress."

FIGURE 51. BOOKER T. WASHINGTON (UNKNOWN)

The trade-off (or Compromise), Washington felt, was that Blacks should avoid further agitation for legal and social equality while Whites should accept responsibility for continuing the general progress made by Blacks toward economic stability and social acceptance.

Although excited white leaders throughout the country felt this "Compromise" was fully supported by most Blacks and that the new legal and social orders were now secure, educated blacks saw Washington's speech as a surrender by Blacks and their acceptance of a future where they would be forever considered inferior to Whites. W.E.B. Du Bois was very vocally opposed to Washington's position and claimed that it represented "in Negro thought the old attitude of adjustment and submission" (W. Du Bois).

FIGURE 52. W.E.B. DU BOIS (PURDY)

In response, Du Bois began organizing black leaders and their supporters who sought civil rights and equality instead of the path advocated by Washington. Du Bois's initiatives eventually led to the 1905 Niagara Movement, a precursor to the NAACP (National Association for the Advancement of Colored People), founded in 1909 (W. E. Du Bois).

Living under Jim Crow Laws in Mansura - Although living as sharecroppers in extreme poverty during most of the Jim Crow era, the average black person in the Mansura area found the strength within their souls to tolerate the harsh conditions under which they lived and to assume some level of dignity when living within their isolated communities.

FIGURE 53. SEGREGATED MANSURA TRAIN STATION[28]

---

[28] This is a copy of a photograph hanging on the wall of the parish courthouse in Marksville.

Whenever it was necessary to venture outside of their home environments and travel to town, however, everything changed. Now, they found themselves having to come face-to-face with those who felt it their jobs to maintain as much dominance over all black people as possible. Although the Jim Crow laws were written to empower the police and other law enforcement entities, in many cases, Whites who had no official authority, still took it upon themselves to develop and enforce rules, practices, and "laws" that permitted them to control and demean the lives of the black people living in the area.

Some examples of these Jim Crow laws and practices that Blacks in Mansura lived under are as follows[29]:

- A black person could be pushed off the sidewalk by a white person for failing to step off the sidewalk and stand facing the ground with his hat in hand until the white person walked by. A black woman could be slapped for this same infraction;
- Blacks were required to address all Whites as Mr., Mrs., or Miss and to always say "Yes, Sir" or "Yes, Ma'am" when spoken to by a white person;
- Any Black caught walking down Main Street after dark could expect to be stopped by the Mansura town police and possibly arrested as a vagrant. Being arrested for vagrancy could lead to being sent to do forced labor for the sheriff or one of the local businessmen or farmers;
- When riding in a car with a white person, the black person had to ride on the back seat or, if in a truck, inside the bed of the truck;
- The Mansura passenger train station (See **Figure 53**) had two sides, one for Whites, and one for "Colored". There were specific passenger cars for "Colored Only";
- In the movie theater, Whites sat anyplace, Blacks were confined to the balcony;
- At St. Paul's Catholic Church, Blacks sat in "Reserved" pews in the back of the building, Whites sat anywhere;
- St. Paul Cemetery was divided into two sections: Whites up front, Blacks in the far back;
- The Avoyelles Parish Fair had a specific day (Thursday) for Blacks;
- All seating inside restaurants and bars was for Whites Only; Blacks could only get served through windows, usually at the back of the building;
- The two Catholic elementary schools in Mansura were segregated even though they were located adjacent to each other, only separated by the Texas & Pacific Railroad tracks;
- Although there was a high school in town for Whites, Blacks who wanted a high school education were forced to travel to either Marksville or Alexandria but with no public transportation provided.

---

[29] Information here was gathered by this author over a lifetime of hearing such stories from his parents, from most Blacks in the area and from his own personal experiences with Jim Crow life.

While few of the "Jim Crow" law are still on the books, some, such as "vagrancy", still remain.

Many of the unofficial practices such a separation of the races under most social and religious circumstances also still remain. For example, despite the extreme shortage of Catholic priests in the U.S., there are two operating Catholic parishes, one mostly Black and one mostly White, immediately adjacent to each other in Mansura, a town of less than 2000 people. None of the local Baptist churches, Black or White, have significant numbers of other-race members of their congregations.

Interestingly, these practices are largely voluntary, with the black and white members, respectively, preferring to continue attending the churches of their youth. This *de facto* segregation is more of a result of everyone being in "comfort zones" where they have spent their lives, not necessarily overt racism.

Most of the newer churches such as Jehovah Witnesses and Assembly of God, however, have members of all races.

Chapter 13 - The New Plantations

As mentioned earlier, the latter half of the 19th century saw the end of the pre-Civil War, slavery-based economy and the rise of a new one based on a new type of economic slavery called "Share-cropping" (H. Staff). Share-cropping, coupled with the so-called "Jim Crow" laws, created an extremely difficult living environment for most black people.

FIGURE 54. RURAL BLACK CHILDREN LIVING IN POVERTY (Eakin)

Origins of Sharecropping (Royce) - Sharecropping was developed as a result of the need for a cheap, available labor supply to operate U.S. farms. **Family Farming** was originally directed primarily towards producing food, tea, tobacco and raw material for clothes and building construction. These early farm products were meant for immediate consumption by a single family or for storage for later use. The amount that a typical, hard-working family could produce was generally sufficient to meet the needs of that family for a year.

The rise of **Commercial Food Production**, as a result of urban growth during the mid-1800's (Edwards), made it possible to produce enough food to feed one family plus sell the excess food commercially. Those small farmers who wished to convert some of their produce into cash, however, soon realized that to be competitive in this new arena, a good, steady labor supply was essential.

While those small farmers attempted to farm the land themselves, the reality was that in a labor-intensive industry such as farming, few families were large enough to supply all of the labor needed for an effective operation that could produce food for consumption and sale. In the majority of cases, the small farmers resorted to hiring farm laborers to perform much of the farm work, thus expanding the scope of their operation and, hopefully, produce cash profits.

Unfortunately, hired laborers usually demanded daily or weekly payment for their work, something that was not possible for farmers who had to wait until harvest time before they acquired cash to pay their bills.

Sharecropping provided a better arrangement. Now the farm laborers owned a share of the commitment and risks, since they were, essentially, borrowing money to support their families while working the farmer's land. The farmers and the sharecroppers ended up settling their financial agreements once the crops were harvested and sold. Unfortunately, the farmers held a distinct financial advantage over the share croppers.

FIGURE 55. SHARECROPPER CABIN NEAR LAKE PROVIDENCE, LA (HATHORN)

Although sharecropping is generally considered a process where Blacks were the key participants, in reality, many poor Whites also found themselves ensnared is this economic servitude with little hope of escape.

FIGURE 56. POOR WHITE FARM CHILD (WALKER)

Some evidence for this comes from 1900 census data for Avoyelles Parish, Ward 3, excluding Mansura (C. Bureau). Here, we find that of the 122 black families listed as farmers, 26 (21 %) owned their own homes while 96 (79 %) were renting. Of the 189 white families listed as farmers, 115 (61%) owned their homes while 74 (39 %!!) were renting. Thus, while it comes as no surprise that such a large percent of Blacks were renters. That almost 40% of the white families were also renters is somewhat of a surprise.

General Share-Cropping Operations[30] - The types of sharecropper plantations that existed in the Mansura area ranged from small, single-family farms to very large, multifamily, commune-style operations. In a common example, an agreement between the farm land owner and the share cropper would stipulate that 25% of the profits from the sale of the crops would go to the share cropper, while the land owner would get 75%. The sharecropper would farm the land using operating funds or credit provided by the land owner to purchase seeds, farm equipment, food, clothing, and other supplies. In most cases, some sort of arrangement was made by the land owner with a local merchant that allowed the sharecropper to make those purchases on credit, pending the sale of the crops in the fall harvest season.

Settling-up occurred once the crops were harvested and sold. The proceeds from each sale were usually sent directly to the land owner, even though it was the sharecropper who actually brought the produce to the gin or mill. Once the harvest was done (usually in the Fall), the land owner would then deduct all his expenses (i.e. seeds, animals, tools, fertilizer, etc.), including all expenses incurred from the local merchant by the sharecropper (i.e. food, clothing, housewares, etc.), from the share cropper's share of the profits (i.e. 25%), pay the share cropper the remainder of his share of the profits and keep all of his own share of the profits (i.e. 75%).

Unfortunately, the generally-illiterate sharecroppers were powerless to monitor the extent of their farming expenses or the charges they and their family incurred with the local merchants. As a result, almost every black family member who lived as sharecroppers, can still tell stories of their father, or grandfather, "Settling up" at the end of the year, **often with a net profit of 50¢ or less**. On the other hand, the land owners and local merchants flourished financially.

Small Share-cropping Operations were the simplest examples of share-cropping. Generally, the land being farmed consisted of a few acres, owned and operated by a single family. Here, that family would contract with one or more sharecropper families to help them farm the land. While the contract may have included some type of lodging for the sharecropper and his family, that was not always the case, and the sharecroppers were often obliged to find lodging at their own expense.

Large Share-cropping Operations were the other extreme. Those consisted of numerous share-cropper families, all farming the same large farm. These type of operations generally included several modest houses for the share cropper families, a "Lot" area where the farm equipment and animals were kept, a common source of water such as a well or cistern, and a common work area that

---

[30] From author's personal experience.

included equipment for grinding grain such as corn into meal and grits or coffee beans into coffee ground. A smoke house for curing meat into bacon and sausage was often included.

In most cases, the land owner lived in a large house near the entrance to the farm or some distance from the farm itself, in a more fashionable area such as L'Eglise Street in Mansura.

FIGURE 57. MAIN BARN OR "LOT" AREA (EAKIN)

The farm workers, both male and females of all ages, generally worked in gangs, just as during slavery. Some of the females, less-able children and older men worked inside the land owner's house as servants or outside the house as gardeners, drivers, etc. School attendance for the black children was generally considered unnecessary by both the sharecropper and the land owner since neither had much education themselves.

The main cotton farming equipment was a plow, a pair of mules with harnesses, a cotton wagon, hoes and cotton sacks. Each worker was issued a hoe at the beginning of hoeing season (Late Spring) and a cotton sack at the beginning of cotton picking season (Early Fall). Sacks ranged from 3 to 9 feet in length based on the age of the picker[31].

---

[31] This author remembers foolishly hoping to be allowed to have a longer sack as a sign of being "Grown".

FIGURE 58. BOY WITH SMALL COTTON SACK[32], (Eakin)

Once the rows were plowed, the cotton seeds were planted, usually by hand, and allowed to grow. When the plants reached about 3-4 inches tall, it became time for hoeing.

Hoeing cotton required a considerable amount of back and arm strength as well as the ability to withstand being outside all day in temperatures approaching 100 degrees F. Each worker was assigned a row that often seemed nearly a mile long. The task was to remove any excess plants (Thinning out) and any weeds growing near the cotton plant and to pull a small amount of dirt to the cotton plant. **Trouble came should a worker accidently cut too many of the cotton plants!**

FIGURE 59. BLACK WORKERS HOEING COTTON (Delano)

---

[32] Sue Eakins Collection

When the cotton plants reached maturity, usually as tall as 3-6 feet, they developed, first, flowers, followed by round bolls. The bolls eventually began to dry and split open, revealing the white cotton fiber inside.

FIGURE 60. BOLLS OF RIPE COTTON (PHOTOGRAPHER)

Picking cotton simply involved pulling the cotton fiber from the dried bolls and stuffing it into a sack hanging from the workers' shoulder or waist. The dried cotton boll had sharp edges that could inflict a vicious tear to the tissue surrounding one's fingernails. Besides the potential for heat exhaustion and stroke, other dangers encountered during the cotton picking activities included stinging caterpillars, wasps and cotton mouth moccasins.

FIGURE 61. TENANTS PICKING COTTON (EAKIN)

When the cotton sack was full, the worker carried it to the cotton wagon where it was weighed, its weight recorded and the cotton dumped into the wagon. A full sack of cotton could weigh as much as 70 pounds and carrying it to the wagon to be weighed could be difficult. Some of the very best Mansura cotton pickers could each pick over 800 pounds of cotton per day.

FIGURE 62. WEIGHING COTTON SACKS WITH SCALE AND PEA (Eakin)

FIGURE 63. COTTON WAGON READY FOR GINNING (Eakin)

The filled wagon was then driven to the cotton gin where its content was weighed and sent through the ginning process to remove the seeds and tie the fibers into bundles for shipping.

FIGURE 64. COTTON BALES READY FOR SHIPPING (Eakin)

A filled cotton wagon weighed about 1500 pounds, enough to produce a ginned bale of cotton. A ginned bale of cotton could weigh about 500 pounds and could sell for $.30/lbs., or $150; a large amount for the times. Thus, a farmer whose farm produced 20 bales of cotton could collect about $3000.

At the end of the cotton harvest, the farmer paid any expenses he owed to the gin and to the local merchants who sold to his sharecroppers on credit during the year. It was never clear how much money actually changed hands but it remains true that by the time the money chain reached the sharecropper, little cash was left[33].

Living and Working Conditions - Farm life was fairly difficult for the black workers who usually were under the command of a white overseer and who could be fired for the slightest reason. Being unemployed and homeless made any black man a prime candidate to be arrested for vagrancy (W. Du Bois). Vagrancy was a concocted set of laws that were part of the Black Codes and were designed to allow local authorities to arrest free people of color and subject them to involuntary labor.

Work hours were long, often from dawn to dusk, and generally included Saturday mornings. Breaks for lunch generally occurred in the fields with the workers simply lying down at or near the end of the rows and eating whatever they happened to have put in their pockets before leaving home in the morning (i.e. sweet potatoes, cornbread, etc.). If the field was close enough to their home, the workers might actually have time for lunch and a quick nap:

FIGURE 65. WORKER ON LUNCH BREAK (EAKIN)

While working in the hot Louisiana sun, one worker was assigned the duty of passing around a bucket of water and everyone drank from the same ladle. The water was usually warm and contained

---

[33] This author vividly recalls how his father, Oliver Prier, felt such pride at producing 10 bales of cotton one year only to have that pride quickly turn to frustration, disappointment and anger when, at **Settling Up**, he received only $0.50 for the year!

dirt, grass, mosquito larva and insects. This was a particularly dehumanizing practice that persisted into the 1970's and greatly resembled the way the farm animals were watered and fed without regard to hygiene, disease transmission or cleanliness.

Chapter 14 - How the Mansura Whites Lived

FIGURE 66. DR. GEORGE DROUIN FAMILY, CA. 1910[34]

By the year 1900 (Mayeux and Decuir), Avoyelles Parish, Louisiana, like the rest of the state and the South, in general, was experiencing an economic boom. That was despite the remnants of the Civil War, with its destruction of so much personal and public property, its huge toll in human life, the dramatic political and economic upheaval resulting from the end of slavery and the adaptation to a new form of racial segregation based of the Jim Crow laws.

The local economy, including that of Mansura, was based on farming cotton, corn, sugar cane, and other crops. Other supporting businesses, such as in the medical field, banks, retail stores, bars, hotels, transportation, etc. had sprung up around the town. Many of the local farmers were experiencing unprecedented success and their ownership of considerable wealth was obvious.

---

[34] Copy of Photograph on Wall of Avoyelles Parish Courthouse on Marksville, LA

FIGURE 67. AVOYELLES PARISH COURTHOUSE[35]

Throughout the parish, there could be found several large public buildings such as the Avoyelles Parish Court House in Marksville; new churches such as St. Joseph's and St. Paul's Catholic Churches in Marksville and Mansura; as well as the Presentation Convent School in Cocoville.

FIGURE 68. ST. PAUL RECTORY, CA. 1890[36]

The Avoyelles Parish School System was now well established with a functioning school board, schools throughout the parish and a paid staff of trained teachers and principals.

---

[35] Copy of Photograph on Wall of Avoyelles Parish Courthouse on Marksville, LA
[36] Copy of Photograph on Wall of Avoyelles Parish Courthouse on Marksville, LA

The Mansura White Upper Class - By the early 1900's (Mansura1900), things had developed to the point that there was, now, a sort of white upper class in the Mansura area that was very similar to what had existed before the Civil War. This group of people was made up of wealthy farmers, merchants, physicians, and politicians, many of whom resided along L'Eglise Street in Mansura.

FIGURE 69. DR. THOMAS A. ROY, SR. HOME, CA. 1901[37]

Many of the members of the "upper class" section of Mansura were the financial beneficiaries of the manual labor of the sharecroppers who resided elsewhere. Most of their homes were large by the standards of the time and had most of the modern conveniences as well as chauffer driven automobiles. All had servants, gardeners and chauffeurs, who were generally black. Their children attended school and many went on to become doctors, dentists, lawyers and other types of business professionals.

These L'Eglise Street denizens included:

- **Alcide and Zoe Normand** (AlZoNormand1900). They were listed in the 1900 census as farmers. Residing with them was **Clara Coco**, Alcide's sister, and her two children, Edward (See Below) and Mercedes. Also present were three black servants: sisters, **Aurelia** and **Sofia Lavalais**, and a widow, **Clarisse Augustine**.
- **Edward Coco.** Edward, Valery and Clara Coco's son, and his wife, **Emma B. Coco** (EdEmCoco1910), were listed in the 1910 census as farmers living inside the town of Mansura. Residing with them

---

[37] Copy of Photograph on Wall of Avoyelles Parish Courthouse on Marksville, LA

were their 3 sons: **Ashton**, **Lysso** and **Lawrence**. They were well known within the Mansura black community since they operated the "Coco Plantation" (See Below), an important factor in the lives of many Mansura Blacks.

- **Fereole and Irma Regard** (FerIrRegard1900). Fereole was a dry goods storekeeper who was born in France. His wife was born in Louisiana and they had 3 daughters (Sydonia, Martha, and Anita) and 2 sons (Fereole, Jr. and Joseph).
- **Dr. Thomas** and **Elise Roy** (ThomElRoy1900). Dr. Roy was one of the physicians practicing in Mansura in 1910. He and Elise were born in Louisiana while Elise's parents were born in France. Their parents were Leandre Francois Roy and Victorine Adeline Cailleteau (See earlier). Living with them were their 4 sons: **Kirby**, **Elmo**, **Clarence and Thomas Jr**. Thomas' mother, **Adeline Roy** also lived with them.
- **Alicia Drouin**. She was the widow of **Leonard Drouin** who had died in 1878. She operated a dry goods store in 1900 (AlDrouin1900). Living with her was her 23 year-old son, **Dr. George Drouin**; her daughter, **Leonce**, a saleswoman; an orphan, **Clemey Mayeux**, a black servant, **Ann Johnson**, and 2 boarders: **Hernandez Ducote** and **Arthur Rabalais**, who were salesmen.

Other white families or individuals residing along L'Eglise Street in Mansura in 1900 included the following (L'Eglise1900):

- **Emile** and **Leonie Berridon** - Dry Goods Grocer
- **Prudent Foucheux** - Dentist
- **Edward** and **Camille Drouin** - Dry Goods Grocer
- **Alphonse Escude** - Hotel Keeper
- **Jules Roule** - Farmer
- Several Saloon Keepers and Bartenders

The Less Affluent White Citizens living in Mansura and the surrounding area led lives that were not nearly as affluent as the denizens of L'Eglise Street. **Table 5**, shown in **Chapter 15** below, lists the various occupations of the Mansura resident in 1900. Note that 49% of the white residents had occupations that were either described as farmers or farm laborers. Equally important is the fact that nearly 40% of the white citizens of Mansura were renting their homes (I. U. Census).

A typical white family lived on a small farm, generally outside the city limits of Mansura. Here they eked out a meager living based on their crops of cotton, corn or sugar cane. While some owned their own land, others were non-resident share-croppers, who were able to live off the farm in rented houses but still were financially committed to the land owner for the expenses of operating the farm.

In some cases, some of the larger farms employed white overseers, many of whom lived on the farm in houses provided by the land owner. Generally, the overseer's house was located away from the black sharecroppers and somewhat larger. These overseers are remembered with the same level of disdain as where the slave drivers of the past.

It was common for white citizens to be engaged in some sort of entrepreneurial activity such as selling vegetables, meat, ice, fish and other wild game from trucks or wagons. Others had service occupations such as bartenders and saloon keepers, seamstresses, and salesmen.

While it is clear that these less-affluent Whites struggled to survive, just as the Blacks did, they were not faced with most of the Jim Crow practices that made lives of the black citizens so difficult. For example, if they could afford it, they could send their children to school or college, they could attend any church they chose, all social activities were open to them, etc. Most importantly, they could vote with no problems.

Chapter 15 - How the Other Half Lived

FIGURE 70. MANSURA BLACK "IN-TOWN" RESIDENCES, CA. 1938[38]

By the year 1900, the white citizens of Mansura had managed to develop an upper class made up of merchants, doctors, farmers, teachers and other types of white collar workers. Many, who lived in large white houses positioned along L'Eglise Street, had servants and their children attended school. This group included some who had farms some distance from town but who preferred the more gentile environment of living in town.

For the black citizens of Mansura and the surrounding area, the situation was much different. Most lived in dilapidated shacks that were located either at the edge of town or as far out as the swamps to the East. Those who did live in town were usually employed by the white citizens as cooks, servants and gardeners. Their standards of living were not much better than those of the black people who lived away from town (See Below).

The economic engine that operated in the Mansura area, as in the rest of the state and the South, was one based on farming. At the base of this engine was the manual labor of the Blacks and poor Whites who worked the farms, converting soil, seeds, fertilizer and manual labor into cash for the land owners and merchants, but little for themselves. Without cash, it was nearly impossible for those types of workers to purchase their own farms or other types of businesses and become economically independent.

---

[38] Enlarged section of picture showing dedication of Our Lady of Prompt Succor Church, ca. 1938

The types of Occupations - The types of jobs performed by black and white citizens of Mansura in the 1900 U.S. census were very different, as shown in **Table 5** below (C. Bureau).

1900 Mansura Occupations by Race						
White Adults				**Black Adults**		
Occupation	No.	%		Occupation	No.	%
Dry Goods Grocer	8	10		Servant	5	5
Salesperson	8	10		Farmer	29	28
Servant	2	3		Farm Laborer	68	65
Dentist	1	1		R/R Laborer	2	2
Hotel Keeper	1	1				
Farmer	18	23				
Physician	1	1				
Laborer	1	1				
Fruit Seller	1	1				
Saloon Keeper	4	5				
Bartender	4	5				
Farm Laborer	21	26				
Seamstress	3	4				
Telegraph Operator	1	1				
Dry Goods Peddler	1	1				
Lumber Dealer	1	1				
Blacksmith	1	1				
Priest	1	1				
Teacher	2	3				
TOTAL	**80**	**100**			**104**	**100**

TABLE 5. MANSURA OCCUPATIONS, CA. 1900

Table 5 indicates that about half of the white citizens living inside the city of Mansura in 1900 held white-collar or skilled jobs (Merchants, doctors, salespeople, seamstresses, teachers, etc.). The remainder held farm-related jobs (Farmer, farm laborer). For the Blacks, nearly 100% worked in farm-related jobs.

During that same year, about 20 white children living inside Mansura were listed as "In school" while no black children were so listed. Also, about 75% of the Whites claimed to be able to read, while only about 20% of the Blacks did so claim.

About half of the white heads-of-households were listed as home owners. Only 7 black heads-of-household were home owners.

The Mansura Geography - The Town of Mansura, in the 1900 U.S. Census, was included as part of the Avoyelles Parish Police Jury Ward 3, Enumeration District 0014 (C. Bureau). As shown in **Figure 71** below, that district, in addition to the "**In Town**" Mansura residents (See Below), also included the areas along the Cocoville Road (Old Highway 1), *Grande Bayou*, *Payee Bas*, *Grande Ecore*, *Boutte de Bayou*, the *Petite Cotes* area, the Long Bridge and Cotton Port Roads and the Hessmer Highway.

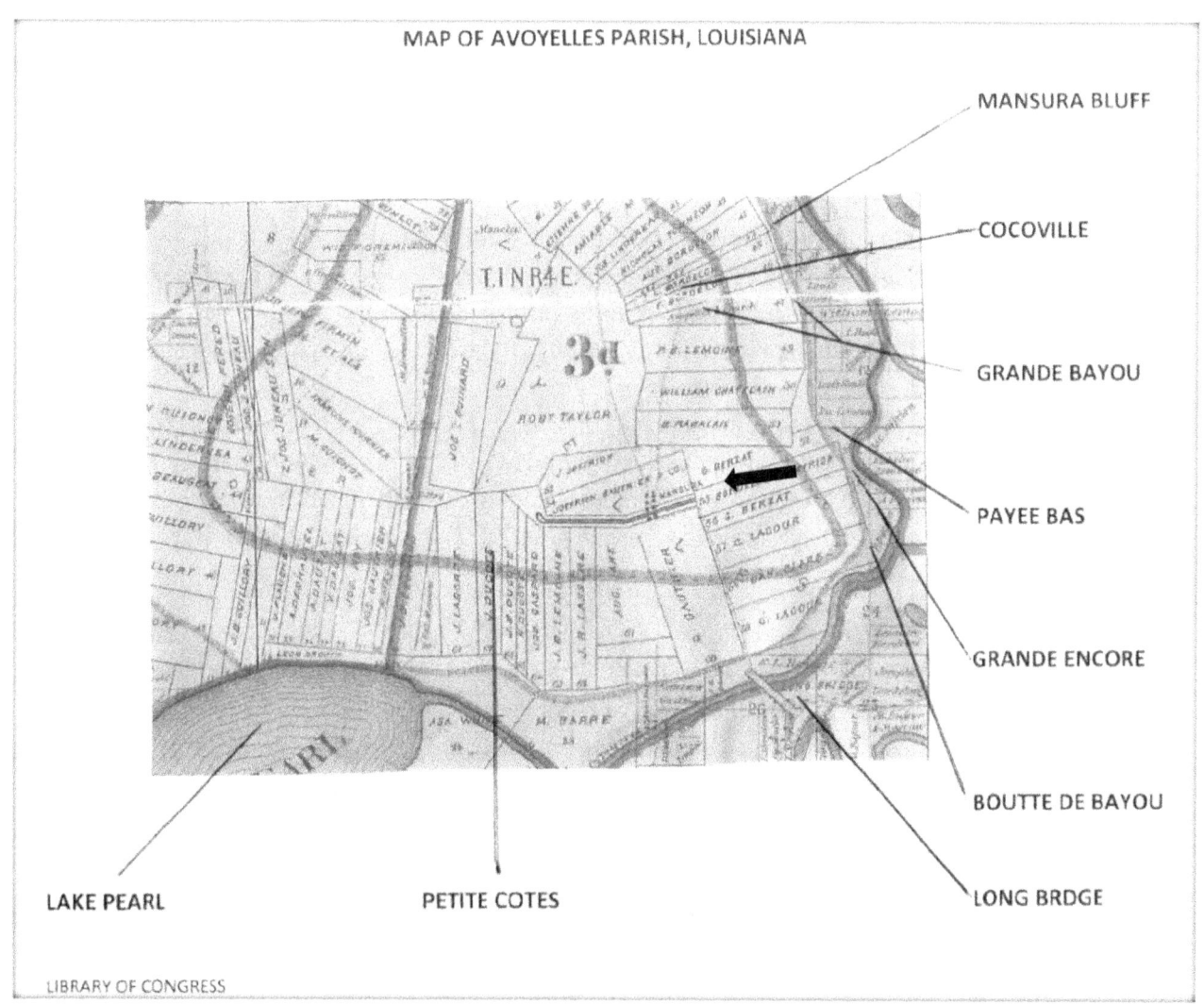

FIGURE 71. 1879 FARM MAP OF MANSURA AREA WITH SOME FEATURES INDICATED (CONGRESS)

The map in **Figure 71**, was copied from a Library of Congress map completed in 1879 and shows the area immediately surrounding Mansura, with Mansura situated to the right of its center.

Shown on this map are the local plantations as they existed before the Civil War. This map has been modified to indicate several important geographical and topographical features[39]:

- **Mansura Bluff** - This contour feature, indicated by a ring of "*//////*" marks nearly surrounding the town, shows the elevation of the town of Mansura above much of the areas to the East and South. This bluff, on which the town of Mansura sits, places the town some 20 feet in elevation above the nearby towns of Cottonport and Moreauville as well as the marshland to the east.

  The areas shown in gray to the east of the Mansura Bluff is the area where some of the current marshland that still surrounds the town lay then. *Bayou de la Cabon, Premiere Bayou* and Old River are currently located within that marshland.

- **Lake Pearl** – This lake and its tributaries, was an important part of the local farming industry, providing a mode of transportation covering a large part of the parish during the 18th and 19th centuries. Several pre-Civil War plantations surrounded Lake Pearl. One of its main tributaries, *Bayou de Cyprierres*, was crossed by the "Long Bridge" and ended at *Boutte de Bayou*.

- ***Bayou Lacombe*** - This small stream, only a few miles long, is shown on the map, just below the name "Mansura". Notice the bridge across it inside the town. The dotted lines "--------", descending from the north and crossing the bridge, are the roads that ran from Marksville, through Mansura and Long Bridge, and on to Moreauville and Simmesport.

- **Avoyelles Church** – This is the past location of St. Paul's Catholic Church in what was called Hydropolis at the time. This is the current location of St. Paul's cemetery along the *Grande Bayou* lane.

- **Long Bridge** - The actual bridge, located near the bottom of the map, is shown where it once crossed *Bayou de la Cyprierres* and the surrounding marsh in 1879. The stream just south of the bridge was part of *Bayou des Glaise*.

The areas identified as *Grande Bayou, Payee Bas, Grande Ecore* and *Butte de Bayou* on the Mansura map in **Figure 71**, were parts of a strip of land lying at the edge of the highlands, or bluff, on which Mansura sits. That bluff formed a boundary between the elevated Mansura farmland and low-lying marshland to the east and south of Mansura. The sloping hillside, from the top of the bluff to the marshland below, required a descent of about 20 feet. A dirt road, located at the bottom of the bluff, ran from *Grande Bayou*, passed under the Louisiana & Arkansas Railroad trestle in *Grande Ecore* and ended in *Boutte de Bayou*.

The strip of land that ran along the edge of the bluff, including the dirt road, because of its location and physical contour, was generally called "**Down the Hill**" by most of the black residents of Mansura (See below).

Down the Hill, at its peak, was a true farming suburb of the town of Mansura, with tenant houses, occupied by black families, extending from *Grande Bayou* to *Boutte de Bayou*. All of the families

---

[39] Items shown in the map were identified by the author based on his own knowledge of the area.

that resided there were sharecroppers, locked in such a cycle of economic slavery that most individuals were never able to escape. Instead, several generations of black families were born, lived their lives farming the land belonging to the white land owners, and died there, in many cases, in the same dilapidated houses.

It is important to discuss the *"In Town"* and *"Down the Hill"* areas as separate entities since so many current and former black Mansura families began and developed their family culture and traditions inside the town while others developed theirs "Down the Hill".

The other locations where large numbers of Blacks lived, e.g. *Grande Bayou, Petite Cote,* Large Lane, etc., will also be discussed, although in much less detail.

"In Town" Black Residents - In 1900, the total number of people living inside the town of Mansura was 408 (C. Bureau). This number did not include the greater portion of the people, who, while living on farms outside the town's city limits, still identified themselves as citizens of Mansura.

Of the 408 people in Mansura, the 1900 U.S. Census listed 189 Blacks and the remainder as White. Many white citizens listed themselves, or one or both parents, as being born in the following countries: France, Italy, Germany or Switzerland. Blacks not born in Louisiana listed their own, or their parents' places of birth, as: Maryland, Mississippi, South Carolina or Virginia, implying that they were people who were brought to Avoyelles parish in bondage from one of those main slave trading sites (Nicholas Boston).

By 1900, no black person remained alive in Mansura who, themselves, had been born in Africa. However, the 189 Blacks living inside the town of Mansura included 37 former slaves[40]. The oldest, by far, was **Ursin Augustine** (See Later and in Book II), who was listed as being at least 100 years old, having lived in slavery from before the arrival of the U.S. government in Louisiana, through the worst of slavery and the Civil War, and then, in freedom.

Some of the Blacks living inside the town of Mansura in 1900 were as follows:
- **Lucien** and **Charlotte Augustine**, along with their 6 sons and 2 daughters;
- **Luke Berzat**, who was a 24-years old head-of-household, along with 3 boarders;

----

[40] People listed in 1900 census who were born before 1865.

- **Edward** and **Emelia Williams** along with 1 daughter, 4 sons, and his sister-in-law, **Ella Wright**;
- **Frank** and **Eulalie Wilson**, 1 son and 1 daughter;
- **Fulgence** and **Fannie Lavalais**, 2 daughters, and 5 sons;
- **Augustine** and **Cleophine James**, 4 daughters, 1 son, and a cousin, **Emma Luke**;
- **Lovincia** and **Florida Sampson**, and 1 son;
- **Henry** and **Jennie Ford**, 2 daughters and 1 son;
- **Simon** and **Mary J. Wilson**, 1 daughter and 1 grandchild;
- **Henry** and **Estella Titus**, 2 daughters and 4 sons;
- **Clarima** and **Olizeane Sampson**, 1 daughter and 4 sons;
- **Joseph** and **Matilda Lavalais**, 1 step-son;
- **Pierre** and **Mary Sampson**, 1 son;
- **Irvin** and **Josephine Sampson**, 2 sons;
- **Oge'** and **Marie Francisco**, 1 son and 1 cousin, **Leonie Luke**;
- **Aimee Croisee** and 3 **Parker** sons;
- **Paul** and **Marie Sampson**, 1 daughter and 5 sons;
- **Marcelin** and **Margarette Celestine**, 2 step-sons;
- **Thomas** and **Emma Sampson**, 3 sons;
- **Jean Pierre** and **Lorenza James**, 6 daughters and 5 sons;
- **Cleophas** and **Mea Francisco**, 2 daughters and 1 son;
- **John Bte** and **Clarisse Joseph**, 1 daughter and 8 sons; 1 boarder, **George Barker**;
- **Provosty** and **Dora Ricard**;
- **Onezime** and **Marie L. Sampson**, 2 daughters, 1 step-daughter, and 4 sons.

Down the Hill - This area was occupied from right after the Civil War, at a time when it was considered safer for a black person to live in a community of other Blacks instead of living near the hostile people in the white community. The remoteness of that community from town gave an added level of safety.

Most families lived *Down the Hill* in small clusters of houses. Those clusters usually represented extended families, where, in many examples, elderly family members either lived on their own but next door to their children or actually lived in the house with their children. For example, in the 1870 U.S. census, Ursin Augustine was listed as a 67 year-old man, married to 65 year-old Therese. They had 5 young people living with them (Sylvest, Perry, Josephine, Herraine and Silas. On one side of their house lived his son, Augustine Augustine, while his other son, Ursin Augustine, Jr. lived one house farther away. On the other side of Ursin Sr. lived his son, Jean Pierre Augustine, while his other son, Andre' Augustine, lived one house farther away. Thus, Ursin Augustine and his sons occupied 5 adjacent houses *Down the Hill*.

Some of the other black residents who worked and lived *Down the Hill*, mostly in the sections called the *Payee Bas* during the 1920's and 1930's, included (Mansura1930):

- **Carrison & Olivia Sampson,**
- **John & Marie Drummer,**
- **Woodruff & Georgia Sampson,**
- **Alfred & Allzane Sampson,**
- **Modella & Heloise Augustine,**
- **Martin & Joyce Sampson,**
- **Widdie & Winnie Walter,**
- **Luther & Lillie Lavalais,**
- **Paul & Julia Jacob,**
- **Jeanpierre & Lorenza James,**
- **Eliza McGlory,**
- **Avit & Mary J Augustine,**
- **Douglas Thomas,**
- **Roosevelt & Nora Sampson,**
- **Peter & Maggie James,**
- **Mathew & Lillian Lavalais,**
- **Lula Augustine,**
- **Willie L. & Mary J. Blackman,**
- **Sostin & Victoria Augustine,**
- **Samuel Augustine,**
- **Pilger & Beatrice Blackman,**
- **Henry & Emma Blackman,**
- **Oliver & Mary Augustine,**
- **Giles & Emma Augustine.**

The *Down the Hill* residents, as mention earlier, lived on a bluff that formed the boundary between the farm lands just outside of Mansura and the large expanse of marshland that extended from east of Mansura to the Mississippi River. Their houses were situated in a row at the top of the bluff that overlooked the marshland, extending for about 3 miles from Grande Bayou to Boutte des Bayou.

FIGURE 72. RAIL ROAD TRESTLE NEAR GRANDE ECORE

The area shown in the circa 1910 picture[41] above (**Figure 72**) shows a scene from a vantage point at the top of the hill near *Grande Ecore*. The camera was aiming down on a section of the dirt road that traveled from *Grande Bayou* to *Boutte des Bayou*. This is near the area where the road passed under the Louisiana & Arkansas rail road trestle and entered Boutte de Bayou. Notice the mule-drawn wagon traveling under the trestle, driven by a black man and carrying a load of sacks, likely cotton. Also, the other four black men, in the foreground, appear to be working on a car parked off the road. There appears to be some sort of garden or other planted area to the extreme left of the picture. The area seen on the right, beyond the tracks, is the easternmost edge of *Boutte de Bayou* (See below).

The dirt road shown in this picture ran along the water's edge at the base of the bluff. It provided the residents living *Down the Hill* with a means to travel within their community as well as into the town of Mansura without going through the fields. Initially, it ran this whole course without any blockages due to fences. Eventually, the fences that crossed the road were added. Vehicle and pedestrian passage through them was still allowed, however, using gates and cattle gaps.

Each of the houses located *Down the Hill* was a small, wood-frame, unpainted or whitewashed house with no more than 2 windows, both located near the front of the house. These wooden windows could be swung outward to allow fresh air to enter the house or swung closed to prevent

---

[41] Copied from a picture inside the Avoyelles Parish Courthouse in Marksville

cold air from entering. The houses generally faced away from the marshland and towards the town of Mansura.

FIGURE 73. HOUSES SIMILAR TO THOSE *DOWN THE HILL* DURING THE EARLY 1900'S (EAKIN)

Each house was constructed from rough-hewn boards that barely fit together well enough to prevent small animals and insects from crawling through. Most tenants resorted to using some sort of newspaper or wall paper, glued on with a paste made from flour, to seal the gaps in the walls. Unfortunately, the flour paste was more of a food for the swarms of rats, roaches and ants that lived nearby, than it was a deterrent.

A typical tenant house consisted of a living room, where the fireplace was situated, one or two small bedrooms and a small kitchen. There was no indoor plumbing, making it necessary to venture outside to use the toilet (Outhouse) or draw water from the well.

The living room nearly always contained a bed and chairs for sitting near the fireplace.

Bedrooms were usually cramped with either a standard bed or bunk beds. In some cases, a small dresser might have been squeezed in.

In the small kitchen, cooking was generally done on a cast iron, wood-burning stove. Preserved salted meat in large crocks (ceramic barrels) and sacks of flour, cornmeal and rice were generally stored on the floor. The walls were lined with shelves holding various jars of preserved fruits, vegetables and meats. Meals were eaten at a small, wooden table or, in the case of small children, on the floor.

Each of the tenant houses had a small yard, enclosed by hog or chicken wire, where they could grow a vegetable garden as well as maintain flocks of chicken, ducks, and geese. Nearly everyone had a "Hog Pen" in their yards where they raised several pigs for butchering during the winter months.

The residents were required to climb up a slanted hillside, from the road at the base of the hill, to reach their homes on the bluff about 20 feet above. In many cases, they constructed crude steps that were built by driving a series of two parallel sets of wooden posts into the ground up to the top of the hill[42]. To the top of each pair of adjacent posts was nailed a wooden board to be used as a step, resulting in a fairly sturdy "Stairway" from the road up to their yards.

Figure 74. TYPICAL CENTRAL LOUISIANA SHARECROPPER HOUSE (Eakin)

---

[42] Oral History Provided by Leanna Sampson, who lived most of her early life "Down the Hill"

FIGURE 75. INSIDE HOUSE ONCE USED BY CENTRAL LOUISIANA BLACK FARM WORKERS (Eakin)

Despite the difficulty of manual farming during the hot and humid days in the Louisiana summer, nighttime was the worst time of all. The location of the *Down the Hill* houses so close to the marshland was an invitation to the huge swarms of mosquitos that resided in the swampland. The residents had a clear choice: Open the windows to let in fresh air and get eaten alive by hungry mosquitos or close the windows and suffocate in the stifling heat. One former resident told of having to sleep with their heads covered all night long to ward off the mosquitos[43].

Most residents who lived *Down the Hill*, instead of traveling around on the dirt road through *Grande Bayou* or *Grande Ecore*, to get to town, preferred to take short cuts through the fields.

Each set of rows in the field ended at a "*Turn row*". This was a narrow strip of land that followed the fence line separating their farm from the adjacent one. It allowed space for the farm equipment being used to work the rows to be turned around and set to work the next set of rows. The *Turn Rows* also served as "roads" to allow movement of produce across the fields and to the market.

The *Turn Rows* that followed the fence lines that headed from *Down the Hill* toward the town of Mansura were convenient roads for the residents to use when traveling back and forth.

---

[43] Oral history from Leanna Sampson

FIGURE 76. WOMAN WALKING ALONG DUSTY TURN ROW (EAKIN)

Members of the black community who made up *Down the Hill* generally lived and worked in groups that were defined by the owner of the land that they farmed. For example, a section of *Down the Hill* that was owned by the Normand/Coco family of Mansura, was generally referred to by the black residents as the Coco Plantation or the *Payee Bas*. In another case, a section owned by the Roy family was called *Grande Ecore*.

These large farms were unique because they employed many black families as sharecroppers during the late 1800s through the 1970s. Their sizes and impact on the black community in Mansura was such that they became almost legendary. These included the Norman/Coco and the Roy farms.

- **The Normand farm**, which later became the Coco farm, or "**Coco Plantation**", was a large portion of land located northward along L'Eglise Street from just north of what is currently Coco Street in Mansura. It extended eastward from L'Eglise Street, where the land owners' homes were located, down to the area called *Down the Hill*, to the east of Mansura. The Texas and Pacific Railroad tracks ran diagonally across the property. The farm was operated by Edward Coco and his family for most of the 1st half of the 20th century.

  It was a large sharecropper operation, with numerous black residents living on site in small, ancient wood frame houses, most of which were never painted. The sharecroppers on the Coco farm lived in two groups of houses: some lived inside the town of Mansura, in a fenced-in "pasture" that was located just behind the Coco family homes on L'Eglise Street while a second group of sharecroppers lived in the area called *Down the Hill*, at the easternmost end of the Coco farm.

The "**Pasture**" contained a row of houses that ran along the Texas & Pacific railroad tracks that crossed through the farm. A second, shorter, row of houses ran along a small dirt road that ran eastward from L'Eglise Street to the center of the pasture. Inside the "Pasture" was the "**Lot**" where the farming equipment, commissary, smokehouse, and other small buildings were located.

Many of the black residents living inside Mansura and listed in the 1900 U.S. census above, were employed as sharecroppers and servants on the Coco farm. **Luke Berzat** and his boarders, the black servants (**Aurelia** and **Sophia Lavalais**, and **Clarisse Augustine**) and **Jean Pierre James** and his family are some examples.

- **The Roy "Plantation",** as it was called by those who lived there during the first half of the 20th century, was generally more remote from the center of Mansura than was the Coco farm, since it did not extend from *Down the Hill* to L'Eglise Street in Mansura. Instead, its black residents lived in small houses that were located from along the southern part of the Down the Hill strip to a point along the current Grande Ecore lane.

Although smaller than the Coco farm, it was also a large sharecropper operation with a large number of black residents living in similar conditions. Also, its version of the "Pasture" was much smaller than the Coco "Pasture". Its version of the "Lot" was similar, with an area for keeping and feeding the farm animals, a large barn for storing tools and farming equipment, and a large bell tower. It's operator for much of the 1st half of the 20th century, T.R. "Teska" Roy, lived on L'Eglise Street in Mansura rather than near the farm itself.

Those who lived on or in the vicinity of the Roy farm, still remember the harsh work conditions and general mistreatment by the owners and overseers. In particular, most remembered the large plantation bell that was rung daily as a signal for the workers to begin their work day, break for lunch, resume the afternoon work and break for the day. That bell was said to have been so large and loud that other local farmers also used its ringing to control their workers' schedules.

FIGURE 77. COMMON PLANTATION BELL (EAKIN)

Just as in the case of the Coco farm, the numbers of black families living *Down the Hill* in Grande Ecore on the Roy farm began to dwindle around the 1920's. For example, in the 1930 U.S. Census, the black families still living in Grande Ecore included the following (1930):

- **Leroy & Irene Augustine** - 1 Daughter (Caroline);
- **Herbert** & **Effie James** - 1 Son (Warren);
- **Clifton Lavalais**;
- **Dave** & **Lou Jones** - 2 Daughters (Lou & May), 2 Step Sons (Aron & Arthur Drummer);
- **Albert** & **Emma Babino** - 2 Daughters (Mary & Octavia), 1 Granddaughter (Hazel Morris), 3 Grandsons (Raymond Alexander, Lenon & Spelman James),
- **Sydonia Augustine** - 1 Adopted Son (Obey Sampson),

By the 1960's, except for a couple of black families living along the "*Grande Ecore* Lane", most had moved away.

Boutte des Bayou was an area located south of the Louisiana & Arkansas railroad tracks, adjacent to *Grande Ecore*. As seen on the map in **Figure 78** (Below), it was a continuation of the strip of land along the marshland referred above as "*Down the Hill*", except that it was separated from the rest of the area by the Louisiana & Arkansas (L&A) tracks (Added to map).

The translated name means "End of the Bayou". The "*Bayou*" part of its name refers to *Bayou de la Cyprierres*, a small stream that began near *Grande Ecore* and flowed into Lake Pearl.

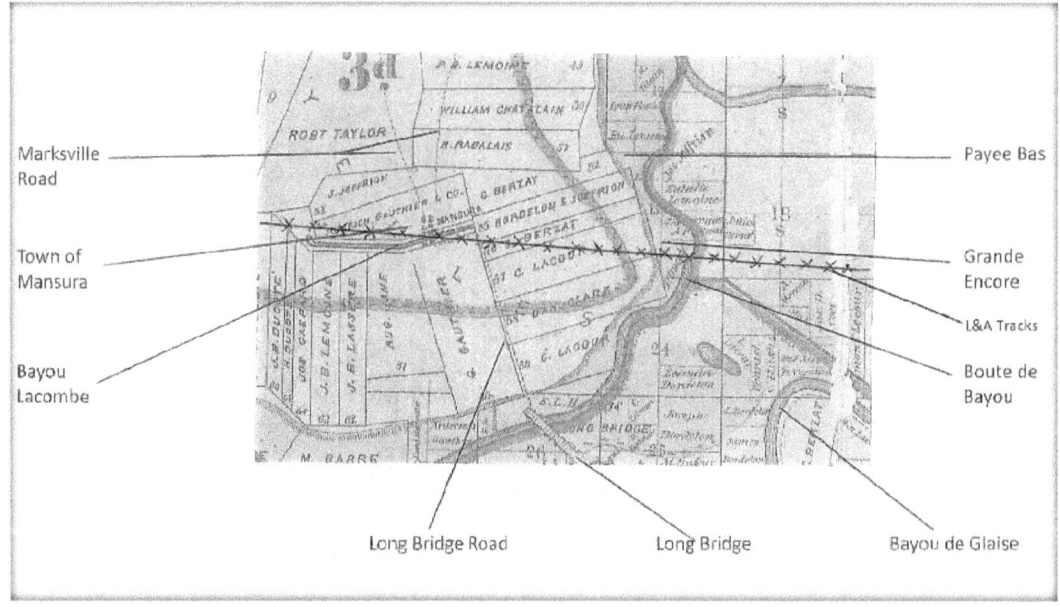

FIGURE 78. MANSURA 1879 WITH LOCAL FEATURES AND ADDED L&A TRACKS

A dirt road that passed under the tracks allowed the residents to travel from *Boutte de Bayou* to the *Grande Ecore*, *Payee Bas,* and *Grande Bayou* sections of "Down the Hill". The current "*Boutte de Bayou* Lane" runs from *L'Eglise* Street in Mansura to its end at *Boutte de Bayou.*

The area called *Boutte de Bayou* was not much different from the other areas that were parts of *Down the Hill* except for the fact that the farms were smaller. Here the land was also farmed by mostly black sharecroppers who were also trapped in the same cycle of economic slavery and poverty as were those who lived in the area called *Down the Hill*.

Some of the farmers owning land in the *Boutte de Bayou* area in the 2nd half of the 19th century included:

- Dan Clark
- Colin Lacour
- Dorcineau Armand
- P. Ducote

During the 20th century, Mo Bordelon's farm is often mentioned as one of the largest in the area, stretching from *Grande Ecore* to *Boutte de Bayou*[44].

Some of the black families who resided in *Boutte de Bayou* during the 1st half of the 20th century included the:

- **Talleys**
- **Sampsons**
- **Blackmans**
- **Berrys**

In 1930, the only black families listed on the *Boutte des Bayou* road were (1930):

- **Teska S. & Lola Williams** - 1 Daughter (Beauty N.), 3 Sons (Sterling J, Chester B. & Wilmer S.), 1 Stepson (William Day);
- **Mary Dorsey** - 1 Daughter (Virginia), 1 Son (Cilton);
- **Thomas & Emma Sampson** - 4 Daughters (Ethel, Mildred, Hazel & Marguerite), 1 Son (Phillip);

While there remain a few black families living on the *Boutte des Bayou* **Lane**, the actual area once called *Boutte des Bayou* no longer exists. The new Louisiana Highway 1 runs through that area now and no black people still live there.

---

[44] Oliver Prier, this author's father, farmed parts of Mo Bordelon's farm during the early 1950s.

The *Cotes* were two roads, between Mansura and Hessmer that joined to form a horseshoe shape south of the Mansura-Hessmer highway[45]. The segment nearest the town of Mansura was called the *Petite Cotes* while the other segment, closer to Hessmer, was called the **Lake Pearl Road** (1930).

During the 1860 - 1880 timeframe, the *Cotes* area included a series of farms that extended south to *Bayou de la Cyprierres* and Lake Pearl (Congress). These farms were owned by a number of white families including:

- J.B. Lassere,
- J.B. Lemoine,
- Joseph Gaspard,
- H. Ducote,
- J.B. Ducote,
- J. Ducote,
- J. Laborde,
- M. Barre.

From as early as the 1880 U.S. Census (1880), the *Cotes* area included a large number of black families, all of whom appeared to be sharecroppers. Some of these families were:

- **Francois & Clementine Francisco**
- **Fulgence & Marie Francisco**
- **Samuel & Julienne Pryor**
- **Jean Baptiste & Josephine Berzat**

Although it is possible that these black families had their origin in slavery on one of the large plantations that existed in the area around Lake Pearl, there is no specific evidence that leads to this conclusion.

Additional black families residing in the *Cotes* by the early 20th century included (C. Bureau):

- **Wade & Manie Prior**
- **Shelby & Rose Francisco**
- **Lucille Francisco**
- **Clarence & Lorina Francois**
- **Emile & Josephine Prior**
- **Preston & Celestine Prior**

By 1930, the black families living in the Petite Cotes included (Cotes1930):

- **Wade & Alberta Prior** - 1 Daughter (**Onelia**), Mother (**Maria**), Cousin (**Evaline Joshua**);

---

45 LA Highway 114

- **Marcelin & Dora Francisco** - Dora's grandson (**Cleveland Murray**), Marcelin's Mother (**Mary Francisco**), Marcelin's niece (**Bernice Francisco**);
- **Kirby & Benita Francisco** - 1 Son (**Louis**);
- **Harry & Louise A. Brooks** - 1 Daughter (**Lucille**), 1 Son (**Mitchel**);
- **Rosina St. Romain** - 1 Daughter (**Celestine**), 2 Grandsons (**Curly Fox & Sidney Murray**);
- **Clifton & Florestine Fox**
- **Clarence & Lorena Francois** - 6 Daughters (**Lessie**, **Effie**, **Bessie**, **Rufy**, **Virginia** & **Dorris**), 3 Sons (**Leroy**, **Spelma** & **Will**);
- **Weston & Delphi Keller** - 1 Daughter (**Loretta**), Niece (**Edlee Kertz**);
- **Frances & Eola Francisco** - 1 Daughter (**Josephine**), 3 Sons (**Alvin**, **Riley** & **Joseph**);

The Petite Cotes area has continued to grow over the years and remains a large community of black citizens. Many of the older names are gone and have been replaced by others.

In 1930, only one black family was listed as residing on **Lake Pearl Road:**

- **Cleavis & Mary Francisco** - 1 Daughter (Sarah)

It still exists today and is populated by several black and white families.

The Mansura-Hessmer Highway was the home to a number of black families during the late 19th and early 20th centuries. Although all were sharecroppers, it's not clear which farmers they were working for since there were no large sharecropping operations in the area similar to those inside of and to the east of Mansura. The sharecroppers appear to have been dispersed among several small farming operations.

By 1930, the number of Blacks living along that road had dwindled to only a few families, all of whom lived off the road, to the north, and near the railroad tracks (Cotes1930). These included:

- **Adelmar & Agnes Prior** - 4 Daughters (**Edna**, **Julia**, **Syble** & **Mariline**), 2 Sons (**Aurelia** & **Albon**),
- **Teska & Della Benjamin** - 4 Daughters (**Viola**, **Ethel**, **Eldie** & **Mabel**), 2 Sons (**Alton** & **Percy**);
- **Leonard & Mathilde Francisco** - 1 Niece (**Therese Batiste**), 1 Nephew (**Herman Francois**),
- **Emile & Josephine Prior** - 1 Daughter (**Mary M**);
- **Oliver & Beulah Prior** - 4 Daughters (**Mary M.**, **Elzica M.**, **Marguerite** & **Louise M.**), 1 Son (**Ury**), Uncle (**John Davis**).

The *Grande Bayou* area extends eastward from the old LA Highway 1, past the St. Paul Catholic Cemetery and ends at the northernmost end of the strip called "Down the Hill". See maps in **Figures 71 & 78**, above.

The black population of *Grande Bayou* is unique for two reasons: 1) a relatively high percentage of that population was listed in the early censuses as "Mulattoes"[46] versus other nearby areas (1880); 2) Many were land owners when most Blacks in the South were not (1880). The origins of these families, how they managed to end up living near each other, and how so many became land owners are 3 questions that require further study.

In the 1880 U.S. census for Avoyelles Parish, several mulatto families were listed as living near each other in the *Grande Bayou* area (1880). These included:

- **Joseph & Virginia Raino** - 4 Daughters (**Marie, Helena, Josephine & Virginie**), Mother-in-law (**Marie Chevalier**), Sister-in-law (**Leontine Berzat**), 2 Brothers-in-law (**Paul & Abel Berzat**);
- **Louis[47] & Marie Olivier** - 4 Daughters (Ernestine, Estelle, Angelica & Flavie), 2 Sons (Jermone & Oliver),
- **Rudolph & Eugenie Berger** - 2 Daughters (**Eleanore & Orare**), 2 Sons (**Pierre & Jules**), Orphan Girl (**Ermentine Berger**);
- **Julian & Lorenza Saucier** - 2 Daughters (**Lorinia & Merente**), 3 Sons (**Jules, Robert & Emile**);
- **William & Laura Allison** - 1 Daughter (**Laura**), 3 Sons (**James, Millium & Spencer**),
- **Prosper & Mary Normand** - 3 Daughters (**Josephine, Leacadie & Lee F.**), 3 Sons (**Joseph, Victor & Simon**).

In the 1910 U.S. census (C. Bureau), people listed as mulattoes who lived near each other in the Grande Bayou area were:

- **Clinton & Elinor Bontemp** - 2 Sons (**Cylton & Sterling**);
- **Joseph Reynaud** - 1 Son (**Ambroise**), Mother-in-law (**Marie Berzat**);
- **Arthur & Eloise Demouy** - 1 Daughter (**Ella R.**), 2 Sons (**Louis E. & Curtis E.**), 2 Granddaughters (**Josephine B. & Rosa B. Berger**);
- **Filmore & Elisou Coco** - 1 Daughter (**Annielou D.**), 3 Sons (**Worthie A., Joseph R. & Filmore E. Jr.**);
- **Rudolph & Eugenie Berger** - 1 Son (**Albert**);
- **Celestine & Leonore Prevot** - 3 Daughters (**Irine, Alzica & Ellen**), 4 Sons (**Louis, Albert, Theophile & Agusta**);
- **Christophe & Lorenia Williams** - 2 Nephews (**Colius Deshautells & Clifton Berzat**);
- **Mary Wallace**;

---

[46] From Wikipedia - The term "Mulatto" is used to refer to a person who is born from one white parent and one black parent, or more broadly, a person of any proportion of significant European and African ancestry. In the broadest sense, it is applied to persons of black and white ancestry. It is not clear what guidance the census takers were given to define whether or not a person was considered a "Mulatto".
[47] Louis was listed as black while Marie and all of their children were listed as mulattoes.

- **Francois** & **Marie Normand** - Granddaughter (**Girtie Simmon**), Orphan (**Felton Voorhies**);
- **Scott** & **Eunice Normand** - 2 Granddaughters (**Sybel** & **Ida Berger**), Orphan (**Walter Arr**)
- **Paul** & **Henrietta Lehman** - 2 Daughters (**Mary L.** & **Emma M.**), 4 Sons (**Walter J.**, **Winston J.**, **Paul M.**, Jr. & **Harvey J.**);
- **Homer** & **Armentine Laurent** - 3 Daughters (**Emma**, **Simonia** & **Rachal**), 4 Sons (**Martin**, **Moses**, **Joseph** & **Samuel**);
- **Eugene Berger**;
- **Henry** & **Rosina Demouy** - 3 Sons (**Carlton**, **Otis** & **Henry J. Jr.**);
- **Oscar** & **Henrietta Prunell** - 1 Son (**Joseph**), 1 Brother (**Overton**), 4 Nieces (**Alice**, **Loucinda**, **Ida** & **Charrie**); 4 Granddaughters (**Mary**, **Odile**, **Viola** & **Hazel**);

Of the 15 families listed above, 9 were identified as farmers who owned their land.

By 1940 (U. C. Bureau), several of the above surnames, (i.e. **Allison**, **Berger**, **Normand**, **Prunell**, **Renaud** and **Saucier**) had completely vanished from the *Grande Bayou* area. In some cases, this was the result of the families moving away. In other cases, the names vanished due to families with mostly females who married and gave up their family names.

In any case, few people still live in the Grande Bayou area who could be described as having the traditional "Mulatto" features.

The Large Lane extended westward from opposite the Coco family homes on L'Eglise Street in Mansura to what is now the Marksville-Hessmer Highway. Its terrain was very different from the other Mansura farming areas in that it consisted of flat prairie land with few large accumulation of trees. There was no noticeable marshland except for a small bayou that flowed into Bayou Lacombe.

The land likely was originally part of the Dominique Coco land grant (Mayeux and Decuir). Some of the white families who managed the land there included:

- **Poret**
- **Mayeux**
- **Normand**
- **Roy**

Some of the black families residing and farming the land there over the years included:

- **Baptiste**
- **Hollis,**
- **Jones**
- **Lee**

- **Sampson**

The Large Lane is still occupied by many black families. They still retain some of the older names such as Sampson, Lee, etc.

The Others - As one might expect, the trauma of living under slavery has to have had some serious mental and emotional damage to many of the people who were forced to endure it. Today, we are all familiar with the concept of PTSD (Post Traumatic Stress Syndrome) that occurs from prolonged exposure to the constant stress, danger, injuries and death in combat situations.

There can be no doubt that the vast majority of black people suffered something similar to PTSD as a result of living in slavery. Unfortunately, the level of interest and the knowledge of this condition was not present in the white community, where most of the doctors resided. In fact, some of the leading white authorities on mental health, at the time of slavery, described mental problems displayed by slaves as being in three categories: *Negritude*, a mild form of leprosy, where the only treatment was to become white; *Drapetomia,* a disease causing "Negroes" to have the urge to run away and *Dysaethesia Aethiopica,* a disease called by the overseers, *Rascality*. Interesting, the recommended cure for all of these "diseases" was whipping. The more severe the symptoms, the greater the applied whippings should be (Randall).

The U.S. census records report nothing about the mental condition of the people being interviewed other than whether or not they could read, write or speak English. However, many stories have been passed down from the African-Americans who resided in Mansura during the early 1900's about people who lived in the swamps far beyond the area called *Down the Hill*[48].

The stories told of old black people who were assumed to be "crazy" at the time because they lived far out in the swamp and never came to town. In fact, they were said to be afraid of anyone who came near them and would hide when approached.

While there is no verification of their identity, some of the names that were repeated were: "*Ole Potch a lafa*" and "*Nonk Tom Chicken*".

Clearly, the passage of time has made it completely impossible to further identify the people who lived in the swamp and whether or not they truly had slavery-related mental diseases.

---

[48] These are stories often told by the author's mother, Beulah Prier

Chapter 16. 1900 - 1940: A Period of Transition

The movement toward some level of racial equality for Blacks living in the South did not begin with the civil rights movement of the 1950's, 60' and 70's. Instead, it occurred over a much longer period of time that stretched from about 1900 and continued through the 1940's and 50's.

Before this "Awakening" occurred, the laws and social rules within the U.S., along with the absence of formal education, prevented most Blacks from seeing Whites as no better than themselves. They rarely saw Whites living in hopelessness as they themselves were. Rarely did black people find themselves in situations where they were comrade with a white person who recognized the need for protecting each other from harm. Rarely did anything happen that allowed Blacks to experience treatment that was similar to that of Whites.

Psychologically, most Blacks saw white people as some sort of special beings who always lived better than themselves, who were smarter than themselves and controlled most events. Most Blacks believed that Whites always had protection from harm by the local and state authorities, their children could get away with anything and had futures that could take them all over the world.

Whites, on the other hand, felt that they had been given some sort of special gift of superiority from God, the so-called White Man's Burden (Easterly). Despite their social or economic condition, they felt that being white always made them superior to any black person, no matter what their social or economic standing in the community might be.

Both sides of the color barrier lived in worlds that were interdependent but as distant from each other as the planets in the solar system.

The True Civil Rights Movement can be defined by a series of events that occurred during the 1st half of the 20th century. Those events, while not changing the laws or improving racial tolerance in the U.S., did, instead, increase the level of awareness regarding what freedom meant for Blacks.

Before these events and their aftermaths occurred, the average black person in the U.S. was in a life that was one step away from slavery. Once those events had occurred, the whole worldview of U.S. Blacks in the South had changed. Now they recognized that they were entitled to the same rights and privileges as Whites because: 1) they had read about freedom and how to obtain it, 2) they had talked about freedom with fellow Blacks who had escaped the South and actually lived a better life "Up North" or in other countries, and 3) they had seen what it was like when Whites experienced disasters so overwhelming that they were literally brought down to their knees, many giving up everything, including their lives.

Their "Veil" was lifted...a bit.

These events in question were: 1) **Establishment of educational opportunities for Blacks**; 2) the **rise of the black religious institutions**; 3) the **Northern Migrations**; 4) **World War I**; 5) the **Flood of 1927** (For Blacks in Mansura and the Mississippi Delta) and 6) the **Rise of Mechanical Farming Technology**.

The Growth of Black Education - As mentioned earlier, one of the first objectives of Blacks following the end of the Civil War and the arrival of Emancipation was the establishment of schools for the education of the Freedmen (W. Du Bois). Most Blacks recognized the value of education as a key to real freedom and emancipation. Also, an educated black person was always regarded as a person to be held in great esteem by members of the black community.

Once the Civil War was ended, the period of Reconstruction, especially via the Freedman's Bureau, resulted in a huge proliferation of black educational institutions throughout the country, especially the South (W.E.B.Dubois). Many of the Historically Black Colleges and Universities that exist today were started during this period.

The Atlanta Compromise (Harlan) made the white citizens more relaxed regarding the issue of black education once it was clear that the level of that education would be more of a rudimentary nature. Teaching Blacks basic reading, writing and math skills became acceptable once these were seen as necessary to become more adept at needed skills such as farming, brick masonry, carpentry, etc. By the 1920's, the slate of school topics had expanded to include topics more related to home making such as canning, cooking, sewing, needle point, etc. (Whitehead).

With this new level of acceptance, the education of Blacks flourished throughout the South. In the Mansura vicinity, the addition of the "Colored Convent School" in 1910 filled a large void. Prior to that time, those Blacks who valued education, were forced to attend one of the church-sponsored schools held at the somewhat remotely-located, Jerusalem and Little Zion Baptist churches and at St. Paul Lutheran Church. The result of this was that none of the black children who lived "In Town" or "Down the Hill" attended school since none of the three schools were near their homes. On the other hand, the black children who lived in the vicinity of Jerusalem (Petite Cote and Hessmer-Mansura Highway), Little Zion (Boutte de Bayou and Long Bridge) and St. Paul Lutheran (Grande Bayou and Cocoville) did attend school.

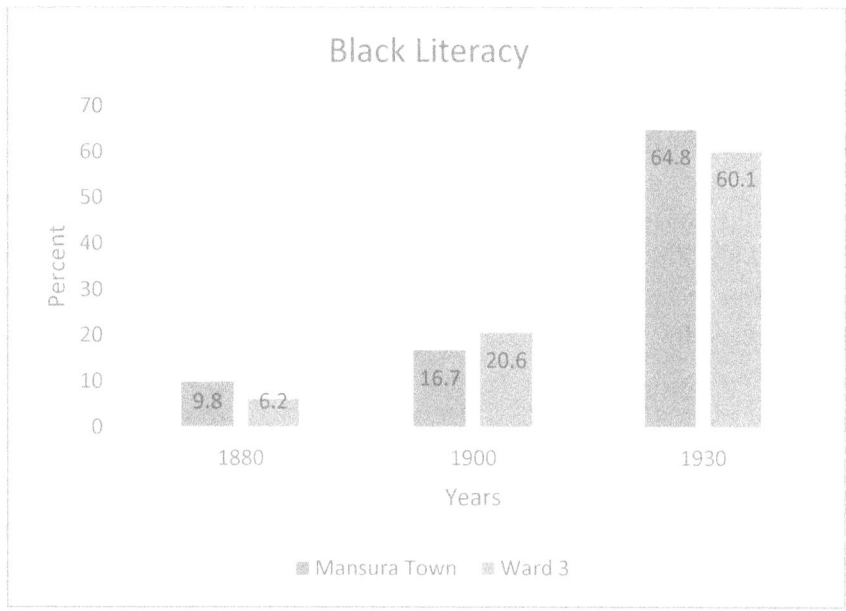

FIGURE 79. BLACK LITERACY TRENDS IN MANSURA & VICINITY (Government)

As can be seen in **Figure 79** above, the establishment of the four church-supported schools in the Mansura area had a profound effect on the educational levels of local Blacks. Included in the data are the following observations:

- **Only a few Blacks were literate in Mansura in 1880**. Included in that number were Joseph Laurent, his wife, Eliza, and two of his children, Joseph and Oscar. The Laurents, headed by Joseph's father, Joseph Sr., were carpenters and brick masons who were listed as Free People of Color in 1860 (Census). It's not clear how or when they acquired their skills at building or at reading but it did occur during slavery.

  Outside of the town of Mansura were small pockets of Blacks who could read, although they were school children and not adults: John Thomson's family had three members in school who could read; Martin Benjamin's family had three children in school who could read and Joseph Prunel's family had three children in school who could read. The rest were scattered individual adults who had, somehow, acquired reading skills earlier in their lives.

- **The effects of the new education initiatives** were slowly beginning to be seen by 1900. By then, 22 small schools for Blacks were scattered around Avoyelles Parish with as many as 1700 students enrolled (Saucier). Records indicate that Blacks had taken over the teaching responsibilities in most of those schools. Unfortunately, these were part-time jobs and few non-farm jobs were listed as held by Blacks.

  By 1930, most Blacks still identified their profession as farm-related (i.e., farmer or farm laborer). There were two, however, who said that their jobs were white collar (i.e., one teacher and one nurse) and several listed theirs as rail road workers and servants (1930).

- **Catholics**, including black Catholics in the Mansura area, greatly outnumbered the other religious groups in Louisiana because of the historical French and Spanish influences (Saucier). The lack of a school for the black Catholics living in Mansura during the late 1800's and early 1900's created a large population without formal education.

  Those black Catholics who happened to live within a reasonable distance of one of the three schools based at Jerusalem, Little Zion Baptist Church or at St. Paul's Lutheran Church were able to send their children to one of those schools. Since all three were so remote, the black Catholic population inside Mansura remained generally illiterate.

  The effect of the new Mansura Colored Convent School on the educational levels of Blacks in Mansura could be clearly seen in 1930. By then, hundreds had attended either one of the public schools based in one of the three churches or the Mansura Colored Convent School. Also, a considerable percent of black children between the ages of 8 and 16 were listed as being in public school in the 1930 U.S. Census (Saucier).

  The Mansura Colored Convent School added a significant number of Blacks to the literacy roles. The school became a part of the Our Lady of Prompt Succor parish when it was formed in 1938. It remained the premier educational institution for Blacks in Mansura until it was shut down and replaced by Cardinal Cushing Elementary School in 1962.

Over the 50 years surveyed in this work, the black school system that developed inside of Mansura and its surrounding areas, including Cocoville, Long Bridge and the Petite Cotes made significant changes in the lives of most Blacks in the area. Later, the expanded public school system, the further development of the Catholic Church schools and mandatory school attendance greatly aided in the growth of the educational level of the black citizens in the Mansura area.

The Role of Black Churches in Building a Cohesive Community

- The church in any community serves several purposes: a place of worship; a sanctuary of peace and inspiration; a healing place for souls needing balm, etc. Throughout history, irrespective of beliefs or culture, churches have also been a place of community, a place where members and visitors could feel a sense of belonging and support, a place where people could join together and, as a group, achieve much more than one might achieve as an individual (McMickle).

Often, this latter function has manifested itself in the form of organizations that, while supported by the church, actually performed more secular activities. Such activities have ranged from addressing the needs of the poor and destitute, upgrading the educational levels of the church members and members of the surrounding community and getting involved in political activities.

As mentioned earlier, throughout slavery, many Slave Holders provided opportunities for the slaves to participate in some sort of religious activities, especially of Sundays. In most cases, the religious activities took the form of a gathering of the slaves on the plantation with the Slave Holder taking an active role in the service. The message given was usually one where the slaves were told of the rewards they would receive in the next life. But to get there, they much adhere to the principles of hard work and obedience to their master. The subject of equality among men was carefully avoided.

It was a common practice for slaves, not able to buy into the messages given by the Slave Holders, to hold their own secret religious gatherings (Maffly-Kipp). These meetings were often held (H. Staff) late at night in secret places away from the plantation house. The information regarding the planned meetings was often given out using secret passwords, signs, song lyrics and other methods.

In those meetings, a more acceptable message could be developed among the members that included the biblical concepts of all men being created in the image of God with the same basic rights as their Slave Holders. It was likely that in those meetings was where the desire for freedom was born and nurtured among those held in bondage.

Another, and probably the most important, aspect of the secret meetings was the opportunity for individual black men and women to exercise leadership skills that they were not allowed to ever display in their normal roles as slaves. In addition to being discussion leaders, some of the slaves were responsible for organizing the meetings, acting as lookouts and other roles. Interesting, several slave uprising, e.g. Nat Turner's, appeared to have developed using a structure very similar to these meetings (McMickle).

Thus, it should be no surprise that no sooner than the black churches in the Mansura area were founded that they turned their attention to opening schools, improving the lives of black people in the local communities, assisting others who were without churches to organize themselves and form their own and to engage in political activities that were perceived to be of value to black people in the area (McMickle).

These activities included the following:

- Eventually, all three black protestant churches plus St. Paul's Catholic Church developed their own schools for black children (Saucier);
- In addition to the basic reading, writing and arithmetic, the schools also stressed Victorian mores that taught young black men and women proper etiquette (James), (Augustine);
- St. Paul's Lutheran Church obtained funding to teach basic homemaking skills such as canning food, a skill that became critical to survival during the Great Depression (Whitehead);

- The black churches, through their organizational structures (i.e. Minister, Deacons, Church Mothers, Secretaries, etc.) provided important opportunities for Blacks to hold leadership roles in their religious communities. Here, they developed skills that would ultimately benefit the larger, non-religious black community (McMickle).
- Under the leadership of Reverend Calvin Peter Thompson, Reverend Prudent Guillory, and Reverend Pilger Blackman, the Avoyelles Chapter of the National Association for the Advancement of Colored People was formed and worked diligently to increase black voting power in the parish (Whitehead).

There is no question that the black churches in Avoyelles did make a significant contribution to improving the lives of Blacks within the local community. They provided the first community gathering places, first schools, first chances for Blacks to become leaders and first nuclei for Blacks to develop personal support for political and other community action. Interestingly, Reverend Charles Guillory, the son of Reverend Prudent Guillory, pastors a church in Marksville, LA that is named St. John **Community** Church-Baptist and whose vision is "To be a Christ-Centered body, impacting the community, resulting in a transformed community for Christ." (Guillory).

The Catholic Church, at the time, was more restrictive in the roles that their non-clerical members might exercise. Very little community or political action developed for Blacks within the Catholic Church in the era of U.S. slavery or Jim Crow. Only over the past few decades, since Vatican II (Pope), has it expanded the role of lay people and allowed more direct participation in the operation of the church. Political activity by clerical and lay church members remains outside the church's mission.

The "Great Migration" was one of the largest voluntary movement of people in history (Great Migration). As shown graphically in **Figure 80**, it occurred in two waves between 1900 and 1970, with the first wave happening between 1900 and 1940 and the second between 1940 and 1970. When it was done, about 7 million U.S. Blacks had moved to the North, mostly from southern farms to northern cities. Between 1910 and 1930, the black population in the North increased by 40%, mostly in cities such as Detroit, New York, Philadelphia, Baltimore, Chicago and St. Louis. During the second wave, cities in California were added as destinations.

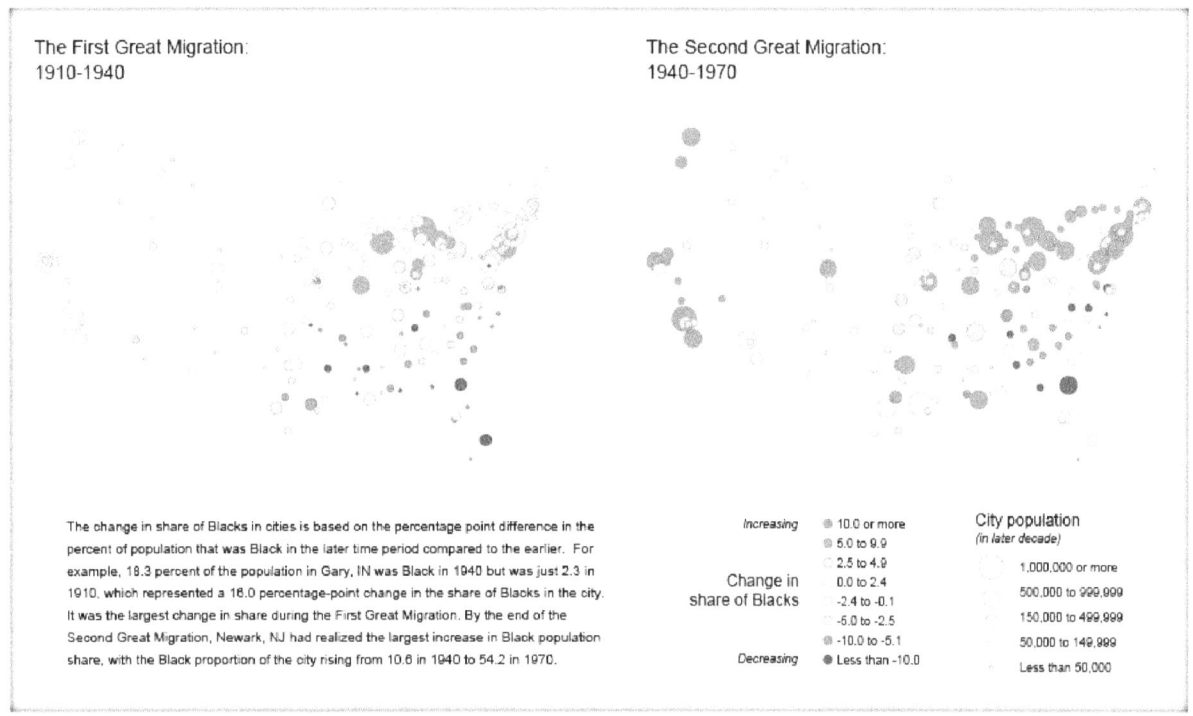

FIGURE 80. THE GREAT BLACK MIGRATION (GREAT MIGRATION)

There were two principal sets of drivers for the migration: 1) Harsh treatment of Blacks under Jim Crow laws and open terrorism by Whites in the South and 2) A strong desire by Blacks to take advantage of new job opportunities resulting from America's involvement in the two World Wars. The net effect was to change the lives of nearly 80% of the U.S. black population from rural to urban.

The plots in **Figure 80** show one interesting piece of information - New Orleans, Galveston and Corpus Christy were the only traditional Southern cities to show increases in their black population during the First Wave, while all of the other formerly Confederate cities showed dramatic declines in their black populations. The growth in black population in those three cities was generally due to job opportunities:

- **New Orleans** was rapidly developing into a major port, transporting everything from cotton and corn to the large and growing supply of lumber (Kendall).
- **Galveston**, following the hurricane of 1900, was in the process of reinventing itself as a sort of "Sin City of the South" where it took advantage to the Prohibition era to openly market everything from underground liquor to prostitution. (Galveston)
- **Corpus Christi** opened its deep water port in 1925 and created many needed jobs that attracted workers from around the country (W. Staff).

Interestingly, there is little evidence that many Blacks from the Mansura area joined in the first wave of Black migrants headed to Northern cities as occurred in so many other Southern rural towns.

NAME	DESTINATION	OCCUPATION
Bontemp, Clinton	Alexandria, LA	Ticket Collector (Theater)
Laurent, Moses	Alexandria, LA	Saw Mill Worker
Demouy, Henry T.	Alexandria, LA	Laborer, Odd Jobs
Morris, Isreal	Alexandria, LA	City Laborer
Berger, Albert	Beaumont, TX	Laborer
Lavalais, Willie	Cheneyville, LA	Building Laborer
Alexander, Joseph	Chicago	Porter
Talley, Wilson	Ft. Worth, TX	Laborer
Joseph, Martin	Galveston, TX	Laborer
Lehman, Harvey	Inglewood, CA	Minister
Prier, Sam	Lake Charles, LA	Laborer
Demouy, Curtis E.	New Orleans	Grocer
Coco. Worthie	New Orleans	Laborer
Prevot, Albert	New Orleans	Taylor
Augustine, Harrison	New Orleans	Cook
Prunell, Oscar	Pasco, OK	Farm Laborer
Sampson, Preston	Port Arthur, TX	Oil Refinery Laborer
Lehman, Paul	Selma, AL	Lutheran Minister

TABLE 6. MIGRANTS FROM MANSURA AREA, 1910-1930

Instead, as shown in **Table 6**, the most common destinations for black families leaving Mansura for better jobs and lives during the First Wave were likely to be Alexandria and New Orleans[49].

During the Second Wave, a far greater number of Blacks from the Mansura area moved to Northern cities such as Chicago, New York and Detroit; to Midwestern cities such as St. Louis and Kansas City; and to Western cities such as Los Angeles and San Francisco.

It remains unclear why those leaving the Mansura area, during the time period from 1910 to 1930, chose to stay closer to home than those from other areas of the South. Some possible reasons could be:

- **Fear of moving so far away, e.g. to Chicago** - Since this was the First Wave of black migrants, they likely did not have families who had made the long trip earlier and had established homes there and could provide them with temporary shelter. This meant moving to a distant place with no clear idea of where to live, work, eat, etc.

---

[49] This data was obtained from the 1910 and 1930 U.S. Censuses by comparing the people living in Ward 3 of Avoyelles Parish, Louisiana for those 2 dates and tracking the new locations of those who had left.

- **The French culture could have been a major barrier** - By 1910, most Blacks in the Mansura area spoke English. However, their predominant language was French with its strong accent influencing their speech. Also, their entire culture was based on French or African traditions, including cooking, music and, in some cases, religion. The Voodoo religion was fairly common then and was feared by many people throughout the U.S. Many held beliefs that all Blacks from Louisiana were Voodoo practitioners. Gaining acceptance among other Blacks in Northern cities could have been made much more difficult as a result of these factors.

- **Not having sufficient resources to fund such a long bus trip** - In 1910, nearly all Blacks in the Mansura area were sharecroppers. They lived in an essentially cashless economy and rarely possessed any amount of money above the few cents that could be obtained by doing odd jobs, working in and around the homes of the wealthier Whites in the area or by peddling anything from turtles to black berries.

  The price of a set of bus tickets from Mansura to Chicago for a whole family was likely much more difficult to accumulate than a similar set from Northern Mississippi, Arkansas or Georgia.

- **Mulattoes were not happy in their home town of Mansura** - From the names shown in **Table 6,** it is clear that the majority of the Blacks leaving the Mansura area were either mulattoes, those who lived near them in the area along Highway 1 or Grande Bayou or those who had married into mulatto families.

  The mulattoes tended to live in tight-knit communities, generally socializing and marrying other mulattoes (mulattoes). They considered themselves more kin to their white ancestors than to Blacks. Unfortunately, most Whites considered them to be Blacks.

  Consequently, the mulattoes were a group living among the Blacks but who were not connected to them or to the Whites in the community. Thus, it comes as no surprise that they were moving away from Mansura as early as 1910. As mentioned earlier, few mulattoes still live in the Mansura area today.

- **Fewer Blacks were lynched in Avoyelles Parish than in the Northern parts of Louisiana** (Finley)- Although there were many stories of Blacks being beaten, chased from their homes, illegally arrested, etc. by local Whites, there are few accounts of actual lynchings in the Mansura area.

- **The U.S. Gulf Coast Provided Jobs** - The state of Louisiana is situated in the center of the U.S. Gulf Coast, an area that was just beginning to develop significant industries during the early 20th century. A combination of the new oil and gas industry, shipping ports and tourism lead to the creation of a tremendous number of new jobs. Although Blacks were not able to acquire the better jobs since they were not allowed to become members of the various craft and trade unions, the lower level jobs they could acquire were considered much better than their former farm-related jobs.

As Blacks ventured away from their cashless, sharecropping lives in Mansura, they learned how to manage money, buy houses and cars, travel to more distant locations, and, most importantly, serve as informal "Educators" to those who stayed behind. Those who stayed behind were able to see, firsthand, how their lives could be better, how money could make their lives better, and their own potential might be achieved. This all helped them get a better view of what freedom looked like.

World War I was a terrible and depressing war (Rosenberg)- It was a global war, centered in Europe, which began on July 28, 1914 and ended on November 11, 1918. By the time it was over, more than 9 million military members and 7 million civilians had died, making it one of the deadliest conflicts in history.

The U.S. entered the war on April 6, 1917 after remaining neutral until then. It declared war against Germany and participated as an independent power, not joining the Allied Power group.

Initially, the U.S. provided supplies, raw material and money. However, in the summer of 1918, a major contingent of U.S. troops under General John J. Pershing began arriving at the Western Front where they played a major role until the Armistice in 1918.

During the course of the war, the U.S. mobilized over 4 million troops and suffered over 110,000 deaths due to combat and a terrible flu pandemic called the Spanish Flu (Rosenberg), which killed 43,000 American soldiers.

A key part of this mobilization was the Selective Service Act of 1917, a.k.a. Draft, which registered over 24 million men. Of these, nearly 3 million were inducted into the U.S. military services. In this new draft, men, ages 21 to 31, were selectively drafted beginning June 27, 1918. In the selection process (i.e. lottery) , each registered man had a specific draft number and Secretary of War, Newton D. Baker, pulled draft numbers out of a fishbowl . The eligibility age was extended in August of 1918 to include any man who was between the ages of 18 and 45.

As part of the war effort, Congress authorized President Woodrow Wilson to create a bureaucracy of 500,000 to 1 million jobs to attract workers from the Midwest and South to the war industries in the East (W. Staff).This became one of the key drivers that led so many Blacks from the Southern farms to move up north seeking jobs and a better life.

Despite massive chaos on the part of the U.S. government (Staff-Wikipedia), the citizens remained enthusiastic in their support for the war effort. Eventually, things began to line out and arms production soared. Food management was very successful and gross farm income increased more than 230%

from 1914 to 1919. Rationing ranged from "*Wheatless Wednesdays*" and "*Meatless Tuesdays*" due to poor harvests in 1916 and 1917, to "*Fuelless Mondays*" and "*Gasless Sundays*" to preserve coal and gasoline.

Although the U.S. armed forces remained segregated, many Blacks eagerly volunteered to serve once America entered World War I (Williams). By the end of the war, over 350,000 black Americans had served with the American Expeditionary Force on the Western Front.

Since most black American units were denied opportunities to engage in combat and assigned to support roles, most U.S. black soldiers did not see combat. Instead, they found themselves in units such as Butchery Companies, Nos. 322 and 363; Stevedore Regiments, Nos. 301, 302 and 303 and Engineer Service Battalions, Nos. 505 to 550, all of whose roles are obvious.

One notable exception was the 369th Infantry Regiment, known as the "***Harlem Hellfighters***" (Williams). That all-black combat unit was kept on the front lines for six months, longer than any other American unit in the war. For their bravery in combat, 171 members of the 369th were awarded the French Legion of Merit.

Only one black American, **Corporal Freddie Stowers** (Henry) of the 371st Infantry Regiment, was posthumously awarded the U.S. Medal of Honor for his heroism against the Germans. Unfortunately, his nomination was supposedly "Lost" until an investigation lead to his award by President George W. Bush, 73 years after he was killed in action.

FIGURE 81. SOLDIERS OF THE 369TH, WHO WON THE CROIX DE GUERRE IN 1919 (U. A. PHOTOGRAPHER)

In the area around Mansura, all citizens, black and white, supported the war effort through rationing, community volunteerism, and military service.

Of the 350,000 black Americans who served in World War I, only about 11 from the Mansura area can be positively identified[50]:

- **Fred Batiste,**
- **Horace Boston,**
- **McKinley Bowman,**
- **Wallace Dupas,**
- **John Francisco**
- **Clifton Lavalais,**
- **Luther Lavalais,**
- **Mathew Lavalais,**
- **Adelma Prier,**
- **Eddie Taylor,**
- **Alfred Williams**

Only one black soldier, **Paul Dupas** from Long Bridge, was said to have been wounded (Saucier).

As in previous wars, black Americans, including many from Mansura, provided strong and courageous support in several areas, including combat. In World War I, their heroism was recognized by foreign governments, e.g. the French Croix de Guerre. And yet, in the only case where there was a recommendation of a black soldier for the U.S. Congressional Medal of Honor, the paperwork mysteriously vanished for seven decades.

The Great Flood of 1927 (Bradshaw) was, arguably, one of the worst natural disasters in U.S. history, rivaling the Johnstown, Pennsylvania Flood of 1889 (McGough), the Galveston, Texas Hurricane of 1900 (Cline), the San Francisco earthquake of 1906 (USGS) and the more recent Gulf Coast hurricanes, Camille and Katrina (NHC-NOAA). The flood was a bellwether event for most Blacks in the U.S. that resulted in a permanent shift in their political beliefs and support.

Prior to the 1927 flood, the U.S. Army Corp of engineers had constructed a complex series of levees all along the Mississippi River in, what it believed, would be a final solution to the hundreds of flooding episode that had so often occurred (S. Wikipedia). The extensive levee network, however, did not include avenues to allow excess water in the Mississippi River to be diverted into other flood plains and reservoirs along its route.

---

[50] This information was obtained from the column in the 1930 U.S. Census for Avoyelles the identified those who were veterans. There were likely some individuals who served in the war but who died prior to the 1930 Census and, therefore, not listed.

During the winter of 1926-27, the Mississippi River Valley experienced some of the most intense rainfall ever, overflowing the levees in several locations and sending flood waters into Illinois, Kansas, Kentucky and Oklahoma.

On Good Friday, April 15, 1927, the skies over much of the Southern U.S. seemed to open up, releasing rain in intensity and area never seen before. It covered nearly all of Arkansas, Illinois, Kansas, Kentucky, Louisiana, Mississippi, Missouri, Oklahoma, Tennessee and Texas. New Orleans reported a rainfall of over 15 inches in 18 hours.

As the waters continued to rise, the Corp of Engineers confidently attempted to maintain control by increasing the height of the levees in several locations. Unfortunately, this did not work. Ultimately, breaches, or *crevasses*, began to occur and water spilled through openings over 25 feet wide.

Ultimately, over 145 breaks in the levee system occurred and 25,000 square miles were covered with water up to 30 feet deep. The Mississippi River south of Memphis grew to almost 60 miles wide.

When the levee north of Greenville, Mississippi gave way, as shown in **Figure 82** (Frankenfeld), sheer panic was the order of the day. Thousands of people needed to be evacuated, mostly by an insufficient number of barges and other small river vessels.

FIGURE 82. LEVEE BREACH NEAR GREENVILLE, MISSISSIPPI (A. L. FRANKENFELD)

In the panic of the hasty evacuation, local authorities, at the urging of white politicians and farmers, insisted that the first evacuees be white. For example, in Mississippi, around 13,000 Blacks were stranded on a levee that was 8 feet wide and 5 miles long without food or water for days after the white planters persuaded the Red Cross leader to focus his attention on saving the white women and children.

FIGURE 83. 1927 FLOOD REFUGEES RECEIVING WATER (U. PHOTOGRAPHER)

Once it became apparent that the Mississippi Delta area, the source of a large portion of the cotton grown in the South, was likely to be flooded, thousands of Blacks, who made up 75% of the delta's population and 95% of its farm labor force, were herded into work camps, mostly against their will (**Figures 83** and **84**). Their unpaid jobs were to fill, haul, and stack sand bags to contain the rising water and, thus, save the crops. In some cases, the black workers were held there at gun point and there was a report of one black man being shot by a white police officer for refusing to help unload a relief boat (Percy).

FIGURE 84. GROUP OF AFRICAN-AMERICAN MEN FILLING SANDBAGS (U. ARTIST)

In the areas of Southeastern and Northern Louisiana that were included within the Mississippi River delta, the flooding and the reaction of the people to it was not much different than in Mississippi and other states in the Mississippi delta. Gangs of black workers, most living in squalid tent cities, fought back against the river as it flooded towns from Tallulah to Melville and along the various tributaries of the Mississippi river including the Atchafalaya and Red rivers.

In Avoyelles Parish, the flooding created a strange situation (Mayeux and Decuir). As mentioned earlier, Mansura lies on an elevated prairie that ends at a bluff that overlooks the swampland and towns such as Bordelonville, Moreauville, Long Bridge and Cotton Port. When the waters arrived, the Mansura Bluff was converted into a sort of lakefront with all of the lands to the east and south either under water or nearly so. Soon, large barges and boats of every size began to arrive, carrying refugees from the flooding. Grande Ecore became the main landing point for the refugees[51].

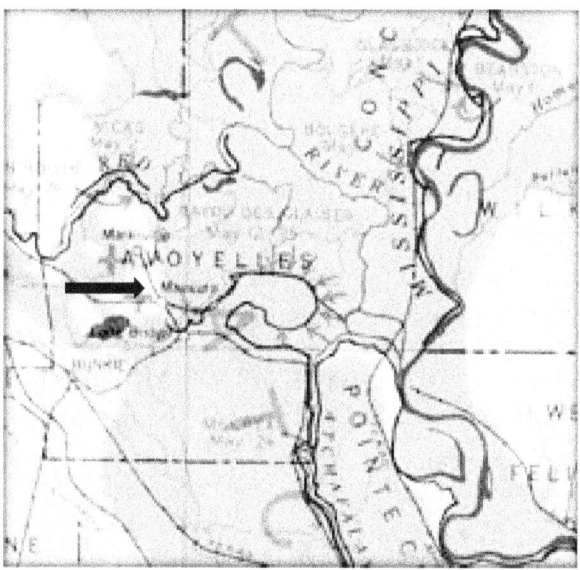

FIGURE 85. CLOSE-UP MAP OF FLOODING NEAR MANSURA

In **Figure 85** (Survey) , the gray area is the flood zone, while the whitish area is generally dry land (Note that Mansura was right at the edge of the flood zone). The gray arrows show the locations of the numerous breaks (i.e. breaches) in the levee along Bayou Deglaise, which lies to the east of Mansura, near Moreauville and Long Bridge. The crosses, indicate Red Cross relief stations in Mansura and Marksville[52].

---

[51] Information from oral histories retold many times by local people who lived through the flood.
[52] Additional pictures of the flood in the Mansura area can be seen on the Facebook page: National Archives on Facebook".

FIGURE 86. 1927 BLACK REFUGEES AT HAMBURG, LA (U. PHOTOGRAPHER, REFUGEES AT HAMBURG)

Once relief supplies arrived by train from Alexandria, tent cities were erected in various parts of Mansura as well as along the bluff at Grande Ecore and Long Bridge (Mayeux and Decuir).

The effect on the lives those who lived "Down the Hill" was disastrous and permanent. The road that traversed the bottom of the Mansura Bluff, from Grande Bayou to Boutte de Bayou, went under water, leaving the black residents with no effective means to get to Mansura unless they traveled through the muddy fields that separated them from the town.

Numerous stories have been carried down from those who were alive then[53]. Stories of caskets floating out of the ground and landing in trees; stories of strange objects seen floating in the flood waters including one that appeared to be some sort of "Creature" with long black hair mixed in with the driftwood and mud.

The anger over the harsh treatment that Blacks experienced during the 1927 flood at the hands of the white farmers and the lack of humane intervention by the Republican leaders in Washington was slow to subside (Barry). Numerous officials and politicians came to assess the situation, arriving by train at the Mansura Depot. **Herbert Hoover**, then Secretary of Commerce under Republican President Calvin Coolidge, was the highest profile visitor to Mansura during the flood aftermath.

Hoover did nothing of substance to relieve the sufferings of the black residents who were being victimized during the flood and its aftermath (Barry). A "Blue Ribbon" panel of black leaders, headed by **Robert Moton** (Heinnemann), **Principal of Tuskegee Institute**, was appointed to perform inspections of the black concentration camps. In its first report, the "Colored Advisory Commission" made it appear that Blacks were treated the same as the white refugees in the camps (Moton). Hoover's refusal to allow the publication of a second report by this same panel that told of Blacks

---

[53] As told by Herman Augustine, Sr.

being mistreated during the flood[54] and his broken promises to support reform in the country regarding black civil rights gained him the ire of several black leaders, including Moton. These, in turn, actively helped change support of the black community from Republican to Democratic.

Hoover was able to use the event as a major public relations opportunity and he was an easy victor in his 1928 bid for the U.S. presidency.

Once the flood waters began to subside in the summer of 1927, the high racial tension between the Whites and Blacks, especially in Mississippi, continued (Barry). As hundreds of former black farm workers tried to leave the Mississippi delta for better lives in the large cities in the North, they found themselves faced with threats of violence from roaming gangs of local Whites, attempting to prevent their departure. Blacks, attempting to escape from virtual bondage on the farms of the Mississippi delta to better lives up North, found themselves in situations that closely resembled escaped slaves trying to find freedom prior to the Civil War (Gazit).

It was not until the early 1940's that Blacks felt free to leave the South (Holt). As World War II began to seem certain, the growth of the new war industries began to create new job opportunities in the North. This, combined with the dramatic disappearance of historic manual labor jobs on the southern farms, further stimulated the desire of southern Blacks to move to the North, thus creating the second wave of the Great Black Migration.

The Great Mississippi River Flood of 1927 is now a fading memory to most Blacks in the U.S. as those who experienced it continue to pass away. And yet, the Republican Party remains an object of contempt to most Blacks, including those who are now several generations removed from that terrible event in American history.

The Decline of Black Farming was, without doubt, one of the main drivers that led Blacks in the South to leave their historical homes for new lives in urban areas far to the north. Three main factors that contributed to this decline were (Bellis): 1) **The Rise of Mechanical Farming Technology**; 2) **The Reduction in the Land Available for Sharecropping** and 3) the nearly complete **Loss of Black Farmland Ownership**. These, taken together, forced Southern Blacks from the farms and into the towns and cities, both in the South and North. These trends, although not pleasant at the time, did give southern Blacks the chance to escape the economic bondage known as sharecropping that had persisted for nearly a century and to finally exercise some level of self-determination for themselves and their families.

- **The Rise of Mechanical Farming Technology** - Prior to the 18th century, the technology used in U.S. farming consisted of wooden plows pulled by either horses, mules, or oxen. The material being grown

---

[54] Robert Moton's Second Report, November 1927

was seeded by hand. Weeding and harvesting required the use of hoes and sickles. Most of the food produced was enough for the farmer and his family, with any excess sold in local markets.

Improvements in farm productivity began during the late 18th century with the patenting of the cotton gin in 1793 (Lakwete) and the cast iron plow in 1797 (J. H. Moore). By 1850, U.S. farming, using new technology such as factory-produced equipment, grain elevators, fertilizers and irrigation, had made it possible to produce 100 bushels of corn using only 75-90 hours of labor. However, throughout much of the U.S. South, where the main crop was cotton, the basic farm technology was a plow and mule, manned by legions of black slaves.

FIGURE 87. BLACK SHARECROPPER PLOWING WITH MULES (U. G. PHOTOGRAPHER)

By the end of the Civil War and loss of the slave labor force, Southern farmers had to find new and more efficient ways to produce their main crop, cotton. While the labor problem was partially solved by the use of sharecropping, the free labor was gone and now the farmers had to include some type of financial payments to the sharecroppers as part of their farming expenses. The need for new and less expensive farming processes became more and more urgent.

U.S. agriculture became increasingly mechanized during the latter part of the 19th century and the use of fertilizers more than doubled between 1890 and 1900. Between 1900 and 1920, large gas-operated tractors appeared on the scene and the use of commercial fertilizers reached over 6,000,000 pounds/year (Wattenberg).

A pivotal point was reached in 1954 when the number of tractors exceeded the numbers of horses and mules for the first time. By 1965, only 5 hours of manual labor was required to produce 100 pounds of cotton using a tractor and its associated mechanical equipment. Clearly, the days of manual farming were almost over.

- **The Reduction in Land Available for Sharecropping** - As the U.S. farm productivity continued to increase through the use of mechanized equipment and fertilizer, the need for large numbers of manual farm laborers declined. U.S. Sharecropping reached its height during the early 1930's when there were about 5.5 million Whites and 3 million Blacks farming land under some sort of land rental, tenant, or sharecropping agreement (Bolton).

The Great Depression (Staff-About.News), which lasted from 1929 to the late 1930's, was one of the worse economic disasters in history (**Figure 88**).

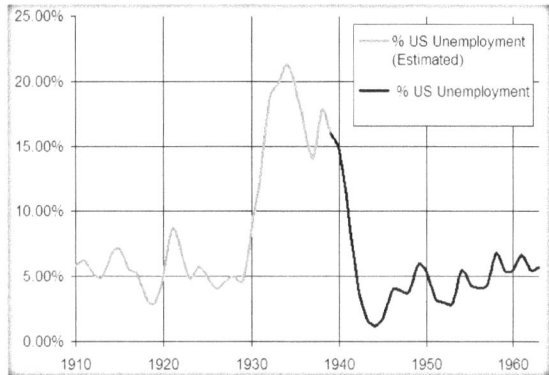

FIGURE 88. U.S. UNEMPLOYMENT HIGHLIGHTING DEPRESSION PERIOD (STAFF-ABOUT.NEWS)

Before things began to show signs of improvement, U.S. unemployment had reached 25%, over 5000 banks had failed and hundreds of thousands of Americans found themselves homeless and living in shanty towns called "Hoovervilles".

FIGURE 89. HOOVERVILLE, PORTLAND, OREGON, 1938 (MUSEUM)

FIGURE 90. PUBLIC HEALTH NURSE (MUSEUM).

While its devastating effects were mostly felt in the financial sector and in primary industries such as mining and logging, the U.S. farm industry was dramatically impacted (S. Moore). The U.S. farm industry began a perilous decline at the end of World War I, well before the Great Depression. U.S. farmers, at the urging of Food Administrator Herbert Hoover, engaged themselves in a state of gross overproduction in order to satisfy the food shortages in Europe as a result of the war. At that time, credit was easy to acquire and farmers made huge investments in the new, mechanized farm equipment to combat the still high labor costs. Farm mortgages soared.

During the 1920's, European farm production stabilized and reached a point where small amounts of exports became possible. The U.S. farm industry was too large and too much in debt to avoid the inevitable collapse that occurred when the Great Depression hit.

The Great Depression, combined with the terrible Midwest drought of 1933 - 1939, called the "**Dust Bowl**" (H. Staff, Dust Bowl), resulted in a protracted period of staggering unemployment and tens of thousands of farm bankruptcies. Many farmers and their families, especially in the Midwest, simply abandoned their land and headed for California, seeking any work they might find. Others were fortunate to live on farms since they could go back to basics and grow enough food to survive even though there were no markets available for large amounts of their produce.

For the sharecroppers and tenant farmers, the effect was worse. Not only were they impacted by the low crop prices, but were also at the mercy of the land owners who could not provide them the credit they needed to purchase food and clothing for their families or seeds and feed for the farm animals. As a result, millions of sharecroppers and tenant farmers found themselves being forced off the land they had farmed for generations.

Interestingly, one of the key U.S. government programs that was instituted to aid the farm industry, the Acreage Adjustment Act, added to the plight of black sharecroppers. As it turned out, the acreage that was "adjusted" away from farming was nearly always that being farmed by the sharecroppers (Bolton), (J. e. Gilbert).

- **Loss of Black Farmland Ownership** - Landownership is an important form of wealth, both financially and psychologically. A land owner is much more likely to feel a sense of independence and well-being than someone who is not. Black landowners have always acted as community leaders who were willing to stand up for what they believed in, willing to support political causes that benefit the black community, and willing to provide meeting locations and financial support for local, state and national black organizations.

During the 1920's, black farmers totaled nearly 900,000 (Boyd), representing 1 out of every 7 farmers. Today, that number is around 18,000 or 1 out of every 67 farmers (C. Gilbert). The erosion of this important resource over the past 90 years has played a major part in depriving Blacks of their rightful place in the leadership of their communities, states, and country.

The reasons for the decline of black farmers are many with some very clear and others not so clear. However, a few have been studied (USDA). These include:

> **Sub-optimization of Farm Sizes** - Because of the reluctance of Whites to sell prime land to Blacks following the Civil War, the average black farmer ended up buying land that seldom was more than 40-50 acres and was usually the least fertile land around. As a result, they generally were some of the first to fail when prices dropped or when the weather didn't cooperate.

> These black farmers, often because of their small farm sizes, could not 1) meet eligibility requirements for federal support programs; 2) garner political strength in the midst of the much larger, white-owned farms; 3) acquire emergency bank loans when their crops failed and 4) find legal assistance when they were the victims of the misuse of federal assistance by local officials.

> **Partition Sales** - Partition sales occurred when a land owner died without a will. Then, each heir, who had a share of the estate, could, at their discretion, sell their share to a non-heir. Also, anyone owning a share of the estate could force a sale of the entire property at any time. In most cases, the non-heir was a white person who, then, forced a sale of the property, usually at a very low price and bought it him/herself. Few Blacks were aware that selling a share of their inherited property could lead to the whole property being sold.

> **Financial Manipulation by Local Officials** - Farming has historically always been linked to financial institutions. In most cases, the financial institutions existed in the form of local banks and other lending businesses. Ultimately, the decision to lend financial support to farmers who need it rested with local white citizens. The results were often discriminatory behavior where approved loans arrived long after the planting season, arbitrary reduction in loan amounts and a much higher pattern in loan rejection rates for minority farmers than for Whites.

> **Racism within USDA** - Many of the problems experienced by black farmers were the result of overt and covert racial discrimination within the USDA. They were accused of ignoring complaints

made by black farmers, processing those types of complaints slowly or not at all and proceeding with foreclosures even after a valid complaint had been filed.

Although a class action law suit that was filed by 15,000 black farmers in 1998 resulted in cash settlements of $50,000 to each family and forgiveness of loans owed USDA, the damage was done.

➢ **Departure of Young Black People from Farming** - Finally, for all black people, irrespective of where they were born or grew up, farming and slavery are forever linked. Beginning with the runaway slaves before and during the Civil War, through the mass displacements after the war and the waves of the Great Migration that occurred throughout much of the 20th century, black people in America have always been trying to get away from the farm.

The urban life that appealed to so many Blacks from the early 20th century is still present and appealing today. The idea of moving from the city to a farm is considered absurd, at best. As a result, the few remaining black farmers are generally older, less educated in the use of modern technology and have never lived in an urban environment.

However, there is a small, but growing trend of younger, better educated Blacks choosing farming as a livelihood. Their approach, however, is more from a business operation perspective than from the labor-intensive life we all are aware of. Also, many black farmers who have left the profession still yearn to return if given better tools, farming strategies and financial support. The involvement of a more supportive USDA and Black Land Grant Universities are keys to success.

By 1940, some of the historic black areas, such as the northern edge of the "Down the Hill" area, i.e. Payee Bas, were no longer occupied. Although many black families still lived in the Grande Ecore and Boutte des Bayou areas, many had moved either nearer or into the town of Mansura.

By 1970, the whole black settlement known as "Down the Hill" was no more.   Similarly, other areas such as the Petit Cote and Grande Bayou had lost most of their black farmers. Those Blacks who still participated in farming did so only as hired hands who caught "**The Truck**"[55] every day and worked on large, white-owned farms.

---

[55] Many farmers used hired hands to perform specific jobs such as planting sweet potatoes, hoeing and picking cotton, picking corn, and cutting sugar cane. Generally, a truck traveled to the areas where these hired hands lived and hauled them to and from the fields every day. All who rode these conveyances called them "The Truck."

Chapter 17 - Our Lives and Culture

FIGURE 91. CLEMENTINE HUNTER MURAL AT AFRICAN HOUSE - WEDDING (HUNTER AND ROSENTHAL)

Despite having lived under the harsh conditions in slavery and the Jim Crow laws and in a state where nearly 400 lynchings occurred from 1886 to 1939, life in early 20th century Mansura was relatively peaceful for most Blacks.

By then, there was a rudimentary school system with classes held at the small Baptist churches in the area around Mansura as well as at a small Catholic elementary school in town.

Blacks freely attended services at the various black churches in the area and many served as ministers, deacons, teachers, and other church leaders. Black members of St. Paul's Catholic Church attended mass under very restricted conditions, as mentioned earlier, and held no meaningful positions in the church until the establishment of the Our Lady of Prompt Succor Catholic Church in the late 1930s.

Most black families were large and stable, providing a considerable "free" work force to the sharecropper. Male and female workers of all ages could be seen chopping and picking cotton in the large fields around Mansura from Monday morning through noon on Saturday.

Saturday afternoons and evenings were a time to get caught up on chores around the sharecropper's home, work in the vegetable garden, go hunting and fishing, and get cleaned up for Sunday.

Saturday were also a time when neighbors went to assist others who might need some type of help either preparing their gardens for planting, canning fruit or vegetables, repairing damage to their homes, splitting wood or participating in quilting bees. This voluntary activity was called a Coup d'Main (Helping Hand). Rarely was it necessary to hire anyone to do this sort of work since the neighbors were always willing to help.

Saturday nights were a time for fun, especially for black men. There were always night clubs, called "Blue Moons" by those who frequented them. Local musicians provided the music, usually some variety of the Blues. Dancing and drinking was the order of the day. Fried fish dinners and pickled pig feet were usually sold by the proprietor. Invariably, a small gambling shack, located in the rear of the building, attracted those who had the misfortune of bringing their hard-earned cash to the club.

Unfortunately, in some cases, drinking, gambling and too much frivolity led to violence. In many cases, the perpetrators ended up being arrested and spending the night in jail. Usually, by Sunday evening, one of the local white business owners were contacted and the prisoners released on bond to them. A common condition of the bond was that the person released was now obligated to work off the cost of the bond, i.e. they were once more in slavery!

Sundays were days of worship and relaxation. After attending church, everyone went home and cooked a large Sunday dinner. Fried chicken was a staple in most houses, often accompanied by potato salad, greens, and candied yams.

FIGURE 92. SEAFOOD GUMBO (HUNTER AND ROSENTHAL)

As a result of their living so near to the marshland, hunting and fishing was a major part of Mansura sharecroppers' daily lives. Nearly everyone became an expert fisherman and hunter before becoming teenagers. Common tools used to catch some of the plentiful wildlife included turtle and rabbit traps, fish nets called *seines*[56], and, of course, good old shot guns and fishing poles. The abundance of squirrels, rabbits, raccoons, and other wild animals made it possible to feed the tenants' families, especially during the winter months.

When the hunting trip was especially successful, the dinner might include a wildlife gumbo consisting of birds such as *gros beck*, *grande heron*, and various black birds (Now all illegal to hunt!!). Stories carried down through the ages told of late-night hunting trips where the meat brought home was described as being from a "P.I.G. Rabbit"[57].

FIGURE 93. SWAMPS IN LOUISIANA (Haklai)

With the emergence of baseball, Sunday afternoons were often the occasion for a baseball game, featuring some of the local athletes competing against nearby rivals such as Marksville, Moreauville, or Cottonport.

Winter was the time for the boucherie (Tyrr), when several families got together and helped kill and butcher one or more of the large hogs that one of their neighbors had raised.

Nearly every bit of the hog was used. The bulk of the meat was cut up and set aside for salting. The skin was cut into small squares and made into crackling. The intestines were cleaned and cooked as chitterlings. Most of the spare meat and the blood were combined with rice and spices to make a type of sausage called *boudin*. The head became hog head cheese. Even the feet were pickled for later eating. It was traditional to give the helpers a piece of the pork to take home along with some of the crackling and boudin.

---

[56] Floridagofishing.com, 2015
[57] "P.I.G. Rabbit" was a secretive term for pigs, usually stolen, butchered and cooked in the middle of the night.

FIGURE 94. COOKING CRACKLING (PRIER)

Although many of the surviving elderly residents of Mansura who experienced the harsh times living Down the Hill and the other remote areas, would not want to ever return to those days, they still look back with some level of fondness. Unfortunately, most of those wonderful people have departed this life, hopefully for a much better one. As time goes by, the memories they shared with us of those special times **become more and more covered by a veil.**

CONCLUSION

In this book, we explored some of the historical events that have occurred over the past 200 years in North America, the state of Louisiana, the parish of Avoyelles, and the town of Mansura, Louisiana.

Mansura, Louisiana and the surrounding area is a microcosm of African-American history. From its beginnings in the late 18th century, the area was the site of strong economic growth based on the terrible institution of slavery. Here, Africans, who were captured and transported by the French to the Americas under the harshest conditions, were forced to toil in the hot Louisiana sun. They farmed land that was infested with deadly snakes, alligators and other wild animals along with mosquitoes and other insects. Their offspring spent their entire lives under the same conditions.

The French version of slavery was much more relaxed than the stricter form that existed following the Louisiana Purchase by the U.S. in 1803. The conditions under which slaves in central Louisiana (and the rest of the South) lived under the U.S. were nothing short of hell. Thousands of African slaves died due to disease and inhumane working conditions.

Numerous records, both public and private, exist that provide critical information that could possibly allow African-American descendants of Mansura-area slaves to identify their ancestors and which Slave Holders were keeping them captive against their will.

In the New Orleans area, mulattoes and other free people of color (FPC) lived lives that were much less restricted than for those who lived in the Mansura area. Here, the lives of the FPCs were not much better than those of the slaves. Many descendants of those people remain in the Mansura area today.

The slaves in the U.S., including Louisiana, were not content with their lives in captivity. Various rebellions and slave uprisings occurred throughout the history of slavery, with some as nearby as Pointe Coupee Parish and Cocoville. As the anti-slavery movement gained momentum, slaves increasingly were involved in slowed productivity, work stoppages, running away and violence.

Once the Civil War began, slaves began fleeing their bondage at plantations in the immediate vicinity of the Union army. Mansura was no different. The passage of the Union army near Mansura resulted in a mass escape of slaves from local plantations. Many of those escaped slaves joined the Union army and fought for their own freedom. Eventually, over 180,000 former slaves, including about 25,000 from Louisiana, fought in the Union army, losing about 36,000 to combat, disease, accidents and a few executions.

The Reconstruction period, following the Civil War, was a roller coaster ride for former slaves. First came empowerment, voting rights, land ownership and protection by the military. The renewed control of state government by the white citizens, with support from a Southern-leaning president, lead to nearly complete loss of African-American voting power. This was followed by a century of Jim Crow living for most African-Americans. Their lives were always in peril from lawlessness by racists Whites who, with support from local authorities, committed thousands of beatings, lynchings, illegal or frivolous imprisonments, and forced many African-Americans from their homes.

Nevertheless, these former slaves were able to establish stable lives, get basic education, and develop church-based cultures that have persisted to this day. Part of this "Stable" lifestyle was the system called *sharecropping*, a form of economic slavery that remained into the 1970s.

The lives of African-American sharecroppers contrasted sharply with those of the white Mansura elite, many of whom lived in an upscale section of L'Eglise Street. They included rich farmers, merchants, doctors and other business owners. However, the lives of other whites were not much different from the African-Americans.

African-Americans, however, generally lived in areas remote from the town itself. There, they lived in desperate poverty and, yet, managed to develop a set of long-lasting communities (i.e. *Grande Bayou, Down the Hill, Grande Ecore, Petite Cote* and the *Large*), whose culture and impact remain today.

Several important events (World War I, 1927 flood, the Great Depression, etc.), occurring during the first half of the 20th century, had a dramatic effect on the worldview of many Mansura African-Americans. The result was a vast migration away from Mansura to other cities in the state, the South and the North.

Today, the remnants of the past, described in this book, remains very visible in Mansura. There is a deep, but weakening divide between the black and white citizens of the town. Blacks now occupy the offices of the mayor, the chief of police and a majority of the town council. Interracial couples are common. Public schools were integrated long ago. No businesses openly seek to exclude Blacks.

However, much of the historical farm land remain in the hands of the white citizens, although Blacks have begun to own small portions of land, generally inside the town. There are few black farmers. The older religions (i.e. Catholic, Baptists) have slowly begun to have mixed-race congregations, while the newer ones seem to be more inclusive.

Nevertheless, the future of Mansura seems bright for all of its citizens, both Blacks and Whites. The diverse heritages of the citizens is beginning to be seen as an asset to the town (e.g. Cochon du Lait

Festival, tourism, etc.). New business growth along State Highway 1 appears to be accelerating, providing the prospect for more jobs and a better future for all.

And, yet, the thinly-veil attempts to restrict minority voting power (i.e. Voter ID, Gerrymandered all-white districts, Denial of citizenship to legal immigrants, etc.) across the country clearly are moving us dangerously closer to the place where we were prior to the beginning of the Jim Crow era. **Without the Right to Vote, we are basically back in slavery.**

The tense relationship between minorities and the police is a manifestation of the issues we face when change is occurring and those opposed to change try to take a stand to prevent that change.

In the end, we are all Americans and have faced strong challenges to our democracy before. We must learn to do our best to legally influence the outcome of national (and local) debates and then accept the results once the issues are settled.

APPENDIX A.

Early Slave Transactions in Avoyelles Parish

Slave Transactions - In "Mixed Notarial Acts", In Avoyelles Parish Courthouse (Saucier)							
Slave Name	Seller	Purchaser	Date	Price, $	Age	Gender	Notes
Unknown	Gme. Gebere	Dominique Coco	12/17/1805				Congo Negro
Baptiste	Tessant Juneau	Dominique Coco	4/8/1809	900.00	20	M	
Geoffrey	John Brown	Dominique Coco	5/24/1808	600.00	30	F	
Adam	John Brown	Joseph Coco		600.00		M	
11 Slaves:	Jesse Benton	Pierre Lemoine	9/9/1809	4,000.00			
Solomon	"	"			8	M	
Adam	"	"			21	M	
Sara	"	"			13	F	
Charlotte	"	"			21	F	
Jack	"	"			4	M	
Petis	"	"			2	F	
Nancy	"	"			20	F	
Benny	"	"			4	M	
Dixie	"	"			21	F	"Quadroon"
Jack	"	"			4	M	Her children
Charles	"	"			1	M	Her children
Saroh	Wd. George Baron	Pierre Lemoine	12 Jun 1815	1343.00	50	F	In Group of 9 Slaves. "Mande" Language, From "Bamana"
Hagen	Ben Miller	Baptiste Rabalais	8/4/1809	380.00	12	F	
Francois	Andre Dupre	Joseph Joffrion	2/28/1793	360.00	25	M	Congo Negro
Jacque	Julian Poydras	Niette Rabalais	1800	Gift	18		
Unknown	Elizabeth Rabalais	Joseph Coco	3/1810	1,300.00	40	M	Dominique Coco, Security
Louise	Elizabeth Rabalais	Unknown	3/1810	?	?	F	
Fanny	Elizabeth Rabalais	Pierre Laborde	3/1810	?	?	F	
Baptiste	Thomas Olivier	John Evans		400.00	11	M	
Daniel	John Evans	Thomas Olivier		700.00	36	M	
Judy	Susanna Purvis	George Purvis			35	F	Children: Bill, 5; Milinda, 3
Marie	Fochin Feallien	Joseph Ferret		800.00	25	F	

Margaret	Amore Dupuy	William Gauthier		800.00	13	F	
Garri	Goeau Duief	Joseph Joffrion	9/5/1797	530.00	40	F	"Guinea Woman"
Marie Louise	Baptiste Lemoine			450.00			Inventory of Genie Lemoine
Charriet			3/2/1801			F	FWC, shot a man, wounding him slightly
Fatty	Marie Leblanc		7/16/1803	600.00	30	F	
Palglet	Daniel Gaspard	Augustine Juneau	10/19/1803	400.00		F	
Marie	Mrs. Rivet	Pedro Lemoine	1/7/1797	500.00	30	F	Has 1-year old child named Henry
Garisse	Alex Oulalet	Baptiste Mayeux	10/31/1795	400.00	25	M	Member of " Maniga" Tribe
Marie Louise	Marc Eliche	Gideon Walker	5/16/1796	150.00	17	F	
Annette, Marie	Poiret	Thomas Poisant	9/30/1797	3,000.00			Marie's child: Mardit
Judy	W.T. Henderson	Amable Couvillion	6/23/1808	400.00	18	F	Seller from Tennesee
Manet	Robert Deselle	William Collins	5/8/1809	700.00	29	F	
Ellender	Will Rusty	John Ryan	4/29/1809	230.00	9	F	
Unity	Will Marshal	Will Rusty	4/29/1809		11	F	
4 Slaves:	Will Marshal	Will Rusty	4/29/1809	1,150.00			
Milley							
Cupid							
Ellender							
Mack							
Carolina							

APPENDIX B.

Free People of Color in Avoyelles Parish, 1860

Avoyelles Free People of Color - 1860						
Last Name	**First Name**	**Others in Household**	**Color**	**M/F**	**Age**	**Trade**
	Magloire		M	M	34	Carpenter
	Harriel		B	F	25	None
		Elmira	Y	F	17	
		Polk	Y	M	15	
		Cass	Y	M	11	
		Pierre	Y	M	8	
		Jefferson	Y	M	5	
		Daniel	Y	M	3	
Dubal	**Celestine**		M	F	43	None
		Clina	M	F	26	None
		John	M	M	2	
Rapelier	**Marlin**		B	M	35	
		Joseph	M	M	17	
		Eugenie	M	F	15	
	Lucy		Y	F	25	
		Mary	Y	F	10	
		Sarah	Y	F	8	
		Sennie	Y	F	6	
		Jane	Y	F	5	
		Sam	Y	M	2	
		David	Y	M	1	
		Marguerite	B	F	50	
		Eveline	Y	F	19	
		Polk	Y	M	15	
		Scott	Y	M	13	
		Jeff	Y	M	12	
		Samuel	Y	M	10	
		Davis	Y	M	8	
Lavaley	**Eloise**		M	F	26	
		Octave	M	M	8	
		Azima	M	F	6	
		Paul	M	M	3	
		Varielle	M	M	11 m	
	Lucile		M	F	35	
		Jean	M	M	15	
		Ardoin	M	M	14	
		Barthelemy	M	M	13	
	Bazile		B	M	40	Servant

Bontemps	**Neel**		M	M	50	Farm Laborer
		Hyppolite	M	M	25	Carpenter
		Rouisere	M	M	20	Day Laborer
		Dejantille	M	M	18	Brick Mason
		Emile	M	M	20	Carriage Driver
		Louisa	M	F	23	Servant
		Lucille	M	F	8	
		Mary	M	F	6	
		Jean	M	M	4	
	Louis		M	M	40	Servant
Vrelle	**Arsine**		M	M	28	Servant
		Corine	M	F	9	
		Laurent	M	M	7	
		Auguste	M	M	5	
		Adolphe	M	M	3	
		Marie Magloire	M	M	54	
Dauzat	**Evariste**		M	M	42	Farm Laborer
Laurent	**Joseph**		M	M	41	Carpenter
		Marie	M	F	38	
		Joseph	M	M	25	Brick Mason
		Sylviendri	M	M	23	Carpenter
Laurent	**Daclair**		M	M	38	Brick Mason
		Julia	M	F	21	
		Marie	M	F	6	
		Lucile	M	F	4	
		Joseph	M	M	2	
		Lursin (sp.?)	M	M	1	
	Louisiana		Ind.	F	23	
		Euphennie	Ind.	F	20	
		John	Ind.	M	17	
		Samuel	Ind.	M	15	
	Heloise		M	F	41	
	Esther		M	F	43	
		Louisa	M	F	20	
		Marielouise	M	F	18	

References

1880, U.S. Census. *U.S. Federal Census, Avoyelles Parish, LA, Ward 3*. Census Report. Washington DC: `U.S. Census Bureau, 1880.

1930, U.S. Census Bureau. *U.S. Federal Census, Avoyelles Parish, LA, Ward 3, Dist. 8*. Census Report. Washington DC: U.S. Census Bureau, 1930.

Ad, Commercial. *Cochon De Lait Festival*. Mansura Chamber of Commerce, Mansura, LA. Advertising Poster.

Affairs, Records of the Department of Veterans. "1890 Veterans Schedules for Louis Olivier, Family Number 66." 2005. *Ancestry.com.*

AlDrouin1900. *U.S. Federal Census, Avoyelles Parish, Ward 3, Dist. 0014, Family No. 8*. Census Report. Washington DC: U.S. Census Bureau, 1900.

AlZoNormand1900. *U.S. Federal Census, Avoyelles Parish, Ward 3, Dist. 0014, Family No. 17*. Census Report. Washington DC: U.S. Census Bureau, 1900.

Ancestry.com. n.d. <http://www.ancestry.com/>.

Ancestry.com. "Lucien Dominique Coco." *Hunting For Bears, comp.. Louisiana, Marriages, 1718-1925*. Ancestry.com Operations Inc. Provo, 2004.

Anonymous. *Purchase of Christian captives from the Barbary States*. Wikipedia.org, Unknown. Painting. <https://en.wikipedia.org/wiki/Catholic_Church_and_slavery#/media/File:Purchase_of_Christian_captives_from_the_Barbary_States.jpg>.

Archives, National. "U.S., Colored Troops Military Service Records, 1863-1865." 2007. *Ancestry.com/National Archives and Records Adminsitration.*

Artist, Our Special. *Our colored troops at work -- the 1st Louisiana native guards disembarking at Fort Macomb, Louisiana*. WikiMedia.org. *OurColoredTroopsFortMacomb.jpeg*. 1863. Engraving. <https://commons.wikimedia.org/wiki/File:OurColoredTroopsFortMacomb.jpeg>.

Artist, Unknown. *American Civil War Scene - Our colored troops at work - the 1st Louisiana Guard Disembarking at Ft. McComb, Louisiana*. <https://commons.wikimedia.org/wiki/File:OurColoredTroopsFortMacomb.jpeg>.

Artist, Unknown. *Co. E, 4th US Infantry, Ft. Lincoln, Defense of Washington*. Library of Congress. *Images of War, Vol. 3, p 235*. Washington, DC, n.d.

Artist, Unknown. *The Atlantic Slave Trade and Slave Life in America: A Visual Record*. University of Virginia Library. *Slaves Baptized in a Monrovian Congregation*. n.d. Image ID: NW0174.

Artist, Unnown. *Aerial Photograph of Flood, Unidentified Stretch of Lower Mississippi River (ARC No. 285959)*. National Archives and Records Administration, Washington DC. Photograph. <https://commons.wikimedia.org/wiki/File:Aerial_photograph_of_flood,_unidentified_stretch_of_lower_Mississippi_River._-_NARA_-_285959.jpg>.

Artist, Unnown. *Funeral of Andre Cailloux in New Orleans, July 29, 1863. Harper's Weekly*. New York: Harper's Weekly, 1863.

Artst, Commercial. *Broadside advertsing sale of slave with 10 individuals listed*. New Orleans, LA, 1835.

Ashur772. "Sullivan Family Tree." 2011. *Ancestry.com.*

Augustine, Laura. Interview. D.G. Prier. Mansura, 1990.

Avoyelles, La Commission des. *Avoyelles: Crossroads of Louisiana Where All Cultures Meet*. Ed. Sue Eakins. Gretna: Pelican Publishing Company, 1999.

Barry, John M. *Rising Tide: The Great Mississippi Flood of 1927 and How It Changed America*. Touchstone, 1997.

Bellis, Mary. "A History of American Agriculture 1776-1990." 2015. *About.com.*

Berry, Mary F. "Negro Troops in Blue and Gray: The Louisiana Native Guard, 1861-1863." *The Louisiana Purchase Bicentennial Series in Louisiana History - The African American Experience in Louisiana*. Ed. Charles Vincent. Vol. XI. Lafayette: Center for Louisiana Studies, University of Louisiana at Lafayetter, 2000. 21-38. Book.

Berzat. *1930 United States Federal Census*. Census. Washington, DC: United States Government, 1930.

Biard, Francois Auguste. *The Slave Trade (Slaves on the West Coast of Africa)*. Wilberforce House Museum. Oil Painting.

Blake, Tom. "Avoyelles Parish. Louisiana: Largest Slaveholders from 1860 Census and Surname Matches for African Americans on 1870 Census." 2001. *Rootsweb.com.* 2015. <http.//freepages.genealogy.rootsweb.com>.

Bolton, Charles C. "Farmers Without Land: The Plight of White Tenant Farmers and Sharecroppers." 2004. *Mississippi History Now*. Mississippi Historical Society. 15 May 2015. <http://mshistory.k12.ms.us/index.php?s=extra&id=228>.

Bordelon, Jerry. "Dominique Coco II (1785-1864)." *Find A Grave*. Find A Grave Memorial# 32782056. Ancestry.com Operations, 9 January 2009. <http://www.findagrave.com/cgi-bin/fg.cgi?page=gr&GRid=32782056>.

—. "Leandre François Roy in the U.S., Find A Grave Index, 1600s-Current, Grave Memorial Number 58410445." *Find A Grave Index*. Ancestry.com Oerations Inc., 9 September 2010. <http://www.findagrave.com/cgi-bin/fg.cgi?page=gr&GRid=58410445&ref=acom>.

—. "Lucien Dominique Coco, III." *U.S., Find A Grave Index, 1600s-Current*. Comp. Find A Grave. Find A Grave. http://www.findagrave.com/cgi-bin/fg.cgi. Find A Grave.com. Provo: Ancestry.com, 10 August 2010.

—. "Valery Coco." 7 August 2010. *Find A Grave.com.* Ancestry.com Operations Inc. <http://www.findagrave.com/cgi-bin/fg.cgi?page=gr&GRid=57244032&ref=acom>.

Bordelon, L. *1850 US Census for Avoyelles Parish, Louisiana*. Census Record. United States Census Bureau. Washington, DC: Ancestry.com, 1850.

Bordelon, L. *Joseph Laurent in 1850 US Census*. Census Report. US Government. Avoyelles Parish, LA: Ancestry.com, 1850.

Boucher, Jack E. *Magnolia Plantation, Slave Quarters*. Cane River National Heritage Area Commission; National Parks Service, Natchitoches, Louisiana.

Boyd, John Jr. "High Price of Monopoly: Why American Farmers Must Buy From Just One Seed." *National Black Farmers Association* 2012.

Bradshaw, Jim. *Great Flood of 1927*. Ed. David Johnson. 13 May 2013. 9 May 2015. <http://www.knowla.org/entry/763/>.

Britannica, Encyclopedia. "African Religions." 4 February 2016. *Encyclopedia Britannica On-Line*. On-Line Document. <http://www.britannica.com/topic/African-religions>.

—. *1900 U.S. Federal Census, Avoyelles Parish, LA, Ward 3, District 0014*. Census Report. Washington DC: U.S. Census Bureau, 1900.

Bureau, U.S. Census. *1810 United States Census for Avoyelles Parish, Louisiana*. Washington, DC: U.S. Government, 1810.

—. *1810 United States Federal Census*. Provo, UT: Ancestry.com, n.d. Microfilm - Record Group 29; NARA microfilm publication M252, 71 rolls.

—. *1810 US Census for Avoyelles Parish Louisiana*. Census Report. Washington, DC: US Census Bureau, 1810.

—. *1820 United States Census for Avoyelles Parish, Louisiana*. Washington, DC: U.S. Government, 1820.

—. *1830 United States Federal Census for Avoyelles Parish, LA*. Provo, UT: Ancestry.com Operations, Inc, 1830. <http://search.ancestry.com/cgi-bin/sse.dll?indiv=1&db=1830usfedcenancestry&gss=angs-d&new=1&rank=1&msT=1&gsfn=p&gsln=normand%2c+norman&msrpn__ftp=Avoyelles+Parish%2c+Louisiana%2c+USA&msrpn=213&msrpn_PInfo=7-%7c0%7c1652393%7c0%7c2%7c3246%7c21%7c0%7c213%7c0>.

—. "1850 U.S. Census for Avoyelles Parish, Louisiana." *1850 U.S. Census*. Washington, DC: U.S. Government, 1850.

—. *1860 U.S. Federal Census - Slave Schedules*. Provo, UT: Ancestry.com Operations Inc., 2010.

—. "1860 United States Federal Census for Avoyelles Parish, Louisiana." 1860.

—. *1870 United Census for Avoyelles Parish, LA Division 5, Family No. 631*. Census Report. Provo, UT: Ancestry.com Operations, Inc., n.d. <http://interactive.ancestry.com/7163/4269407_00216/30550307?backurl=http%3a%2f%2fsearch. ancestry.com%2f%2fcgi-bin%2fsse.dll%3fdb%3d1870usfedcen%26indiv%3dtry%26h%3d30550307&ssrc=&backlabel=ReturnRecord#?imageId=4269407_00215>.

—. "1910 United Federal Census for Avoyelles Parish, LA, Ward 3." Ancestry.com Operations, Inc., n.d.

Bureau, United States Census. "1850 U.S. Federal Census - Slave Schedules ." *Bureau of the Census. Seventh Census of the United States, 1850*. Ancestry.com. Washington, DC: Ancestry.com Operations Inc., 1850. <http://search.ancestry.com/cgi-bin/sse.dll?gss=angs-c&new=1&rank=1&msT=1&gsfn=lucien+dominique&gsln=coco&mswpn__ftp=Avoyelles+Parish%2c+Louisiana%2c+USA&mswpn=213&mswpn_PInfo=7-%7c0%7c1652393%7c0%7c2%7c3246%7c21%7c0%7c213%7c0%7c0%7c&MSAV=1&msbdy=1812&cpxt>.

Bureau, US Census. "1840 U.S. Census for Pointe Coupee Parish, Louisiana." *U.S. Census*. U.S. Government, 1840.

—. *1840 U.S. for Avoyelles Parish, LA*. Provo, UT: Ancestry.com, n.d. <http://interactive.ancestry.com/8057/4409529_00572/1310161?backurl=http%3a%2f%2fsearch.ancestry.com%2f%2fcgi-bin%2fsse.dll%3fgss%3dangs-g%26new%3d1%26rank%3d1%26msT%3d1%26gsfn%3dlaurent%2bsr.%26gsln%3dnormand%26mswpn__ftp%3dAvoyelles%2bParish%252c%2bLouis>.

Calvin Peter Thampson. Dir. Tom Whitehead. Prod. W. Belton. Townsend Foundation, 1979.

Car, The Little Black. *Slave cabins at the Audubon State Historic Site in Louisiana*. Audubon State Historic Site. <http://www.flickr.com/photos/littleblackcar/4815714757/>.

Census, 1900 U.S. "1900 U.S. Census for Avoyelles Parish." *1900 U.S. Federal Census*. Washington, DC: U.S.Census Bureau, n.d.

Census, US. *1860 US Census*. Census. Washington DC: US Department of the Census, 1860.

Church, St. Paul Catholic. *Early Baptism Records: St. Paul the Apostle Catholic Church 1824-1844*. Ed. Alberta Rousseau G.R.S Ducote. Mansura, LA: St. Paul the Apostle Catholic Church, n.d.

CJ. "Jean Pierre Normand." 10 September 2012. *Find A Grave Memorial*. Ancestry.com. <http://www.findagrave.com/cgi-bin/fg.cgi?page=gr&GRid=96846810&ref=acom>.

Cline, Isaac M. "SPECIAL REPORT ON THE GALVESTON HURRICANE." 4 February 2004. *NOAA History - A Science Odyssey.* 6 March 2016. <http://www.history.noaa.gov/stories_tales/cline2.html>.

Cockrone, E.E. *Joseph Laurent in 1860 US Census for Avoyelles Parish, LA.* Census Report. Census Bureau. Provo, UT: Ancestry.com Operations, 1860. <http://interactive.ancestry.com/7667/4231218_00425?pid=38462247&backurl=http%3a%2f%2fsearch.ancestry.com%2f%2fcgi-bin%2fsse.dll%3findiv%3d1%26db%3d1860usfedcenancestry%26h%3d38462247%26tid%3d%26pid%3d%26usePUB%3dtrue%26rhSource%3d7163&treeid=&personid=&hi>.

Committee, Avoyellean of the Year. "Dominique Coco I, Avoyellean of 1786." n.d. *Avoyelles.com.* Ed. Randy Decuir. <http://avoyelles.com/Avoyelleans/1786-DominiqueCoco/bio.html>.

Congress, Library of. *Map of Avoyelles Parish Louisiana.* Washington DC, 1879. Library of Congress Document.

Contributors, H-Net. "African Muslim Slaves in America." 5 February 2016. *H-Net.org.* <http://www.h-net.org/~africa/threads/muslimslaves.html>.

contributors, Wikipedia. "Battle of Fort De Russy." 28 July 2015. *Wikipedia, The Free Encyclopedia.* <https://en.wikipedia.org/w/index.php?title=Special:CiteThisPage&page=Battle_of_Fort_De_Russy&id=673440145>.

—. "Battle of Mansura." 10 September 2013. *Wikipedia, The Free Encyclopedia.* <https://en.wikipedia.org/w/index.php?title=Special:CiteThisPage&page=Battle_of_Mansura&id=572272371>.

Contributors, Wikipedia Staff and. "Siege of Port Hudson." n.d. *Wiipedia.com.* <https://en.wikipedia.org/wiki/Siege_of_Port_Hudson>.

Cotes1930. *U.S. Federal Census, Avoyelles Parish, LA, Ward 3, Dist 8.* Census Report. Washington DC: U.S. Census Bureau, 1930.

Court, Avoyelles Parish Clerk of. "Lousisiana Marriages, 1718-1925." *Hunting for Bears.* Ancestry.com Operations Inc., 2004. <http://search.ancestry.com/cgi-bin/sse.dll?gss=angs-c&new=1&rank=1&msT=1&gsfn=Edgar&gsln=Francisco&mswpn__ftp=Avoyelles+Parish%2c+Louisiana%2c+USA&mswpn=213&mswpn_PInfo=7-%7c0%7c1652393%7c0%7c2%7c3246%7c21%7c0%7c0%7c213%7c0%7c0%7c&MSAV=1&msfng=Francois&msfns=>.

Daggett, US Army Copyist. *US Colored Troops Military Service Records, 1863-1865.* Provo, UT: Ancestry.com/National Archives and Records Administration, 1864. On-line Database.

Database, US Government. "U.S., Civil War Pension Index: General Index to Pension Files, 1861-1934 for Jean B Berzat." 1901.

Dauphine, James G. "The Knights of the White Camelia and the Election of 1868: Louisiana's White Terrorists; a Benighting Legacy." Vincent, Charles. *The African American Experience in Louisiana; Part B: From the Civil War to Jim Crow*. Lafayette, Louisiana: Center for Louisiana Studies, University of Louisiana at Lafayette, 2000. 223-238. Hardcover Book.

Davis, Burke. "The Civil War, Strange and Fascinating Facts." 1 Nvember 2004. *CivilWarHome.com*. <http://civilwarhome.com/casualties.htm>.

Davis, Theodore R. *The riot in New Orleans – murdering negroes in the rear of Mechanics' Institute. Harper's Weekly*. New Yor, 1866. Engraving.

Decuir, Randy. "Avoyelles Almanac." *The Bunkie Record, The Marksville Weekly News* 20 March 2014.

Delano, Jack. *Sharecroppers chopping cotton on rented land near White Plains, Greene County, Ga*. Library of Congress Prints and Photographs Division, Farm Security Administration, Washington DC. Photograph.

Dethloff, Henry C. and Jones, Robert R. "Race Relations in Louisiana, 1877-98." Vincent, Charles. *The African American Experience in Louisiana, Part B: From the Civil War to Jim Crow*. Lafayette, Louisiana: Center for Louisiana Studies, University of Louisiana Studies, 2000. 501. Hardcover Book.

Dobak, William A. "Buffalo Soldiers." 2015. *HistoryNet*. <http://www.historynet.com/buffalo-soldiers>.

Dodd, Jordan R and et. al.. *Early American Marriages: Louisiana to 1850*. Bountiful, UT: Precision Indexing Publishers, 1824.

Dodd, Jordan R. and et al. "Early American Marriages: Louisiana to 1850." *Elza Bordelon*. Bountiful: Precision Indexing Publishers, 30 July 1829.

Dodd, Jordan R. et al. *Joseph Laurent in Louisiana Marriages to 1850*. Database. Provo, UT: Ancestry.com Operations, n.d. <http://search.ancestry.com/cgi-bin/sse.dll?indiv=1&db=eamla&h=101346&tid=&pid=&usePUB=true&rhSource=8054>.

Dodd, Jordan R., et al. "Clara Normand." n.d. *Louisiana Marriages to 1850*. Ancestry.com Operations Inc. <http://search.ancestry.com/cgi-bin/sse.dll?gss=angs-g&new=1&rank=1&msT=1&gsfn=clara&gsln=normand&mswpn__ftp=Avoyelles+Parish%2c+Louisiana%2c+USA&mswpn=213&mswpn_PInfo=7-%7c0%7c1652393%7c0%7c2%7c3246%7c21%7c0%7c213%7c0%7c0%7c&MSAV=1&msbdy=1834&cpxt=1&cp=12>.

—. "Joseph Dominique Coco." 1997. *Early American Marriages: Louisiana to 1850*. Ancestry.com Operations inc. <http://search.ancestry.com/cgi-bin/sse.dll?gss=angs-c&new=1&rank=1&msT=1&gsfn=joseph+dominique&gsln=coco&mswpn__ftp=Avoyelles+Parish%2c+Louisiana%2c+USA&mswpn=213&mswpn_PInfo=7-%7c0%7c1652393%7c0%7c2%7c3246%7c21%7c0%7c213%7c0%7c0%7c&MSAV=1&msbdy=1827&cpxt>.

douetk. "Lemoine Family Tree." *Ancestry.com.* Ancestry.com Operations Inc., n.d. <http://trees.ancestry.com/tree/50013383/person/28206360913>.

Du Bois, W.E.B. *Black Reconstruction in America: 1860-1880.* New York, NY: Atheneum, 1972. Paperback.

Du Bois, W.E.Burghardt. *The Souls of Black Folks.* Chicago, IL: A.C. McClung & Co., 1903.

Du Bois, William Edward Burghardt. *The story of the Niagara Movement and the N. A. A. C. P.* Amherst, MA: University of Massachusetts Amherst ; Special Collections & University Archives : University Libraries, 1945.

Dubose, William E. B. *The Georgia Negro.* African American Photographs Assembled for 1900 Paris Exposition. *Negro Exhibit of the American Section at the Paris Exposition Universelle in 1900.* Paris: U.S. Library of Congress, 1900. <Image download: http://lcweb2.loc.gov/master/pnp/ppmsca/33800/33863a.tif>.

Ducote, Alberta Rousseau. *Early Baptism Records, St. Paul the Apostle Catholic Church, 1824-1831, 1832-1844, 1845-1850.* Mansura, LA: St. Paul the Apostle Catholic Church, n.d. Book.

Ducote, Willie J. *Avoyelles Parish- St. Paul, Mansura, Louisiana Burial Register.* Trans. Willie J Ducote. Vols. 4, 5. Mansura, LA: St. Paul the Apostle Catholic Church, 1998. 5 vols.

Eakin, Sue. *Sue Eakin Papers.* University Archives and Central Louisiana Collection, James C. Baldwin Library, Alexandria . Photograph.

Eakins, Sue. *Calvin Peter Thompson.* James C. Bolton Library, Louisiana State University, Alexandria. Sue Eakins Papers Collection, Central Louisiana Collection.

EdEmCoco1910. *U.S. Federal Census, Avoyelles Parish, LA, Ward 3, Dist. 0016, Family No. 436.* Census Report. Washington DC: U.S. Census Bureau, 1910.

Editor, Obit. "Lucien Dominique Coco, III." *Marksville Bulletin* 12 September 1879: 3.

Edwards, Everett Eugene. *Bibliography of the History of Agriculture in the United States.* University of Michigan, 1930. Book.

Ehret, Christopher. *The Civilizations of Africa: A History to 1800.* Richmond, VA: University of Virginia Press, 2002.

Faber, Lo and Charles Chamberlain. "Spanish Colonial Louisiana (1763 - 1802)." 7 February 2014. *KnowLa: Encyclopedia of Louisiana.* Ed. David Jihnson. Louisiana Endowment for the Humanities. 30 May 2015. <http://knowla.org/entry/773/>.

Faragher, John Mack. *A Great and Noble Scheme: The Tragic Story of the Expulsion of the French Acadians from Their American Homeland.* New York, NY: WW Norton & Company, 2005.

Fatal Flood, The American Experience. By Chana Gazit. Dir. Chana Gazit. Prod. Chana Gazit. n.d.

Fauburg Treme - The Untold Story of Black New Orleans. By Lolis Eric Elie. Dir. Dawn Logsdon. Prod. Dawn Logsdon & Lolis Eric Elie Lucie Faulknor. PBS.org, HBO, n.d. Television. <http://www.tremedoc.com/>.

FerIrRegard1900. *U.S. Federal Census, Avoyelles Parish, LA, Ward 3, Dist. 0014, Family No. 2*. Census Report. Washington DC: U.S. Federal Census, 1900.

Finley, Keith. "Lynchings." 21 December 2012. *KnowLa Encyclopedia of Louisiana*. Ed. David Johnson. Louisiana Endowment for the Humanities. 8 February 2016.

—. "Lynchings (ca. 1860 - 1940s)." *KnowLa Encyclopedia of Louisiana* (2012).

Fort, Bruce. 10 August 1996. *American Slave Narratives - An Online Anthology*. American Hypertext Workshop at the University of Virginia, Summer 1996. <http://xroads.virginia.edu/~hyper/wpa/wpahome.html>.

Fortier, Alcee and James McLoughlin. "Louisiana." *The Catholic Encyclopedia* 1910. <http://www.newadvent.org/cathen/09378a.htm>.

Foundation, Constitutional Rights. "A Brief History of Jim Crow." 2014. *CRF-USA.org*. 11 February 2016. <http://www.crf-usa.org/black-history-month/a-brief-history-of-jim-crow>.

Frankenfeld, A. L. *The Floods of 1927 in the Mississippi Basin*. NOAA - Historic NWS Collection. *1927 Monthly Weather Review*. Silver Spring, and Suitland: Wikimedia Commons, n.d. 13 March 2016. <http://www.photolib.noaa.gov/htmls/wea00733.htm>.

Frankenfeld, H.C. *The Floods of 1927 in the Mississippi Basin*. Vol. Supplement No. 29. 1927 Monthly Weather Review, 1927.

French, B. F. "Louisiana's Code Noir (1724)." 1851. *BlackPast.org*. <http://www.blackpast.org/primary/louisianas-code-noir-1724>.

Galveston. *History of Galveston, Texas*. Wikipedia, 1915.

Gates, Henry Louis Jr. "Did Black People Own Slaves?" 4 March 2013. *The Root*. 30 May 2015. <http://www.theroot.com/articles/history/2013/03/black_slave_owners_did_they_exist.html>.

Gates, Henry Louis, Jr. "Did African-American Slaves Rebel?" 2013. *The African Americans, Many Rivers to Cross*. PBS.

General view looking from the north along west row of cabins - Magnolia Plantation, Slave Quarters, LA Route 119, Natchitoches, Natchitoches Parish, LA .

GenevaSwis. "Notes on Joseph Joffrion II." 7 November 2007. *Ancestry.com*. <http://trees.ancestry.com/tree/3454724/person/-1613111471/story/bbdd9def-2996-471f-999b-ecfbed30d84a?src=search>.

Gibson, James F. *Cumberland Landing, Va. Group of "contrabands" at Foller's house*. US Army. *Photograph from the main eastern theater of war, The Peninsular Campaign, May-August 1862.* . Library of Congress, n.d. <http://hdl.loc.gov/loc.pnp/pp.print>.

Gilbert, Charlene. *Homecoming: The Story of African-American Farmers*. 2002.

Gilbert, J et al. *The Decline (and Revival?) of Black farmers and Rural Landowners. A Review of the Research Literature"*. . Land Tech Center, University of Wisconsin, 2001.

Gladstone, William A. *United States Colored Troops, 1863-1867*. Gettysburg, PA: Thomas Publications, 1996.

Government, US. "US Census." 1880, 1900, 1930.

Great Migration. By History.com Staff. History Channel, 2010. <http://www.history.com/topics/black-history/great-migration>.

Gremillion, L.V. "Estate of Julien Goudeau, deceased." Trans. PeteNormand1949. Bayou Rouge Prairie, Avoyelles Parish: Ancestry.com, 16 January 1858. <http://mv.ancestry.com/viewer/742266b3-285f-47f4-80f9-8e8c574ccdb5/7048077/-1175110605?_phsrc=opB2&usePUBJs=true>.

—. "Inventory of the Estate of Julien Jules Goudeau I." Trans. PeteNormand1949. Bayou Rouge Priarie, Avoyelles Parish: Ancestry.com, 12 January 1858. <http://mv.ancestry.com/viewer/1e4aa80e-591d-4ac4-810e-2bd637ccd51a/7048077/-1175110605?_phsrc=opB2&usePUBJs=true>.

Guillory, Reverend Charles. *St. John Community Church-Baptist is on Facebook*. n.d.

Haley, Alex. *Roots: the Saga of an American Family*. New York, NY: Vanguard Books, 1974. Book.

Hall, Gwendolyn Midlo. *Africans in Colonial Louisiana: The Development of Afro-Creole Culture in the Eighteenth Century*. Baton Rouge, LA: Louisiana State University Press, 1995.

—. "Berri in the Louisiana, Slave Records, 1719-1820." n.d. *Ancestry.com*. <http://search.ancestry.com/cgi-bin/sse.dll?gss=angs-g&new=1&rank=1&gsfn=joseph&gsln=joffrion&mswpn__ftp=Avoyelles+Parish%2c+Louisiana%2c+USA&mswpn=213&mswpn_PInfo=7-%7c0%7c1652393%7c0%7c2%7c3246%7c21%7c0%7c213%7c0%7c0%7c&MSAV=1&msbdy=1755&_83004003-n_xcl=>.

—. "Louisiana Freed Slave Records, 1719-1820." *Afro Louisiana History and Genealogy, 1719-1820*. Ancestry.com Operations Inc., 2003. <http://www.ibiblio.org/laslave/>.

—. "Louisiana, Slave Records, 1719-1820." 2009. *Ancestry.com Operations*. <http://search.ancestry.com/cgi-bin/sse.dll?gss=angs-g&new=1&rank=1&msT=1&gsfn=joseph&gsln=joffrion&mswpn__ftp=Avoyelles+Parish%2c+Louisiana%2c+USA&mswpn=213&mswpn_PInfo=7-%7c0%7c1652393%7c0%7c2%7c3246%7c21%7c0%7c213%7c0%7c0%7c&MSAV=1&msbdy=1775&cpxt=1&cp=>.

—. *Louisiana, Slave Records, 1719-1820*. Ancestry.com, Inc. Operations Inc. Provo, 2003. On-Line Database. <http://search.ancestry.com/cgi-bin/sse.dll?gss=angs-g&new=1&rank=1&msT=1&gsfn=magloire&mswpn__ftp=Avoyelles+Parish%2c+Louisiana%2c+USA&mswpn=213&mswpn_PInfo=7-%7c0%7c%7c1652393%7c0%7c2%7c3246%7c21%7c0%7c%7c213%7c0%7c0%7c&msbdy_x=1&msbdp=5&MSAV=1&msbdy=1794&_830>.

Hamilton. Harper's Weekly Newspaper, April 18, 1863 Edition . *Contemporary Newspaper view of the Union fleet passing Port Hudson published by ''Harper's Weekly Newspaper'' April 18, 1863*. New York: Harper's Weekly, 1863. Wiipedia.com. <https://en.wikipedia.org/wiki/Siege_of_Port_Hudson#/media/File:Port_Hudson_Navy_Harpers.jpg>.

Harlan, Louis R. *Booker T. Washington: The Wizard of Tuskegee, 1901-1915*. Oxford, U.K.: Oxford University Press, 1986.

—. *The Booker T. Washington Papers*. Ed. Louis R. Harlan. Vol. 3. Urbana: University of Illinois Press, 1974.

Harper, Douglas. "American Colonialization Society." 2003. *Slavery in The North*. <http://slavenorth.com/colonize.htm>.

Harper's Weekly Newspaper, April 18, 1863 Edition. *Photograph of black soldiers of the Native Guard regiments of the Union army at Port Hudson, Louisiana, 1862-1864*. National Archives, Archival Research Catalog, Washington, DC. Archival Research Catalog, digital images, National Archives, ARC identifier 594179, Local Identifier 165-JT-433B. <https://commons.wikimedia.org/wiki/File:Port_Hudson_Native_Guard.gif#filehistory>.

Harper's Weekly Staff. "The Louisiana Murders—Gathering The Dead And Wounded." *Harper's Weekly* 10 May 1873: 397. <http://blackhistory.harpweek.com/7Illustrations/Reconstruction/Illustrations/0397w500.jpg>.

Hathorn, Billy. *Sharecropper's Cabin, Lake Providence, LA*. Louisiana State Cotton Museum in Lake Providence, LA, Lake Providence, LA. Photograph.

Heinnemann, R.L. "Robert Russa Moton (1867-1940)." *Encyclopedia Virginia*. Virginia Foundation for the Humanities, 2014.

Henry, Ashley. *Medal of Honor recognition long overdue*. 9 May 2008. 9 May 2015. <http://www.army.mil/article/9075/medal-of-honor-recognition-long-overdue/>.

Herbert_Holmes_1. "Oliver Normand and Lucinda Sampson." 2015. *Ancestry.com*. <http://trees.ancestry.com/tree/75282541/person/32316540762/story/e664b873-9e94-479e-9965-e385cb5f4898?src=search>.

Hewitt, Lawrence E. *Port Hudson, Confederate Bastion on the Mississippi*. Baton Rouge, LA: Lousiana State University Press, 1987.

Hollandsworth, James G. *An Absolute Massacre: The New Orleans Race Riot of July 30, 1866*. Baton Rouge, Louisiana: Louisiana State University Press, 2004.

Holmes, Jack D. L. "The Abortive Slave Revolt at Pointe Coupée, Louisiana, 1795." *Louisiana History: The Journal of the Louisiana Historical Association* 11.4 (1970): 341-362. <http://www.jstor.org/stable/4231151?seq=1#page_scan_tab_contents>.

Holt, Thomas C. *The Second Great Migration, 1940-1970*. Ed. Molly Hodgens. Chicago: University of Chicago, n.d.

Hunter, Clementine and Cammie G Henry. *Melrose Plantation, African House, State Highway 119, Melrose, Natchitoches Parish, LA*. Library of Congress Prints and Photographs Division, Washington, D.C. 20540 USA. < http://hdl.loc.gov/loc.pnp/pp.print>.

Hyacinth, Mother Mary. "The Murder of Laurent Normand." McCants, Sister Dorothy. *They Came To Louisiana; Letters of a Catholic Mission 1854-1882*. Trans. Daughter of the Cross Sister Dorothea McCants. LSU Press, 1970. 90-91.

JacqAug1870. "1870 United States Federal Census for Avoyelles Parish, Louisiana, Subdivision 6." *1870 U.S. Federal Census*. Provo: Ancestry.com Operations Inc., 1870. <http://search.ancestry.com/cgi-bin/sse.dll?gss=angs-g&new=1&rank=1&msT=1&gsfn=celeste&gsln=normand&mswpn__ftp=Avoyelles+Parish%2c+Louisiana%2c+USA&mswpn=213&mswpn_PInfo=7-%7c0%7c1652393%7c0%7c2%7c3246%7c21%7c0%7c213%7c0%7c0%7c&msbdy_x=1&msbdp=10&MSAV=1&ms>.

James, Ola. Interview. D.G. Prier. 2014.

Jones, Amara. "Outflow of Africans to the Americas and Europe." 2015. *SlaveryBlog*. <http://slaveryblog.tumblr.com/AboutAdministrator>.

Jones, Terry L. "The Free Men of Color Go to War." *New Yor Times Opinionator* 19 October 2012. <http://opinionator.blogs.nytimes.com/2012/10/19/the-free-men-of-color-go-to-war/?_r=0>.

JosMagPen. *U.S., Civil War Pension Index: General Index to Pension Files, 1861-1934; U.S. Civil War Soldier Records and Profiles, 1861-1865*. 2000.

Katz, William Loren. *Black Indians: A Hidden Heritage*. New York: Atheneum Books, 1986.

Kendall, John Smith. *History of New Orleans*. Chicago: Lewis Publishing Co., 1922.

Kenmayer. S*ites of first operations by African Americans in the American Civil War, 1862-1863*. National Park Service. <https://commons.wikimedia.org/wiki/File:AfricanAmericanCivlWarMap1.jpg>.

Kimball. *Wilson Chinn, a branded slave from Louisiana--Also exhibiting instruments of torture used to punish slaves*. Library of Congress Prints and Photographs Division Washington, D.C. 20540 USA, New York, NY.

King & Baird, engravers. *Emancipation*. S. Bott, Philadelphia. 1 print on wove paper : wood engraving printed in black and rose ; image 36 x 52.1 cm. <http://cdn.loc.gov/service/pnp/pga/03800/03898r.jpg>.

LaCour, Geraldine Dufour. *Brides' book of Avoyelles Parish, Louisiana*. Bunkie, LA: Open Library, 1979. Book.

Laird, Father Martin. "Our Lady of Prompt Succor, Mansura." n.d. *The Diocese of Alexandria*. 2 May 2016. <http://www.diocesealex.org/churches/our-lady-prompt-succor-mansura-mansura>.

Lakwete, Angela. *Inventing the Cotton Gin: Machine and Myth in Antebellum America*. JHU Press, 2003.

Laughlin, S.H. "US Land Office Certificate No. 4685." *Land Office Land Purchase*. Opelousas, LA: US Land Office, January 1849.

—. "US Land Office Certificate No. 4721." *United States Land Office Records, 1796-1907 for Francois Roy*. Opelousas: United States Land Office, 1 January 1849.

Laver, Tara Zachary (Curator of Manuscripts). "Free People of Color in Louisiana - Revealing an Unknown Past." n.d. *LSU Libraries*. <http://www.lib.lsu.edu/sites/all/files/sc/fpoc/index.html>.

Lemoine, Sidney J. "1910 United States Federal Census for Ward 3, District 0016 of Avoyelles Parish, Louisiana." UNited States Census Bureau, 1910.

Leslie, Frank. *Bailey's Dam in Alexandria, Louisiana During the Red River Campaign, 1864*. Wikimedia Commons. *Frank Leslie's Scenes and Portraits of the Civil War (1894*. 1894. Engraving. <https://commons.wikimedia.org/wiki/File:Frank_Leslie%27s_Scenes_and_Portraits_-_Bailey%27s_Dam.jpg>.

Levin, Jeff et al. *Religion in the Lives of African Americans*. Thousand Oaks, CA: Sage Publications, Inc., 2010. Amazon.

Levtzion, Nehemia. *History Of Islam In Africa*. Athens, OH: Ohio University Press, 2012. Project Muse; https://muse.jhu.edu/.

Lewis-Jones, Huw. "The Royal Navy and the Battle to End Slavery." 2011. *History*. BBC. <http://www.bbc.co.uk/history/british/abolition/royal_navy_article_01.shtml>.

Louisiana, State of. "Poste Des Avoyelles." Waymarker.com, n.d.

Lugo, Luis. *Tolerance and Tension: Islam and Christianity in Sub-Saharan Africa*. Study. Washington DC: Pew Forum on Religion & Public Lif, 2010. <http://www.voltairenet.org/IMG/pdf/Islam_and_Christianity.pdf>.

Luttrell, Natalie. "Guthrey Family Tree." n.d. *Ancestry.com*. <http://trees.ancestry.com/tree/72283831/person/32347080106/facts/facts>.

Maffly-Kipp, Laurie F. *The Church in the Southern Black Community, Documenting the American South*. Chapel Hill: University Library, The University of North Carolina at Chapel Hill, 2004.

Management, Office of Land. "U.S. General Land Office Records, 1796-1907." Provo, UT: Ancestry.com Operations, Inc., 2008. <http://search.ancestry.com/cgi-bin/sse.dll?db=BLMlandpatents&h=836402&indiv=try&o_vc=Record:OtherRecord&rhSource=8058>.

Mansura1900. *U.S. Federal Census, Avoyelles Parish, LA, Ward 3, District 0014*. Census Records. Washinggton DC: U.S. Census Bureau, 1900.

Mansura1930. *U.S. Federal Census, Avoyelles Parish, LA, Ward 3, Dist 7*. Census Report. Washington DC: U.S. Census Bureau, 1930.

Martin-Quiatte, Stephenie K. "LOUISIANA SLAVES SALES: 1800-1832." n.d. <http://files.usgwarchives.net/la/state/history/afriamer/slaves/sale.txt>.

Mayeux, Carlos and Randy Decuir. *Mansura: Prairie des Avoyelles*. Mansura: Avoyelles Publications, 2010.

McAllenR14. *Carbo/Jeansonne Family Tree*. Comp. McAllenR14. Ancestry.com . Ancestry.com , n.d. <http://trees.ancestry.com/tree/34736916/person/18689167600>.

McGough, Michael R. *The 1889 Flood in Johnstown, Pennsylvania*. 2002.

McKellar, Ian. *Slave cabin at Destrehan Plantation in Louisiana.*

McMickle, Marvin Andrew. *"The Black Church", A Brief History. An Encyclopedia of African American Christian Heritage*. The Center for African American Ministries and Black Church Studies. Chicago: Judson Press, 2002.

Meeler, Brenda. "Bowman's/Meeler's Family Tree." n.d. *Ancestry.com.* Ed. Ancestry.com Operations Inc. <http://trees.ancestry.com/tree/9645101/family?fpid=6068121037>.

Mertins, J.L. *Henry Smith's lynching in 1893*. Wikimedia Commons, Paris, TX. Photograph. <https://commons.wikimedia.org/wiki/Category:1893_photographs>.

Messner, William F. "Black Violence and White Response: Louisiana, 1862." *The African American Experience in Louisiana*. Ed. Charles Vincent. Vol. 11. Lafayette: Centers for Louisiana Studies, University of Louisiana at Lafayetter, 2000. 18 vols. 39-55.

Midlo Hall, Gwendolyn. *Africans in Colonial Louisiana: The Development of Afro-Creole Culture in the Eighteenth Century*. Baton Rouge, LA: Louisiana State University Press, 1992.

Mitchner, Patsy. "Black Codes (United States)." 1937. *Wikipedia.Com.* Ed. Slave Narrative Collection. Federal Writer's Project of the WPA. <https://en.wikipedia.org/wiki/Black_Codes_(United_States)>.

Mizelle, Richard M. *Backwater Blues: The Mississippi Flood of 1927 in the African American Imagination*. Mineapolis, MN: University of Minneasota Press, 2014. Book.

Moissennet, F. *Well dressed mulatto woman*. New Orleans, LA. 6-Plate Daguerreotype.

Moore, John Hebron. *The Emergence of the Cotton Kingdom in the Old Southwest: Mississippi, 1770-1860*. LSU Press, 1988.

Moore, Sam. *U.S. Farmers During the Great Depression*. Ogden Publications, Inc., 2015.

Moreau, Harry James. *Dr. Edmé Goudeau and his American Descendants*. 2 vols. Baton Rouge, LA: Self, 2006.

Moton, Robert R. *The Final Report of the Colored Advisory Commission Appointed to Cooperate with The American National Red Cross and the Presi-dent's Committee on Relief Work in the Mississippi Valley Flood Disaster of 1927*. Washington, DC, 1927.

Mrsbethbarton. *Slave Cabin Interior*. Booker T. Washington National Monument.

mulattoes. *Mulatoes, Creoles & Mixed Race*. n.d. 2015.

Museum, Franklin D. Roosevelt Presidential Library and. Franklin D. Roosevelt Presidential Library and Museum, Portland, Oregon.

nacu, Andre. *Red River campaign March-May 1864*. Wikipedia. <https://commons.wikimedia.org/wiki/File:Red_River_campaign.svg>.

NHC-NOAA. *Hurricanes in History*. n.d. 6 March 2016. <http://www.nhc.noaa.gov/outreach/history/>.

Normand, Mark J. "The Murder of Laurent Normand." 2012. *Ancestry.com*. Ed. NancyLawrence1217.

Normand, Mark. "The Normand Family of Avoyelles Parish." 3 July 2012. *Ancestry.com*. <http://trees.ancestry.com/tree/7048077/person/-1175429613/story/569db023-a892-43d2-b3d3-66563a859aa5?src=search>.

Northrup, Solomon. *12 Years a Slave*. Ed. David Wilson. Auburn, NY: DERBY AND MILLER, 1853.

Notary, LA. "Louisiana, Slave Records, 1719-1820." n.d.

Office, US Land. "Laurent Normand." *United States Land Office Records, 1796-1907*. Marksville, 1 May 1849.

Oldershaw, J. *Black soldier in Union Army Sergeant uniform 1864*. Beinecke Rare Book & Manuscript Library, Yale University, New Haven, CN.

Operations, Ancestry.com. *U.S. General Land Office Records, 1796-1907*. Land Office Record. Provo, UT: Ancestry.com, 2008.

Original, New York Public Library Scan of. *Sweet angel, whisper low*. New York Public Library, New York. <https://commons.wikimedia.org/wiki/File:Sweet_angel,_whisper_low_(NYPL_Hades-609036-1257198).jpg>.

Ott, Thomas O. "The Haitian Revolution (1791-1804)." 1973. *BlackPast.org*. PBS.org.
    <http://www.blackpast.org/gah/haitian-revolution-1791-1804>.

Painter, Nell. "Modern Voices - Nell Irvan Painter on soul murder and slavery." n.d. *Africans in America*.
    PBS.org. <http://www.pbs.org/wgbh/aia/part4/4i3084.htm>.

Pastor, Church. "Our Lady of Prompt Succor, Mansura." n.d. *The Diocese of Alexandria*. 5 February 2016.
    <http://www.diocesealex.org/churches/our-lady-prompt-succor-mansura-mansura>.

patsybaker19. "Our Family Through the Years." n.d. *Ancestry.com*.
    <http://trees.ancestry.com/tree/6657845/family/familygroup>.

Percy, William Alexander. *Lanterns on the Levee: Recollections of a Planter's Son*. Louisiana State
    University Press, Baton Rouge. 1998, 1941.

Photographer, Our Lady of Prompt Succor Church. *Our Lady of Prompt Succor*. Mansura, LA. Church
    Bulletin.

Photographer, Unknown Army. *Soldiers of the 369th (15th N.Y.) who won the Croix de Guerre for
    gallantry in action, 1919*. U.S. National Archives, Washington DC. Photograph.

Photographer, Unknown USGS. *Refugees at Hamburg*. U.S. Geologic Survey, Washington DC.
    Photograph.

Photographer, Unknown. *Workmen repair levees near Geismar during the Mississippi River flood of 1927*.
    Baton Rouge Advocate, Baton Rouge. Photograph. 7 March 2016.
    <https://www.facebook.com/theadvocatebr/photos/br.AbrH03lSq9Zr0gcGce-
    SQR070EOCskS4q3jQ_yqRZQN2a_u_IJ3wC_c8hjwx76kifqRUSYH282pfsXp86MWp0YdqYcE
    mP4GpukN6LR0Glzn-A-
    oA2R806SELygUU7v0_oiI/10153247145322524/?type=1&opaqueCursor=AbqGEVFDZTjrjZkM
    PvhjfPqWXXeO-cZghAI>.

Photographer, Unknown Government. *Sharecropper plowing. Montgomery County, Alabama*. United
    States Library of Congress's Prints and Photographs division under the digital ID fsa.8b36026.,
    Washngton DC. Photograph.
    <https://commons.wikimedia.org/wiki/File:Sharecropper_plowing_loc.jpg>.

Photographer, Unnown. *Refugees at Hamburg*. National Archives, Washington DC. Photograph.

Photographer, USDA. *Cotton Plant, Texas*. USDA Natural Resources Conservation Service, Washington
    DC. Photograph. <http://photogallery.nrcs.usda.gov/Index.asp ==Licensing== {{PD-USGov-
    USDA}}>.

Photographer, USGS. *Refugees Receiving Water*. U.S. Geologic Survey, Washington DC. Photograph.

pinkladyrider59. "Coco Family Tree." n.d. *Ancestry.com*.
    <http://trees.ancestry.com/tree/58787125/family/familygroup>.

Pope, John. "Huff Post Religion." 11 October 2012. *Huffington Post.* 6 May 2015.
<http://www.huffingtonpost.com/2012/10/11/vatican-ii-catholic-church-changes_n_1956641.html>.

Press, Columbia University. "Abolishionists." 2012. *Infoplease: The Columbia Electronic Encyclopedia, 6th ed.* Columbia University Press.

Prier, Donald G. *Cooking Cracklings at Home of Benjamin Jean's Residence*. Rosharon, Texas. Photograph.

Prier, Donald G. *Desfosse' House*. Mansura.

Prier, Donald G. *Down Town Mansura, LA*. Katy, TX. Photograph.

Project, WPA Writers. "American Life Histories: Manuscripts from the Federal Writers' Project, 1936-1940." n.d. *Library of Congress.* <http://www.loc.gov/collection/federal-writers-project/about-this-collection/>.

Purdy, James E. *W.E.B. Du Bois*. United States Library of Congress's Prints and Photographs division under the digital ID cph.3a29260, Washington DC. Photograph.

Raper, A.F. *The Tragedy of Lynching*. Chapel Hill, NC: University of North Carolina Press, 1933. Book.

Recorder, Marriage. "US and International Marriage Records." 1851. *Ancestry.com.* <http://search.ancestry.com/cgi-bin/sse.dll?db=WorldMarr_ga&h=251958&indiv=try&o_vc=Record:OtherRecord&rhSource=7163>.

Recorders, Land Office. "U.S. General Land Office Records, 1796-1907." Accession Numbers: LA1290_.292; LA1330_.161; LA1350_.324; LA1350_.331. Ancestry.com Operations, 2008.

Ripley, C. Peter. "Confederate Slavery." *The Louisiana Purchase Bicentennial Series in Louisiana History - The African American Experience in Louisiana*. Vol. XI. Lafayette: Center for Louisiana Studies, University of Louisiana at Lafayettr, 2000. XVIII vols. 7-20.

Robertson, S. B. "Map of Avoyelles Parish, Louisiana." 1879. *Library of Congress.* 1 map on 2 sheets : col. ; 107 x 101 cm., each sheet 58 x 103 cm. <http://www.loc.gov/item/2012592318/>.

Rodriguez, Junius P. ""We'll Hang Jeff Davis on the Sour Apple Tree" - Civil War Resistance in Louisiana." *The Louisiana Purchase Bicentennial Series in Louisiana History - The African American Experience*. Ed. Charles Vincent. Vol. XI. Lafayette: Center for Louisiana Studies, University of Louisiana at Lafayette, 2000. XVIII vols. 95-106.

Rosenberg, Jennifer. *1918 Spanish Flu Pandemic*. 2015. 9 May 2015. <http://history1900s.about.com/od/1910s/p/spanishflu.htm>.

—. *World War I*. 2015. 9 May 2015. <http://history1900s.about.com/od/worldwari/p/World-War-I.htm>.

Sacher, John M. "Civil War Louisiana." 6 January 2011. *KnowLA Encyclopedia of Louisiana*. Ed. David Johnson. Louisiana Endowment for the Humanities. 10 September 2015. <http://www.knowla.org/entry/536/>.

Saucier, Corinne L. *A History of Avoyelles*. Louisiana State Normal College. Natchitouches, LA, 1943.

Shellystafford. "FGW's Family Tree." n.d. *Ancestry.com*. Ancestry.com Operations inc.

Slavery and the Making of America. By M.S., Jennifer Hallam, Ph.D., Kimberly Sambol-Tosco, M.A. Nicholas Boston. Prod. David McCarty Brian Brunius. PBS.org, 2004. <http://www.pbs.org/wnet/slavery/about/credits.html>.

Slavery and the Making of America: Education, Arts & Culture. By Kimberly Sambol-Tosco. Thirteen/WNET New York. PBS, 2004. Television.

Slavery in America. Prod. History.com. 2009. <http://www.history.com/topics/black-history/slavery>.

Sorrels, D.G. "Where the Family Came From." 10 August 2012. *Ancestry.com*. <http://trees.ancestry.com/tree/2229227/person/823733837/story/23c6e271-7e2b-4162-b311-240b91f1ccc4?src=search>.

Staff, Biography. "William Lloyd Garrison, Biography." n.d. *Biography.com*. A+E Television Network. <http://www.biography.com/people/william-lloyd-garrison-9307251>.

Staff, Black History in America. *Black History*. 2010. <http://myblackhistory.net/Jim_crow.htm>.

Staff, Catholic Church. "Pierre Normand's Date of Birth." *Sacramental Records of the Roman Catholic Church of the Archdiocese of New Orleans*. Vol. 3. Ancestry.com, n.d. 224.

Staff, Civil War Trust. "United States Colored Troops (USCT)." 2014. *Civil War Trust - Saving America's Civil War Battlefields*. <http://www.civilwar.org/education/history/usct/usct-united-states-colored.html>.

Staff, Civil-War.net. "The Civil War Home Page." n.d. *Civil-War.net*. 10 September 2015. <http://www.civil-war.net/>.

Staff, History Channel. "Slave Rebellions." 2009. *History.com*. 2 September 2015. <http://www.history.com/topics/black-history/slavery-iv-slave-rebellions>.

Staff, History.com. "Abolishionist Movement." 2009. *History.com*. A+E Networks. <http://www.history.com/topics/black-history/abolitionist-movement>.

—. *Black Codes*. 2010. A+E Networks. <http://www.history.com/topics/black-history/black-codes>.

—. "Brown versus Board of Education." 2009. *History.com*. A&E Networks. 18 February 2016.

—. "Dust Bowl." 2009. *History.com*. A+E Networks. 15 May 2015. <http://www.history.com/topics/dust-bowl>.

—. "Freedmen's Bureau." 2010. *History.com.* A+E Network. <http://www.history.com/topics/black-history/freedmens-bureau>.

—. "Sharecropping." 2010. *History.com.* A&E Network. <http://www.history.com/topics/black-history/sharecropping>.

—. "Sharecropping." 210. *History.com.* A&E Networks. 18 February 2016. <http://www.history.com/topics/black-history/sharecropping#section_1>.

Staff, Hunting for Bears. "Louis Olivier in Louisiana Marriages, 1718-1925." 2004. *Ancestry.com.*

Staff, Louisiana Freedmen's Bureau. "Miscellaneous Reports and Lists Relating to Murders and Outrages" Mar. 1867 - Nov. 1868." 1868. *Freedmen's Bureau On-Line.* <http://freedmensbureau.com/louisiana/outrages/outrages4.htm>.

Staff, Slave Rebellion Website. "The 1795 Conspiracy in Pointe Coupee." n.d. *Slaverebellion.org.* <http://slaverebellion.org/index.php?page=the-1795-conspiracy-in-pointe-coupee>.

Staff, St. Paul. *Burial Register of St. Paul's Church.* Trans. Willie J. Ducote. Vol. 1. Mansura, 1997.

Staff, U.S. Census. *Slave Inhsbitants in the Parish of Avoyelles, Louisiana.* Washington: U.S. Government, 1860.

Staff, Wikimedia Commons. *Slave bill of sale for Nancy 1816-6-27.* n.d. 2015. <http://commons.wikimedia.org/wiki/File:Slave_bill_of_sale_for_Nancy_1816-6-27.jpg>.

Staff, Wikipedia. *Corpus Christi, Texas.* Wikipedia, n.d.

—. "Louisiana in the American Civil War." 2015. *Wikipedia, the free encyclopedia.* 2 October 2015. <https://en.wikipedia.org/wiki/Louisiana_in_the_American_Civil_War>.

—. "Red River Campaign." 2015. *Wikipedia.Com.* <https://en.wikipedia.org/wiki/Red_River_Campaign>.

—. *War Industries Board.* 2015. 9 May 2015. <http://en.wikipedia.org/wiki/War_Industries_Board>.

Staff-About.News. "The Great Depression of 1929." 2015. *About.com.* AboutNews. <http://useconomy.about.com/od/grossdomesticproduct/p/1929_Depression.htm>.

Staff-WIkipedia. *Great Mississippi Flood of 1927.* 2015. <http://en.wikipedia.org/wiki/Great_Mississippi_Flood_of_1927>.

Staff-Wikipedia. *Hurricane Katrina.* 2015.

—. *World War I.* 2015. 9 May 2015.

Stolp-Smith, Michael. "The Colfax Massacre (1873)." n.d. *BlackPast.org, Remembered & Reclaimec.* University of Washington, Seattle. <http://www.blackpast.org/aah/colfax-massacre-1873>.

Sturgell, Cathy Lemoine. "Joseph D. Coco." 25 December 2013. *Find A Grave.com.* Ancestry.com Operations Inc. <http://www.findagrave.com/cgi-bin/fg.cgi?page=gr&GRid=122137827&ref=acom>.

Survey, Coast and Geodetic. "1927 LA Flood Map." 1927. <http://www.archives.gov/global-pages/larger-image.html?i=/publications/prologue/2007/spring/images/coast-miss-flood-l.jpg&c=/publications/prologue/2007/spring/images/coast-miss-flood.caption.html>.

—. "Mississippi River Flood of 1927 Showing Flooded Areas and Field of Operations." 1927. *Wikimedia Commons.* <http://www.archives.gov/global-pages/larger-image.html?i=/publications/prologue/2007/spring/images/coast-miss-flood-l.jpg&c=/publications/prologue/2007/spring/images/coast-miss-flood.caption.html>.

Taker, 1850 Census. "1850 U.S. Federal Census - Slave Schedules." 2004. *Ancestry.com.* Ancestry.com Operations Inc. <http://search.ancestry.com/cgi-bin/sse.dll?gss=angs-g&new=1&rank=1&msT=1&gsfn=valery&gsln=coco&mswpn__ftp=Avoyelles+Parish%2c+Louisiana%2c+USA&mswpn=213&mswpn_PInfo=7-%7c0%7c1652393%7c0%7c2%7c3246%7c21%7c0%7c213%7c0%7c0%7c&MSAV=1&msbdy=1827&cpxt=1&cp=12&c>.

Taker, 1880 Avoyelles Parish Census. "1880 United States Federal Census for Louis Olivier; Family Number 96." *10 United States Census*. Avoyelles Parish, Louisiana: Ancestry.com/The Church of Jesus Christ of Latter-day Saints, 1880.

Takers, 1880 Census. "Valery Coco." *1880 US Census*. Vol. Roll 448 ; Image: 0124. Marksville, Avoyelles, Louisiana: US Government, 1880. 389B.

Takers, 1910 Census. "Clara Normand Coco." *1910 US Federal Census*. Police Jury Ward 3, Avoyelles; Enumeration District: 0016: Ancestry.com, 1910. Roll: T624_508; Page: 23A. <http://search.ancestry.com/cgi-bin/sse.dll?gss=angs-g&new=1&rank=1&gsfn=clara+normand&gsln=coco&mswpn__ftp=Avoyelles+Parish%2c+Louisiana%2c+USA&mswpn=213&mswpn_PInfo=7-%7c0%7c1652393%7c0%7c2%7c3246%7c21%7c0%7c213%7c0%7c0%7c&MSAV=1&msbdy=1837&mssng0=valery>.

Takers, 1920 Census. "Edward Coco." *1920 US Federal Census*. Mansura, Avoyelles Parish; Enumeration District: 4; Image: 175: Ancestry.com Operations Inc., 1920. T625_605; Page: 1A.

Takers, Census. "Valery Coco." Subdivision 5. Avoyelles Parish, LA, 1870. 420B; Image 216. Family History Library Film: 552005.

Takers, US Census. "1870 United States Federal Census." 2009. *Ancestry.com.* Ancestry.com Operations, Inc., Provo, UT. <http://search.ancestry.com/search/db.aspx?htx=List&dbid=7163&offerid=0%3a7858%3a0>.

Talbott, William F. "$1200 to 1250 Dollars for Negroes." 1853. <http://www.nytimes.com/2014/03/30/books/review/the-problem-of-slavery-in-the-age-of-emancipation-by-david-brion-davis.html>.

Tarver, A.B. *Mansura, LA*. Library of Congress on Facebook. *Flood of 1927-Avoyelles Parish Tarver Photos*. Mansura, LA, 1927. Phitograph. <https://www.facebook.com/photo.php?fbid=10205582294850818&set=a.10205582294050798.1073741869.1056279623&type=3&theater>.

Tate, Albert Jr. and W.N. Sr. Gremillion. "1785 Census of Avoyelles Post, Avoyelles Parish, Louisiana." *Louisiana Genealogical Register* (1981): 121-125.

Taylor, James E. *African American Students in Classroom with Teachers*. Freedman's Bureau. *The Misses Cooks School*. Richmond, VA: Library of Congress, Illustration in AP2.L52, 1866. Sketch.

Terry, E.S. "US Land Office Certificate No. 4668." *U.S. General Land Office Records, 1796-1907*. Opelousas: US Government Land Office, 15 May 1852.

Thomas, J. D. "Law of Slavery in the State of Louisiana." 24 August 2011. *Accesible-Archives.com*. 3 September 2015. <http://www.accessible-archives.com/2011/08/law-of-slavery-in-the-state-of-louisiana/>.

ThomElRoy1900. *U.S. Federal Census, Avoyelles Parish, Ward 3, Dist. 0014, Family No. 4*. Census Report. Washington DC: U.S.Census Bureau, 1900.

Turner, Patricia A. *Ceramic Uncles & Celluloid mammies: Black Images and Their Influence on Culture*. University of Virginia Press, 2002.

Tyrr, Tanith. "Processing a Pig for Meat." 1 January 2001. *The Pig Site*. 5M Publishing. Internet. 30 March 2016. <http://www.thepigsite.com/articles/600/processing-a-pig-for-meat/>.

U.S. and International Marriage Records, 1560-1900. "Marriage of Jean Pierre Normand and Marguerite Vicknair." Yates Publishing - Ancestry.com Operations Inc. 2004, n.d.

Underwood, Underwood &. *Cabins where slaves were raised for market--The famous Hermitage, Savannah, Georgia*. Library of Congress Prints and Photographs Division Washington, D.C. 20540 USA , New York. 1 photographic print on stereo card : stereograph.

—. "Anti-Slavery Movement in the United States." n.d. *National Library of Australia*. Lost Cause Press. Collecrtion. <http://www.nla.gov.au/selected-library-collections/anti-slavery-movement-in-the-united-states>.

Unknown. *Booker T. Washington in a poster in 1911*. <https://commons.wikimedia.org/wiki/File%3ABooker_T_Washington_-_1911.jpg>.

Unknown. *Common Street Slave Market*. 1850s drawing from New Orleans Notorial Archives. *Lost New Orleans*. American Legacy Press, 1980.

Unknown. *English: The Church at Eala (Bongandanga district), Congo, ca. 1900-1915. International Mission Photography Archive, ca.1860-ca.1960*. University of Edinburgh, U.K: University of Southern California. Libraries, ca.1900-ca.1940s. lantern slides 8.2 x 8.2cm.

Unknown. *Freedmen Voting in New Orleans 1867*. New York Public Library Digital Collection, New York. This is a faithful photographic reproduction of a two-dimensional, public domain work of art. <https://commons.wikimedia.org/wiki/File:FreedmenVotingInNewOrleans1867.jpeg>.

Unknown. *Horrid massacre in Virginia*. Library of Congress, Southampton County, Virginia. Wood Cut. <http://www.loc.gov/resource/cph.3a39248/>.

Unknown. *Liberators of Cuba, soldiers of the 10th Cavalry after the Spanish-American War*. Wikimedia.com.

Unknown. *Map Showing the Route of the Army During the Red River Campaign in the Spring of 1864*. U.S. National Archives and Records Administration. *Map Showing the Route of the Army During the Red River Campaign*. Washington DC, 1864. Map.

Unknown. *Mississippi River Flood of 1927*. Library of Congress, Washington DC. <https://www.loc.gov/item/2002707619/>.

Unknown. *Slave Market, Common Street*. New Orleans Notorial Archives. *Lost New Orleans by Mary Cable*. American Legacy Press, 1980.

USDA, Staff. "Civil Rights Action Team." 1997.

USGS. "The Great 1906 San Francisco Earthquake." n.d. *USGS Science for a Changing World*. 6 March 2016.

Vincent, Charles. "Black Louisianians During the Civil War and Reconstruction: Aspects of Their Struggles and Achievements." Vincent, Charles. *The African American Experience in Louisiana; Part B: From the Civil War to Jim Crow*. Lafayette, Louisiana: Center for Louisiana Studies, University of Louisiana at Lafayette, 2000. 120-141.

Voltz, Noah Mellick. "'It's no disgrace to a colored girl to placer': Sexual Commodification and Negotiation among Louisiana's "Quadroons," 1805-1860." 2014. *Mixed Race Studies*. Ohio State University. Dissertation. <http://www.mixedracestudies.org/wordpress/?tag=quadroon-balls>.

W.E.B.Dubois. *Black Reconstruction in America, 1860 - 1880*. 1935.

Walker, Evans 1903-1975. *Lucille Burroughs, daughter of a cotton sharecropper. Hale County, Alabama*. Library of Congress Prints and Photographs Division Washington, DC 20540 USA, Washington DC. Photograph. <http://hdl.loc.gov/loc.pnp/fsa.8c52249>.

Warren, Kim. "Seeking the Promised Land: African American Migrations to Kansas." 2015. *Civil War on the Western Border*. The Kansas City Public Library. <http://www.civilwaronthewesternborder.org/essay/seeking-promised-land-african-american-migrations-kansas>.

Wattenberg, Ben J. *Statistical History of the United States from Colonial Times to the Present*. New York: Basic Books, Inc., 1970.

Waud, Alfred R. *The Freedman's Bureau*. Harper's Weekly, New York, NY. <https://commons.wikimedia.org/wiki/File:Freedman_bureau_harpers_cartoon.jpg>.

Wikipedia, Staff -. *Great Mississippi Flood of 1927*. 2015. <http://en.wikipedia.org/wiki/Great_Mississippi_Flood_of_1927>.

Wikipedia, Staff-. *Flood Control Act*. 2015.

Wikipedia-Staff. "Mansura, Louisiana." 2015. *Wikipedia, The Free Encyclopedia*. <http://en.wikipedia.org/wiki/Mansura,_Louisiana>.

Williams, Chad. *African Americans and World War I*. 2015. Schomberg Center for Reseacrh in black Culture - New York Public Library. 9 May 2015.

Williams, Heather Andrea. *Help Me to Find My People*. University of North Carolina Press, 2012.

Writers, WPA. "An Introduction to the WPA Slave Narratives." n.d. *Library of Congress.* Ed. Norman R. Yetman. U.S. Library of Congress . <http://memory.loc.gov/ammem/snhtml/snhome.html>.

Yetman, Norman R. "An Introduction to the WPA Slave Narratives." n.d. *Slave Narratives.* <http://memory.loc.gov/ammem/snhtml/snbio.html>.

Acknowledgements:

- **Dr. Huey L. Perry** for taking the time to not only make excellent suggestions regarding improvements in both spelling, grammar and content, but also writing a very thorough and supportive critique of this work.
- **Dr. Vanessa Jackson** for her painstaking review of this work, her recommendations for improving the many nuances that I tend to include in my writing and for her very thorough and positive critique.
- **Mary Bernell Prier** for the many hours we spent in discussions that allowed me to get a clearer view of what post-slavery Mansura was like. Also for allowing me my "quiet time" in the early morning when I do my most creative thinking.
- **Sue Eakin Family** for allowing me the privilege of using pictures from her personal collection in this book.

About the Author:

Donald Gregory Prier was born in Mansura, Louisiana. He was one of 12 children whose parents, Oliver Prier and Beulah Walter, were born and lived during the most difficult years of the Jim Crow era.

Donald attended Our Lady of Prompt Succor and Cardinal Cushing elementary schools in Mansura. He graduated from Mary Bethune High School in Marksville and from Southern University with a BS in Chemistry and LSU with a PhD in Chemistry. He retired from the Dow Chemical Company in 2009 after 28 years of service.

Donald has been married to Mary Bernell Augustine of Mansura for 46 years. They have three children and four grandchildren.